P9-CRD-772

PRAISE FOR

Boundless Leadership

"This very practical book shows how to optimize your body, mind, and heart for twenty-first century leadership. From two master teachers, it is comprehensive, profound—and extraordinary."

> —RICK HANSON, PHD, bestselling author of *Resilient and Hardwiring Happiness;* Senior Fellow, Greater Good Science Center, UC Berkeley

"In this empowering synthesis of contemplative insights and the science of the brain and mind, Joe Loizzo and Elazar Aslan offer a guide to personal and professional leadership that helps us find deep inner resources of strength in ourselves and others. The approach of this guide to being an impactful, compassionate, and visionary leader is built upon cutting-edge science and inspired by the wisdom of meditative practice, providing us the best of rigorous research and heartfelt truths that can help us all to create a new world of compassion, connection, and creativity."

> —DANIEL J. SIEGEL, MD, bestselling author of *Mindsight;* clinical professor, David Geffen School of Medicine at UCLA; and executive director, Mindsight Institute

"*Boundless Leadership* is a ground-breaking book that redefines what it means to be a true leader today. Rather than a superficial list of mundane and trite qualities found among 'great leaders,' *Boundless Leadership* takes a deep dive into the leaders themselves to identify the critical characteristics that define authentic, mindful, and effective leadership in a world full of sloganeering. This book is as much for the leader as it is for those they lead. A unique and progressive take on the organization of the future, Joe and Elazar are to leadership what Demming was to quality. A must read for both current and aspiring leaders."

> — RON INSANA, senior analyst, CNBC

"A breathtakingly original approach to leadership, both practical and visionary. Anyone who cares about our future and how leaders can help shape a better one will find *Boundless Leadership* a source of inspiration."

—DANIEL GOLEMAN, author of *Emotional Intelligence*

"Have you ever had a workplace that you just couldn't relate to? *Boundless Leadership* provides us with a road map to change—blending the heart, mind, and body to change how we relate to ourselves, bring authenticity, connect with others, and lead in the workplace."

—SHARON SALZBERG, author of *Lovingkindness* and
   Real Change

"In a world increasingly powered by connectedness, interdependence, and networks, the ability to shed historical win-lose thinking and embrace boundless leadership is critical for the success of any leader, organization, or society. The evidence-based approach and pragmatic techniques contained in *Boundless Leadership* combine to create a powerful handbook that guides the reader to successfully achieve this necessary and advanced approach to self-development and leadership."

—BRAD D. SMITH, former CEO and executive chairman, Intuit

"Boundless Leadership builds an understanding that leadership comes from within, that each of us can impact positive change in ourselves, our organizations, our personal lives, and even the world. It doesn't stop there; the book gives practical methods to shift thinking and behavior to achieve success. I cannot help but think how helpful this work would have been for my younger self."

—BETH SHAPIRO, executive director, Citymeals on Wheels

"There has never been a more 'appropriate' time for this book. Leaders today struggle to transform, as they are defined by archaic stereotypes and presented with conventional approaches for improvement. *Boundless Leadership* delivers a path for those ready for self-exploration and to begin their own personal journeys of transformation. The practical methods offered by Elazar and Joe apply to the leaders in all of us and transcend our personal and professional lives. The future of authentic and empathetic leadership starts here. For those who embrace it, the positive impact in your lives, organizations, communities, and the world are endless."

—FIONA BRUDER, president, Americas, George P. Johnson Experience Marketing

"*Boundless Leadership* is a deeply comprehensive and science-backed manifesto for enlightened leadership—an essential manual for leaders, change-makers and anyone who wants to make a difference and develop their full potential."

—EMMA SEPPÄLÄ, PHD, author of *The Happiness Track*

"We take as a given that professional athletes practice their sport based on years of research into the optimal way to build muscle, skill, and motivation. *Boundless Leadership* is the 'training manual' for professional leaders, combining neuroscience and psychology to provide pragmatic and effective skill development that will have a huge impact on you and your organization."

—BRIAN O'KELLEY, Serial Entrepreneur, Technologist, and Angel Investor

"*Boundless Leadership* fearlessly proclaims how to place human dignity and joy at the very center of the twenty-first century workplace. Clear, practical, and seasoned, Elazar and Joe use their decades of business experience and transformational practice to challenge, guide, inspire, and advise. Their guidance is urgent; their insights are vital; their wisdom is refreshing!"

—MICHAEL CARROLL, author of *The Mindful Leader* and
Awake at Work

"Joe and Elazar have written a book that isn't just another leadership manual that offers new wrapping for the same old concepts of how to lead. This book is a guide for how to shift your whole being to uncover the compassionate wise leader within you. They lay out a clear and actionable plan for training the mind, body, and heart, and I am certain it will help all those who read it find the boundless potential they might not have even known they possess."

—ERIN L. OLIVO, PHD, MPH, cofounder and executive
clinical director, Center for Wise Mind Living

"*Boundless Leadership* uses the latest findings in science and a finely engineered architecture along with tools and practices to guide you on a journey of transformation. If you do just some of the work, expect a massive shift in your leadership, of self and others."

—ELENA GRINEV, head of Solution Delivery, Shell New Energies

The Breakthrough Method
to Help You Realize Your
Vision, Empower Others
& Ignite Positive Change

BOUNDLESS
LEADERSHIP

Joe Loizzo
MD, PhD

Elazar Aslan
MBA, PCC

Edited by Alice Peck

Fountaindale Public Library District
300 W. Briarcliff Rd.
Bolingbrook, IL 60440

Shambhala Publications, Inc.
2129 13th Street
Boulder, Colorado 80302
www.shambhala.com

© 2021 by Joseph Loizzo and Elazar Aslan

Cover art: Oleksandr Slobodianiuk/iStock
Cover design: Pete Garceau
Interior design: Kate Huber-Parker

All rights reserved. No part of this book may be reproduced
in any form or by any means, electronic or mechanical, including
photocopying, recording, or by any information storage and retrieval
system, without permission in writing from the publisher.

9 8 7 6 5 4 3 2 1

First Edition
Printed in the United States of America

♾ This edition is printed on acid-free paper that meets the
American National Standards Institute z39.48 Standard.
♻ This book is printed on 30% postconsumer recycled paper.
For more information please visit www.shambhala.com.

Shambhala Publications is distributed worldwide by
Penguin Random House, Inc., and its subsidiaries.

Library of Congress Cataloging-in-Publication Data
Title: Boundless leadership: the breakthrough method to realize your vision,
empower others, and ignite positive change / Joe Loizzo, MD, PhD and
Elazar Aslan, MBA, PCC; edited by Alice Peck.
Description: First edition. | Boulder, Colorado: Shambhala, [2021]
Identifiers: LCCN 2021016137 | ISBN 9781611809213 (hardback)
Subjects: LCSH: Leadership. | Management.
Classification: LCC HD57.7 .L645 2021 | DDC 658.4/092—dc23
LC record available at https://lccn.loc.gov/2021016137

CONTENTS

Part Three
THE DISCIPLINE OF HEART—
TRAIT OF AUTHENTIC ENGAGEMENT

Part Four
THE DISCIPLINE OF BODY, HEART, AND MIND—
TRAIT OF EMBODIED FLOW

Part Five
A COMMITMENT TO PRACTICE

PREFACE

OUR EVOLUTIONARY TIPPING POINT

Joe Loizzo

Leadership—the timeless art of fostering the best in oneself and others—is at a turning point. The landscape we live and work in is evolving rapidly. The digital economy, the global marketplace, unlimited connectivity, exploding interdependence, environmental crisis, the drive toward greater inclusivity and equity each demand meaningful changes in how we conceive, develop, and embody leadership. Yet even taken together, these current trends barely scratch the surface of the deeper tectonic shifts of our pivotal age: the culmination of humanity's incremental progress toward global civilization and the growing maturity in our scientific understanding of human nature and its malleability.

The perfect storm out of which boundless leadership emerges involves the convergence of four historic trends. First, new science shows unmistakably that we're capable of adopting a more social and sustainable way of being leaders and humans. Second, our current age of global interdependence and complexity makes it imperative that we seriously accommodate that new way. Third, the unacceptable cost of business as usual on our well-being as individuals, our social progress toward racial, gender, and class equity, and our environmental crisis all add to the imperative that we develop a new culture of business that is truly healthful, equitable, and sustainable. Finally, the unlikely merging of neuroscience with humanity's most potent contemplative methods of mind/body change—training in mindfulness, compassion, imagery, and breathwork—offers the missing link: an evidence-based method of making a new way pragmatically possible, reproducible, and scalable.

Elazar and I have written this book because everything we've learned in the course of our personal and professional lives has convinced us that a deeper shift in our way of being is not only critically necessary for the challenges we face today but more possible and practical than ever before in history. After spending our early careers facing the growing costs of traditional leadership in our respective fields, we both set out on our search for alternatives wherever we could find them—from current thinking and research to some of the world's oldest traditions of self-transformation. Our shared fascination with the contemplative science and practices of India and Tibet is what brought us together over two decades ago. Over the years our dialogue has deepened to the point where our dual perspectives on how leadership needs to change—mine coming from neuroscience and psychotherapy, his from business consulting and coaching—began converging and allowed us to share clients, teach together, and fine-tune our teamwork.

Boundless Leadership is the fruit of our two converging life journeys—part manifesto, part road map. It makes the case for the fundamentally new way of being and leading we need to navigate this final phase in our collective human transition to truly equitable global interdependence. And it lays out a step-by-step path of transformational learning and practice that can empower us to sustainably be at our best, inspire others to realize their best, and embody new ways of being human that can have far deeper and wider positive impact than any personal best we dreamed possible. Elazar and I have written *Boundless Leadership* for anyone and everyone. Whether you're a CEO, manager, team leader, grassroots organizer, consultant, coach, social entrepreneur, spiritual guide, caregiver, or community activist, this book offers the tools you need to lead yourself, lead others, and transform your whole being and world.

We call this new form of leadership "boundless" for four reasons:

First, because it taps our full human potential for social engagement and harnesses it to the traits of mind, heart, and body—self-awareness, authentic engagement, embodied flow, respectively—which extend human leadership beyond its stress-imposed boundaries.

Second, because its insights and practices, when internalized and embodied, irreversibly shift our minds, brains, and bodies into a mode that empowers our natural competence to communicate, cooperate, and cocreate in equity and interdependence, making our impact as institutional and social leaders potentially boundless.

Third, because it challenges us to conceive and embody a vision, narrative, flow, and manner not limited by our familiar stress-reactive identity or monologue or to the survival-based energy, lifestyle, and embodiment that have driven the natural evolution of life and cultural evolution of civilization until now.

Fourth, and perhaps most powerfully, because it's not limited to scarcity-based hierarchical ideas of leadership as restricted to the elite few who occupy positions of privilege and power in mainstream organizations within industrialized societies but applies equally to the entire field of human beings and groups in any and all life contexts, institutions, and communities around the world. In other words, it expands the domain of leadership to the boundless reservoir of potential innate in humanity.

By cultivating our competence for unbiased, nonreactive, fearless social engagement—through integrated disciplines of mind, heart, and body—then aligning and integrating these into a new way of being and leading, we clear the path to having a boundless positive impact within our family, team, institution, community, and interdependent world.

The history of human civilization and of life on this planet has reached a tipping point. As the heirs of a seventy-million-year explosion in social evolution, in the lightning flash of fifty thousand generations, we humans have gone from being among the most vulnerable life-forms on earth to the top of the food chain, endangering our future and the planet. While our modern forebears assumed the destructive, reptilian side of human nature was fixed and unchanging and taught us to invest in outer material progress at the expense of self-change, science—the vanguard of modernity—has since conclusively found that they were dead wrong. Fortunately, this next enlightenment has come in the nick of time to show us all a way out of the dead end of us-versus-them othering and the dinosaur of stress-driven leadership. Its historic amalgam of social neuroscience and contemplative practice has already begun to act as a catalyst for the deep transformation we need in our way of being as leaders and human beings.

Given the urgency and historic opportunity of our age, Elazar and I are grateful to be able to share our vision and practice of boundless leadership. It is our sincere hope that this book and our Boundless Leadership program will be the catalysts you need to spark your transformation as a leader and help us tip the balance of our future toward sustainably abundant and fully equitable global interdependence. Remember, interdependence doesn't just make things more complex, it also means we each, through our self-transformation, can cause ripple effects that change the course of history and life itself. With our intimate and infinite connectedness, there has never been a time in history when one individual can make such a widespread, lasting difference as we can now. Our humanity need not be an inconvenient truth; with enough awareness, care, and practice we can evolve to have a boundless impact that benefits all life on earth.

PREFACE

OUR MORAL IMPERATIVE

Elazar Aslan

As a born-and-bred marketer, it's second nature for me to create a product or brand with a precise understanding of the overlap between the target audience, the competitive frame, and the value proposition, yet this book eschews those principles, and more than that, it violates the fundamental law of targeting an audience, as *Boundless Leadership* is written to benefit everyone.

Joe and I do not see leadership as an executive position of power or set of skills honed to influence others. We see it as a way of being. A way that manifests a reality born from our authentic aspirations and shaped by fearless grace. Although the traditional view of leadership is defined by the sphere and gravity of influence over others, the power of boundless leadership is sourced from the radical leadership of self. We believe that the real impact of leadership springs not from seeking power over others in a futile attempt to control conditions and out-comes but from clearing, seeding, and cultivating our inner terrain to yield a harvest we can share with everyone.

To be clear, this was not my understanding when I studied at Wharton or when I trained in the upper echelons of corporate Amer-ica or, frankly, even when I founded my own firm. Yet, it was from those experiences that the sobering awareness that the emperor had no clothes dawned. I struggled with all the distractions and wasted energy that plague most business organizations. How could a leader playing by the rules of a zero-sum game create true wealth and abundance? If the big prize is available only to the select few who best separate them-selves from the rest, how could true engagement and collaboration emerge? What was the purpose of a professional "me" and a personal "me" who dressed, spoke, and even acted differently? Why was "Thank God it's Friday" an acceptable mantra for work? Why couldn't our jobs bring meaning and joy as we continue to explore and discover our full potential? Where were the enlightened leaders who wanted to change all that?

I began to ask these questions not just about the organizations I was part of but for myself as an individual, as one human being. Why am I here and what am I supposed to do? What is the meaning of any particular "we," and how do we exceed the sum of its parts? These questions opened up a journey of self-exploration, one that took me to several continents to study with different masters in an effort to un-derstand different beliefs. In the end, I found the path of mindfulness emerging from my encounter with Buddhism to be the most helpful. That journey brought me to Joe Loizzo, who like me was questioning whether the established wisdom of his discipline was actually that wise. Our seemingly incongruent energies began to fuse, and a powerful col-laboration emerged between him, with his keen scholarly and scientific insights into the human psyche, and me, with my growing awareness of the collective scars of my peers, who battled for higher grounds of suc-cess in hopes of capturing happiness. This confusion and disappoint-ment was also expressed by participants in our workshops and retreats.

What began as a shared personal passion became a moral imper-ative. The adolescent years of the digital age had intensified the toxic fallout of the business world and cracked open—perhaps through sheer necessity—a way out. The proliferation of young CEOs who have exceptional acumen and functional capacities but lack the expe-rience of managing emotions—their own and others'—has dramati-cally increased aggressive behavior in the workplace, giving rise to an all-too-common style of leading we refer to in this book as reptilian leadership. The accelerated need for agility and shifting priorities has created greater tension with our instinctive fear-based resistance to change. The information overload across all time zones in an increasingly interconnected world has generated chronic stress beyond what our bodies can bear, setting our inner critic on overdrive as it insists we are not doing enough or achieving enough or, our greatest fear, we are just not enough. Many of us are infected by the epidemic of imposter syndrome as we measure ourselves against overnight billionaires, disruptive innovators, and social media entrepreneurs who are changing the world while still in high school.

Our clients work diligently to earn the time to rest yet have lost the muscle that creates the space to rest. They worry about the sheer quantity of emails left unattended and obsess about the one email that will signal their demise. They've become negativity addicts, wrongly thinking that if they vigilantly focus on what might harm them, they can be immunized from the inevitable downturn. They struggle with balance in their lives and respond to all this pressure by doing more, driven by the delusion that if they run faster and harder, they can reach the horizon sooner. In turn, they try to unreasonably control others as they attempt to ease the overwhelm within. Because the majority of our clients lead others, you can imagine the ripple effect through their organizations.

At times, this pressurized scenario merely serves as a backdrop for personal crises like illness or divorce or even global disruptions such as a pandemic that wreak havoc on our ability to rely on the familiar, creating extremely challenging times to be managing stress and leading others. Yet, whether it's the day-to-day stress of performance or the stress on steroids that we all face at times, this state of affairs is unsustainable, and the path out must be scaled not only for our own peace but so inclusivity, social justice, and economic fairness can cascade throughout our societies.

On the flip side, the evolution of the digital age has created unbounded possibilities. More people are able to retire at forty with the time and money to ask, "What is my legacy?" Companies have been launched with a triple-bottom line that focuses on social impact as well as profits, creating a "virtuous cycle." Disruptive business models are founded on the belief that everyone can win, upending the zero-sum mindset. Age and hopefully soon, gender, race, heritage, religious beliefs, and other demographic distinctions are dissolving under the force of our shared humanity and the single planet we inhabit. Our ability as individuals or small groups to turn ideas into realities has never been greater in the history of humankind.

However, the moral imperative that has driven Joe and me to write this book is not limited to the magnitude of the pain we want to alleviate or the opportunities we want to unleash. It is fueled by the knowledge that the path from our old way of being to the new one, despite the steep learning curve involved, is traversable by anyone and everyone who wishes to walk it.

Over the past decade, we've married the quintessence of the esoteric to a stepped methodology, creating the most direct path to the highest pinnacle of leadership, the methodology we refer to as boundless leadership. The steps have been carved by the sages who walked them, the guardrails have been erected by the cutting-edge neuroscience that informs it, and the trails have been marked by the people who've blazed them. There is no reason for any of us to be hindered by self-doubt, imprisoned by our inner critic, or bound by self-limiting beliefs when we can lead by drawing on the best we have to offer from an integrated mind, heart, and body. One's leadership no longer needs to be guided by the pessimistic projections of a culture of self-limiting beliefs, when we can as easily lead by the boundless imaginings of a world of possibilities—for self, other, and all. And with capitalism itself on trial, and each shareholder relegated to being just another stakeholder, the time is ripe for boundless leaders to arise and create a world we are proud to leave for our children and our children's children.

If the idea of this journey has a modicum of interest for you, then this book is offered to honor the part of you that longs for it.

Happy trails.

Part One

THE TRUTHS OF
BOUNDLESS LEADERSHIP

1 THE SITUATION

We Work Hard and Do Our Best,
Yet We're Still Unfulfilled (and
So Are the People around Us)

The insidious problem with leadership as usual is that the survival-driven way of being forces us to choose between success and happiness. In the competitive, goal-oriented culture we've inherited, most of us are conditioned to think of happiness as an individual status we achieve through our personal accomplishments. We are encouraged to dream up elaborate fantasies of our eventual success and how it will ultimately yield lasting happiness. Typically, we learn to frame our success as the endpoint of a particular time line with specific goals attained—a schedule against which we track our "progress" and compare it to that of other people. Most of us learn to link our progress to reaching financial and professional milestones. Yet as part of this goal-driven framework of happiness, we are trained to dismiss the lack of enduring happiness and rationalize that lack by promising ourselves—or our partners or families—that the inner prize of real happiness will somehow magically be waiting at the milestones' end. We get lulled into a trance, chasing a horizon without noticing it's not getting closer.

In fact, as we become increasingly depleted and isolated by our marathon pursuit, we may become disillusioned and feel that our map is all wrong and leading us further and further away from happiness. While some of us may hit this critical point early in life, many only realize it well into their careers. Whether we sacrificed watching our children grow up, neglected a marriage that required ongoing care, or were driven to hear the stirrings of our deeper longings or feel the warning signs of illness and burnout, we find ourselves in a mid-career or even midlife crisis. And with the ever-mounting complexity and pace of the work world, the crisis point seems to be arriving earlier with each generation. Under the surface story of progress and success, we often find that our clients are not thriving at a deeper, human level. While their careers may be booming, as people and as leaders they're stuck.

This delusion—that the next milestone or landmark is the one that will yield happiness—can be evident in many ways. Elazar recalls being on his way to close a deal with board members at a designated restaurant. It was a time prior to our reliance on GPS, and he'd been given written directions that included a water tower. Fixated on this key landmark, Elazar kept asking for directions to the elusive water tower to orient himself and find the restaurant. His last attempt was at an old Texaco station where he was able to get clear instructions to the water tower. Once rerouted, Elazar eventually made it to the restaurant, only to notice that it was across the street from the Texaco station where he'd stopped for directions. The water tower that was supposed to be merely a milestone to the final destination became such an object of focus that he lost track of the end goal of the restaurant and kept pursuing the marker. Similarly, success as a common strategy for the objective of happiness often becomes the end goal itself, usually at the *cost* of happiness.

Another experience presented an even starker contrast. Elazar met with the lama who headed his meditation center to convince him to accept a raise to his paltry salary for the valued teachings he gave every week. As had happened in the past, the lama politely declined the offer, saying he lacked nothing and the money would be of better use to others. After the conversation, Elazar experienced a contentment and ease that permeated his being. He was holding that feeling as he initiated a scheduled client call. It was a tough call—Elazar's client was livid. Her full bonus had not been approved, and despite her healthy, seven-figure salary she did not know how she could meet her financial obligations. Despite becoming a CEO at a young age and navigating the company successfully, she identified more with the lack and discontentment that permeated her life than any sense of accomplishment. These back-to-back interactions dissipated any lingering thoughts that success may be the proven path to happiness, or even a viable one.

Nor are these discontented executives alone. In our experience, most everyone in a leadership role as well as most everyone around them feels this gap between themselves and success in one way or another. It's not limited to an individual or group—it's everyone. This pervasive, insidious suffering isn't personal but reflects fundamental limits in how we've traditionally approached business and leadership. This is why boundless leadership is the alternative we need to break out of this bind and access our full potential not just for leadership but for our sustained happiness.

In the traditional pyramid design of reptilian organizations—which we define as organizations that run a fear-based focus on survival as opposed to a collaborative focus on thriving—we consistently reinforce two underlying premises that are at odds with psychological and social safety, the fundamental requirements for happiness. First, we pair success with upward movement—promotions, raises, advancements, upgrades—to a more thinly populated level, thus creating a false sense of scarcity. Confined to the limits of a zero-sum game, we become burdened by the belief that there isn't room at the top for most of us, never mind all of us. Like we do in musical chairs, we obsess about making sure we are not the one left out.

Second, our primal human need for connection and the avoidance of exclusion or isolation are in direct conflict with a system that uses reward and punishment to weed out those "unworthy" of the next rung up the ladder of success. This constant threat is perhaps why so many people are shaken or even devastated by seemingly innocuous events like being left out of a meeting, being overlooked in a memo, or being disregarded by someone higher up. Never mind the impact of stressful events like reporting to a new outside hire for the position we felt should have been ours or an unfair performance evaluation that doesn't reflect the facts. Constantly on the lookout for inequity, power plays, and unspoken biases, the path to success is more about self-protection and survival along the way than arriving at happiness.

The good news is that not all organizations and business cultures function in the extreme version of these scenarios. The bad news is that even though it inevitably locks our minds and brains into survival rather than thriving mode, the mainstream culture of business presupposes the pyramidal structure, scarcity mindset, and the exclusivity ethos of the reptilian organization. These two stressful forces—a lack of psychological safety and a perceived scarcity—converge in the constant threat of exclusion, which not only makes pursuing success in the context of business as usual incompatible with real happiness, it makes it an inevitable source of unhappiness.

This dynamic is not exclusive to large organizations. Individual entrepreneurs and small limited partnerships are shaped by the same forces. Safety, connection, and inclusion are the requirements of our psychoemotional makeup that are so easily triggered by the external activity that is prevalent in any relationship and implicit contract. The myth of modern business, in fact the myth of modern colonial culture, is that the system works for the winners, the few who deserve greater happiness because of their hard work and who are blessed even before they do things "right." But our experience, along with decades of happiness research by psychologists, sociologists, and historians, debunks this myth. It exposes the sobering truth that our winner-take-all business culture, embodied in the reptilian organization, leaves even the biggest winners less happy than people who live and work in the more network-based, egalitarian, and democratic environment of mammalian cultures and organizations.

2 THE PROBLEM

Our Conditioned Way of Being: Surviving versus Thriving

The hierarchical and limiting structure of our modern colonial culture and reptilian organizations exacerbates underlying stressors that characterize our survival-based mind and brain. We struggle because we are driven by archaic, stress-reactive instincts and conditionings that we try to alleviate by focusing on external challenges or opportunities, but to no avail. Modern culture has taught us a series of myths about stress that keep us from facing our part in the problem. We've been taught that stress cannot be eliminated from human life; that some stress is good or even necessary for us to perform optimally; that "embracing the suck" or pushing through stress with brute force, "grit," or "toughness" is what allows some to be more resistant to stress; and that because stress comes from the oldest "reptilian" part of our brain our stress reactions are hardwired into our neurons and genomes so they cannot be consciously unlearned or changed. More than half a century of stress research has essentially debunked all these myths and dramatically upgraded modern science's assessment of our human potential to reduce, and even eliminate, the impact of stress and trauma on our lives.

To begin with, we've learned that the three main systems of our human brain—vertebrate (reptilian), limbic (mammalian), and neocortical (primate)—have survival biases and reflexes as default settings, comprising what we call our "survival" mode. Just as importantly, it turns out that our brains come equipped with an equally natural and robust set of social capacities and responses embedded in all three systems—what we call our "thriving mode." While our survival mode is responsible for more illness and suffering than we are often taught, our built-in thriving mode enables us to heal, grow, and change in safe connection and community with other individuals and groups. In fact, mounting evidence from research in positive psychology and optimal health suggests that our thriving mode gives all humans the capacity to drastically reduce and eventually eliminate stress reactions from our minds, brains, and lives.[1] This research has increasingly shown that our thriving mode supports more exceptional and sustainable performance at all mind/brain levels, in large part because—unlike grit—it fosters resilience as the flexibility to bounce back from stress and shift reactivity to responsiveness.

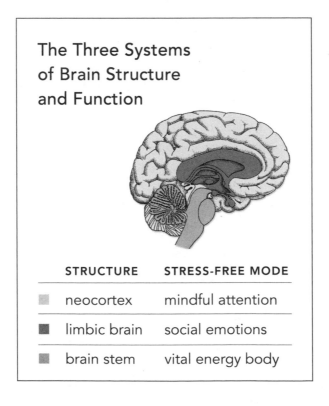

The Three Systems of Brain Structure and Function

STRUCTURE	STRESS-FREE MODE
neocortex	mindful attention
limbic brain	social emotions
brain stem	vital energy body

NEGATIVITY BIAS

If our thriving mode is natural and much more beneficial to our health and well being, why do we so easily get stuck in survival mode—living from goal to goal, crisis to crisis, trauma to trauma? And why is it so hard to shift from that default mode into thriving? Here's where nature—and culture again—get in the way. Not only is our survival mode the natural default setting we are born with as vulnerable mammals, it is held in place by what researchers call negativity bias. Negativity bias is the five- to ten-fold bias preset into our minds and brains at all levels to pay more attention, give more weight, and hold tighter to negative events and inputs we experience as threatening than to positive events and inputs we experience as safe, rewarding, or meaningful.

The popular expression "Our brains are wired like Velcro for suffering but like Teflon for happiness" holds truth. We've all experienced it. For example, the odds of being in a plane crash are about one in ten million, a fraction of the odds of a car crash, but since we hear about every plane crash via the media, many people have more fear of flying than of driving. Most of the time humans will dwell on the negative, not the positive, and routinely get stuck there. This evolutionary default is why we need to put in real effort, repeatedly over the long haul, to override our default survival settings and access our thriving mode. Our negativity bias makes perfect sense when we consider the primary importance of survival in evolution—prehistoric humans couldn't assume that a saber-toothed tiger was a potential friend—as well as when we reflect on how we would never want to override safety settings prematurely or by accident. Here is where culture can play a key role in encouraging or discouraging our capacity for change. If we live in cultures that minimize or even deny the possibility and benefits of consciously choosing and cultivating thriving mode, the stress-driven way we learn to think and live cancels out our natural potential for self-healing and optimal well-being.

Two recent breakthroughs—one in neuroscience, one in molecular biology—have increased interest in the potential benefits of stress reduction and self-healing. Neuroscience's *neuroplasticity*—the discovery that our brains are not hardwired by genetics or childhood—has been a game changer, showing that we have much more power to transform how our minds and brains work than science ever dreamed possible. Likewise molecular biology's *epigenetics*—the discovery that our genes can be accessed and interpreted in different ways based on our current experience or the experience of our ancestors—has boosted our understanding of how learning can fundamentally restructure our brains and bodies from the molecules up.

Although genetics and environment play powerful roles in shaping our mind, brain, and body, implicitly learned habits of thinking, feeling, and acting are even more critical determinants of our well-being. Such acquired habits, conditioned and reinforced by constant repetition, become so ingrained and resistant to change that even science has long assumed they are determined by nature or character. But by learning to pay close attention to familiar habit patterns in our lives, we can slow and stop the mindless repetitions that are needed to keep unhealthy habits installed as default traits. Since much of the neural wiring that supports these habits is plastic and can be reshaped by the repeated practice of healthy alternatives, as we'll demonstrate, mindfulness practices can help us remodel our minds, brains, and consequently our lives.

While stressors from work, family, and even the environment can be very real, the impact they have on our minds and bodies depends on how we perceive and respond to them. We are more likely to be harmed by stressors if we exaggerate the threats they represent and/or minimize our capacity to cope; if the challenges we face trigger reactive emotions like fear, shame, isolation, or rage; if we feel so gripped and threatened by them that they trigger visceral fight-flight-faint-freeze reflexes; and if we are stuck in a way of life wherein the burden of stress reactivity exceeds our opportunities for restoration and our capacities for resilience. When we unwittingly engage our habitual stress reactions because our culture has not taught us to accurately appraise and thoughtfully respond to a challenge, we get stuck and feel locked into the cycle of stress and trauma.

NEUROPLASTICITY

The idea of neuroplasticity was introduced in the 1940s by psychologist Donald Hebb, who proposed that the ability of nerve cells to support learning and growth is directly related to how we use them. His formula for how this use-dependent growth process of plasticity works—"neurons that fire together, wire together"—has become a mantra for the new paradigm that has emerged over the past few decades. According to this new model, when we pay attention, the network of neurons that support that attention fire, stimulating blood flow and cellular growth that the cells in the network use to sprout new branches, which connect them together.

What does this mean in terms of learning and development? What it means is that the brain grows when we use it. This is one of the most powerful and even revolutionary neuroscientific concepts in recent decades, overturning centuries of thought about how the brain and neurons work. Until recently, most people, even researchers and doctors like Joe, were trained to believe that our brains are hardwired based on a genetic blueprint. Childhood programming and a few other factors like diet, illness, and injury were taken into account, but essentially who we became as adults was thought to be written in stone. The belief was that we were born with a limited number of brain cells that never grew and weren't added to, which meant that we were at our full mental capacity in childhood, and we slid downhill as we aged. Fortunately for us all, this conventional wisdom was wrong.

In the 1980s studies were published that challenged and redefined this "we are what we are" belief. Mark Rosenzweig, a researcher at University of California, Berkeley, developed one of Joe's favorite studies. He discovered that the lab rats he brought home for his daughter to raise as pets (which put them in an enriched environment where they were petted, played with, and nurtured) turned out to be smarter than the ones that never left the lab or their cages even though they were genetically identical. When he reproduced this "enriched environment" in the laboratory, he found that the brains of rats raised in more nurturing environments with positive stimulation were consistently 10 to 15 percent larger than their conventionally caged cousins and that everything about their brains—the mass of brain tissue, the number of brain cells, the number of connections, the sizes of cell nuclei—had grown. All the parameters got a boost through something that happened between the rats and their environment—the tincture of nurturing stimulation replicating his daughter's love. It was a revolutionary discovery!

From an evolutionary point of view, if you think about how humans wound up with such big brains, it makes sense that this nurturing treatment was so helpful. Because an infant is born with a proportionally huge brain that's like a sponge and is very much in proximity to the caregiver, the baby can learn a lot more about its environment than you could ever put in a genome, especially if there's affection and positive interplay. So it makes sense that neuroplasticity would be stimulated and grow from nurturing treatment.

Rosenzweig and his colleagues' research blew open our understanding of the brain. Instead of being a hardwired machine, they showed that it was a dynamic organ like a muscle that will grow if you exercise it. Whatever neurons are used by our experience, action, intellectual exercise, or meditative practice enjoy greater electrochemical activity and blood flow and as a result begin not only to grow but to grow together as a network. Hence the mantra of neuroplasticity, "neurons that fire together, wire together."

Whether in rats or humans, the capacity for higher awareness is dependent on a sense of safety and connection. When humans feel threatened or alienated—under attack in the battlefield or the conference room—our neocortex, which is normally led by the central executive network including parts of our prefrontal cortex, shifts our awareness and brain activity into a narrow self-protective mode run by the default-mode network. The result is a more "self-enclosed" awareness that is tunneled by hypervigilance and self-referential processing and hence limited in its capacity by obstacles to clarity like distraction and negativity bias. A nurturing experience of safety, connection, and positive task engagement tends to produce the opposite result.

FOURFOLD CYCLE OF STRESS AND TRAUMA

Current stress researchers including Sheldon Cohen[2] have divided the process of stress and trauma into four phases. These phases are less about the specific external or internal stressors in our lives than how we read, react, and respond to the challenges we find stressful. Once a challenge is perceived as a threat we cannot handle, the experience triggers our stress reactivity, setting in motion a cascade of internal events that wreaks havoc on our minds, brains, bodies, and lives. It is these four phases that make up the spectrum of stress and trauma, including the wear and tear they impose on our minds, bodies, and lives. These phases are as follows:

1   Cognitive appraisal
2   Emotional reaction
3   Visceral reflex
4   Cumulative impact

Cognitive Appraisal

The first line of defense in our response to a stressful challenge (including an opportunity we see as scarce—perhaps a big job interview or a new client) is a snap judgment about the nature of that challenge, the level of threat it poses, and our capacity to successfully meet it. This appraisal typically privileges default instincts we hold about ourselves and the world. These instincts are shaped by implicitly learned perceptions, emotions, and tendencies including attitudes like self-confidence versus self-doubt. In this phase, your appraisal of a stressor occurs in a flash, before you even know it. Your assessment routinely arises less as a conscious thought than as an unconscious bias, shaped by forces like default self-protective instincts, innate stress-reactive emotions, and ingrained beliefs and habit patterns internalized from your caregivers, ancestors, and the culture you're born into.

One all-too-familiar sign of this first phase of the stress cycle is the intrusion of obsessive, worst-case thinking. We get caught up in negative thought spirals way before our higher consciousness has a chance to assess the facts or check our findings. One example is our panic response to a new deadline. Already overwhelmed by hearing we have one more challenge, we jump to the worst-case fear, "I'll never make that!" And our stress response embellishes the negative narrative, "I'll get into a fight with my boss, get fired, wind up homeless, get sick, and die!" In less than a heartbeat, a deadline has become a death threat. This miscalculation enlists our traumatic memories and sense of learned helplessness and hopelessness.

Emotional Reaction

Compounding our worst-case appraisal, the second phase in the cycle of stress and trauma is how that appraisal triggers an embattled sense of self, including stress-reactive emotions and compulsions. Once we perceive ourselves as powerless to some degree in the face of an overwhelming challenge, our instinct is to regress to the survival mindset, emotions, and reactions of a frightened child or cornered animal. Given our early memories as totally dependent social animals, we often experience feeling overwhelmed through the filter of a small child's worst-case social fears: feeling all alone, abandoned, or victimized by the world. Psychologists call this threatened condition of body and mind a traumatic self-state.

Since these experiences of social rejection or neglect feel to human infants and children like life-or-death nightmares, they trigger our social survival emotions: fear-based anxiety, panic, or clinging; reactive anger, resentment, or rage; and self-pity, self-aggrandizement, isolation, or shame. These emotions in turn trigger three kinds of instinctive reactions: to anxiously cling to what seems lifesaving; to angrily push away what seems threatening; and to isolate by ignoring everything in between. Even if our early experiences were not ones of what we nowadays call parental abuse or neglect, painful emotional memories are inevitable and universal. Given our default negativity bias, they tend to hold center stage in our emotional processing, and once they are triggered, they push our minds, brains, and bodies to the next phase in the cycle of stress and trauma.

Visceral Reflex

Once emotional stress reactivity has put us in a state of feeling alone and unsafe, it triggers the third phase of the cycle: the visceral stress response that locks us into the compulsive repetition of stress-reactive habits and traumatic experiences. Triggered by the raw sensation of hurt, fueled by shame, pride, fear, and rage, we feel toxic inside, craving a conquest or an escape and driven to spring into action. Here is where our most primitive survival instincts kick in, locking us into a neurochemical suit of armor that serves to tune every organ system to the demands of physical combat, retreat, or shutdown. Escalating the fight-or-flight mode of sympathetic alarm, our bodies pump adrenaline and corticosteroids that surge into every tissue and cell, kicking us into life-or-death overdrive. Or, if the threat feels so overwhelming or immediate that no fight or flight seems possible, our systems shift into the faint-freeze mode of primitive parasympathetic shutdown, pumping out acetylcholine and endorphins to anesthetize us into a self-protective paralysis wherein our system plays dead to lock down life-death terror.

With either one of these two potent neurochemical cocktails coursing through our brain and body, we are in fact completely mismatched to the real-life challenges we face. With our higher social faculties for communication, empathy, and judgment switched off, along with our capacity to learn, grow, and change, all that is left to us is to compulsively act out the asocial survival programs of our primal brain. Our main survival programs include prowling, scavenging, or hunting for prey on the one hand and hiding or playing dead to evade predators on the other. Either way we are locked in the self-defeating overdrive of obsessive, addictive, and compulsive behaviors or parked in a paralyzing mode of evasion or lockdown. It is this recurrent nightmare of being locked by our worst-case reflexes into an extreme and archaic survival mode of being and living that exposes us to the chronic wear and tear we see in phase four.

Cumulative Impact

It helps to compare the cumulative effect of stress and trauma on human development to balancing a bank account. Each time we revert to stress, given its high cost in energy and the havoc it wreaks on our lives, we dip into our mind/body reserves, effectively withdrawing funds from our bio-bank account. Each time we recharge in rest, relaxation, or play, we replenish our mind/body reserves, effectively making a deposit in our bank. If, over time, we spend more time and energy in stress and trauma than in rest and regeneration, our withdrawals effectively exceed our deposits, leaving us bankrupt in body, mind, and spirit. This is the origin of the various syndromes of chronic fatigue, burnout, and stress-related mental and physical illnesses that result from a way of life stuck in the four-fold cycle of stress and trauma.

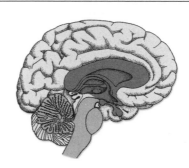

How Stress Impacts the Three Levels of Brain

	STRUCTURE	STRESS RESPONSE	STRESS-PRONE MODE
	neocortex	perceptual stress	scarcity thinking
	limbic brain	emotional stress	harsh inner critic
	brain stem	embodied stress	defensive stance

If the phases of this cycle sound bleak, we must recall they represent only one element of human experience. We each have a unique capacity for conscious self-regulation and change as part of our natural equipment for lifelong development. This points to the fact that we each have the ability to adapt and overcome life stressors when we engage our prosocial mind and brain networks, which we'll explore in these pages, especially in the practices. Attention-training practices like mindfulness can help us exercise our learning muscles and override the automatic habit patterns set up and reinforced in the past. *Body mindfulness* can help us stop and notice our fear-based appraisals by balancing our worst anticipation with attention to what is right with us here and now. *Nonreactive mindfulness* can empower us to bear with our vulnerability instead of being triggered into reactive emotions. *Mindful awareness* can free our minds to step back when we're being flooded by visceral stress states and ride out the body's stress reflexes until we can restore calm. *Mindful insight* enables us to bring the clear discernment we need to opt out of stress-prone habits and lifestyles and choose a self-healing life.

THE REAL SOURCES OF HAPPINESS, RESILIENCE, INSPIRATION, AND CREATIVITY

As we said, our brains are wired with a dominant negativity bias that makes them Velcro for suffering and Teflon for happiness. This is evolution's way of sharpening our attention to learn from negative experiences. To ensure negative experiences register strongly in our circuitry, they are installed deep in our long-term emotional memory, capturing the majority of our attention and energy and keeping us caught in the cycle of stress and trauma. Positive experiences, on the other hand, do not get the special attention that negative events do and are generally allotted a spot in our short-term memory. To be moved into our long-term memory repository, positive experiences need to be consistently felt over longer periods of time.

One of the main ways in which our survival mode keeps us locked into reinforcing the cycle of stress and trauma is by a system of default reactivity designed to protect us from the predictable threats of life in the wild. While we are capable of rising above the struggle for survival, our minds and brains are preset to be constantly on guard for life-threatening danger or lifesaving opportunities and ready to dismiss everything in between as irrelevant to our survival. Under the surface of our higher consciousness, unbeknownst to us, the older emotional part of our brain is getting its own stream of data from sensory stimuli without any discerning input from the higher functioning primate part of our brain.

Psychologists call this type of internal data collection "bottom-up" processing. This early warning detection system is constantly scanning our inner and outer worlds with the polarizing hypervigilance of an animal in the wild. But that is not all. This sensory-based defense apparatus is wired into a hair-trigger motivational system set to push us to react without hesitation, thought, or awareness when our scanner detects even a hint of danger or opportunity. It turns out that this unconscious system of hypervigilance and reactivity is the engine that drives the cycle of stress and trauma in real time.

Fortunately, we evolved the higher brain capacity to intentionally bring awareness to this unconscious engine and override its default reactive mode with the help of "top-down" processing. Top-down processing engages the newest part of our brain and brings higher awareness to more clearly assess and skillfully respond to the immediate experience of our inner and outer lives. This capacity, which involves what psychologists call affect tolerance, is vital to our ability to be with and stay with our vulnerable, embodied minds so that we can understand and care for ourselves as we are here and now. We know, thanks to research[3] on the positive neuroplastic effects of meditation, that by paying attention to our survival bias and overreactive stress emotions and habits through mindful attention training, we can more consistently choose and grow the healthy states and traits of nonreactive mindfulness, compassion, and resilience.

Decades of research[4] on stress-reduction practices show that by consciously monitoring and overriding our survival bias, we can gradually change our minds and rewire our brains to unlearn stress habits and learn to live more resilient, connected, and happier lives. And as we said above, the deep reflection we develop through mindfulness practice can even change how our cells read our genetic blueprint, allowing fundamental and lasting shifts in the biochemistry our genes generate that help install and maintain healthy traits of mind, heart, and body. The fact is, as humans we are sitting on a great reservoir of untapped potential for thriving, so with the necessary learning, training, and practice, we can free ourselves from the cycle of stress and trauma.

What would happen if we started looking within for the real sources of happiness, resilience, inspiration, and creativity? We've all been trained to chase the next promotion, a raise, our share of equity, a vacation, the next horizon. But the horizon moves as much as we do because it's a mirage. It isn't only that we'll never get there; it's that we're looking for happiness in the wrong place. Even if we could get there it would never be as satisfying as we imagine or in the way we want it to be.

This never being satisfied is related to scarcity psychology—mistakenly believing material wealth and status are the only sources of power, well-being, and innovation. We now know the real sources of well-being, lasting happiness, and innovation lie in the untapped reservoir of our mammalian capacities for thriving with other people, the ultimate source of all human power. This science explains why our modern culture and especially the culture of business and leadership as usual need to change, along with the culture and structure of our organizations. To reach a type of success and a style of leadership that is truly equitable and sustainable, we must learn to shift out of survival mode and dedicate ourselves to the biology and psychology of thriving. Given that this biology and psychology only emerge when our social brains feel safely connected to others in equitable communities and institutions, the only way forward for us as individuals, leaders, or as a civilization is to learn the art of boundless leadership and create mammalian organizations.

3 THE PROMISE

Unleashing Our Boundless Potential

Embarking on the path of boundless leadership begins with rewiring the default mindset that keeps us from being in the present moment, from knowing how to thrive with others in community, and from adapting to the reality of our civilized lives. It's not merely about changing our behavior but radically changing who we think, say, and feel we are, and thus our fundamental way of being. Since our understanding of who we are is a function of the assumptions, beliefs, and biases that inform how our minds process our experiences, it only stands to reason that our unconscious habits of mind will obscure our unbounded nature or potential. This is why boundless leadership is not predicated upon more skills or better command of business principles but rather upon an unrelenting pursuit of optimizing the inner conditions—the way of being—underlying our thoughts, feelings, and actions. As long as our mind/body state is locked into survival mode and into the habits of stress-prone thinking, feeling, and reacting that drive it, we will necessarily be cut off from our thriving mode as well as all the positive social capacities that sustain well-being and peak performance.

In boundless leadership, we free the mind from the grip of negativity bias—including scarcity thinking, fear of exclusion, and our inner critic—and tap into the clean energy we need to fuel our passions and achieve from a place of excitement and play, rather than stress and trauma. We learn, metaphorically, not to waste our time trying to smooth the rocky road of business but instead equip ourselves with an all-terrain vehicle of fundamental security and resilience. We leverage the people we lead or influence—our greatest asset—by nurturing them to be their best through engagement and inspiration rather than compliance and fear. We learn to be consciously in flow, partnering with the more graceful power of true confidence and trust in ourselves and others.

This process of transformation is gradual, based on our understanding of the art and science of how our business, leadership, and life must be restructured to unlock the promise of a completely different way of working with ourselves, our teams, our companies, and the world around us.

Moving away from a sense of scarcity or lack of psychological safety, even as our organizations are mired in them, we identify with the vision of what is optimally possible, rather than focusing on mitigating the risks of failure or chasing mindlessly after short-term gains that incur long-term losses. Our scarcity-based, self-enclosed narrative is replaced with a more authentic and abundant voice, allowing us to share our vulnerabilities and connect with those around us through empathy and compassion. Thus, cutting through stress and trauma to clear away the shame-based insecurity that binds us, we model for our organization the value of empowered responsibility, transforming a culture of blame and attack to a no-fault collaborative approach to problem-solving that lifts all boats. No longer susceptible to other people's version of who we are and who we should be, we come to be guided by meaning and purpose, thus helping others find their own voice. We not only become leaders others want to follow, but leaders others are inspired to become. And as a result of this fundamental sea change toward a boundless way of being and a mammalian style of leadership, our personal lives thrive along with our companies, contributing to a more equitable and sustainable way of living and working and a better world.

As we transform who we are, our leadership ability and our overall impact on the world become a natural outflow of that self-transformation. But of course the transformative path of boundless leadership cannot be traversed in one leap of faith. It must be traveled through a series of incremental steps that yield progress in a cumulative, systematic way that maximizes impact, while minimizing time and effort.

4 THE PATH

An Optimized and Integrated Mind, Heart, and Body

At its core, boundless leadership is based on the premise that our full potential is most accessible when our mind, heart, and body are each optimized and functioning as one integrated whole that is greater than the sum of its parts. In terms of science, that means deprogramming our default survival mode and accessing our optimal thriving mode at the following three levels:

1   Perception (mind)
2   Emotion (heart)
3   Visceral embodiment (body)

To source our way of being, and thus our leadership, from our potential for thriving requires that we not only experience optimal mind/body states from time to time, but that we cultivate those states often and deeply enough to install them as traits that come to define who we are. Specifically, consistently showing up with a clear and self-aware mind, an authentic and engaged heart, and embodied fearlessness will allow us to be boundless leaders. Yet, developing the optimal states and traits of our thriving mode takes time. This is why the architecture of the path of boundless leadership involves a step-by-step approach to changing our fundamental way of being.

To develop the optimal traits of boundless leadership, we must identify the moment-to-moment state or competency that engenders that particular trait over time. The basic map of the path aligns the three key traits of boundless leadership in the disciplines of mind, heart, and body with the three competencies that engender them as follows:

1   Discipline of mind: trait of self-awareness; competency of clarity
2   Discipline of heart: trait of authentic engagement; competency of compassion
3   Discipline of body: trait of embodied flow; competency of fearlessness

These traits and competencies exist in a synergistic relationship—each feeds and enhances the presence of the other. We identify them as key traits and competencies because they represent the most crucial capacities each human being needs for thriving socially and performing optimally together—capacities that are blocked by stress-prone habits at the level of mind, heart, and body.

Since these traits and competencies require deep understanding, experiential reflection, and repeated practice, even the most ardent transformational leaders can't develop them overnight. This is why we further divide the three competencies into four key facets, which are the qualities we must cultivate to improve our proficiency in the competency within each discipline. Each quality involves a manageable step forward that can be nurtured and combined with the other three qualities to make incremental progress toward the competency.

The qualities can be cross-trained to foster the three competencies and three key traits as follows:

1 Discipline of mind: competency of clarity; qualities of presence, balance, unbiased awareness, discernment
2 Discipline of heart: competency of compassion; qualities of empathy, resilience, engagement, inspiration
3 Discipline of body: competency of fearlessness; qualities of boundless vision, empowering speech, natural flow, fearless embodiment

The best way we've found to develop the qualities, competencies, and traits of boundless leadership is by using a wide range of methods and types of meditation to train our attention and bring contemplation to action. These basic, intermediate, and advanced contemplative practices have proven effective for deep transformation over millennia, and science is now unlocking their mysteries.

Far more than the simple mindfulness techniques being popularized today, these practices have been curated to specifically tap and harness the mind/body states we are sculpting and that support the qualities of boundless leadership we are cultivating. By conditioning our mind, heart, and body with precisely calibrated tools, we incrementally move toward a transformation that is accessible and stable.

These practices also leverage the new mind/body science to address our habits of mind, not just on the most accessible and tangible level, but at subtler, more subliminal levels too, fostering transformation at all levels of our being. Because transformation takes time, in each part of this book we teach everyday work applications designed to leverage the benefits of even the most nascent moves within the mind, heart, and body disciplines.

Ultimately, we hope we will have helped liberate the boundless leader within everyone. That is, we hope that traveling this path will help remove the default limitations imposed on us by stress instincts and habits—by nature and nurture—so we can tap and harness our boundless innate potential for learning and thriving together in mind, heart, and body, awakening as individuals, as equitable communities, and as purposeful stewards of the future and our planet.

The Boundless Leadership Map

Discipline	MIND	HEART	BODY
Intention	Manifesting Your Best	Creating the Conditions for Others to Be at Their Best	Embodying Boundless Leadership
Trait	Self-Awareness	Authentic	Embodied Flow
Competency	Clarity	Compassion	Fearlessness
Qualities	Presence Balance Unbiased Awareness Discernment	Empathy Resilience Engagement Inspiration	Boundless Vision Empowering Speech Natural Flow Fearless Embodiment
Practices	Body mindfulness Mindful Sensitivity Open Awareness Mindful Insight	Equal Empathy Self-Compassion Giving and Taking Emulating Mentors	Role-Modeling Imagery Empowering Narrative Breath-Energy Work Fluid Movement
Application	Aligning Intentions	Empowered Responsibility	Embodying Purpose

Remember, the path to boundless leadership is not about accumulating more knowledge and skill or remedying our deficiencies to improve our leadership. Rather, it's a counterintuitive path that begins with exposing and eliminating self-limiting obscurations, so we can gradually access and develop our unlimited yet dormant potential for thriving. This potential that abides within us is undoubtedly far greater than adequate—it's the greatness innate in each human being. In this book, we are, in effect, providing the science, the tools, and a step-by-step methodology to liberate the boundless leader that is already present. A transformation that is perhaps similar to how Michelangelo described his way of creating sculptures like *David* from a solid slab of marble: liberating the figure by a process of removing (*per via di levare*) all the stone that had been covering up what was already naturally there.

5 THE PRACTICE

The New Science and Timeless Art of Optimizing Mind/Body Systems

Not long after the groundbreaking research on neuroplasticity in the 1990s, psychotherapists began to think about its potential to explain how talk therapy and behavior therapy enhance self-awareness in the neocortex and empower clients to reshape their brains. So did athletes, educators, musicians, and businesspeople. They all recognized that the brain is more malleable than had been thought. We don't have to stay stuck in familial, social, or cultural limits to our capacity for clarity and self-awareness. We can transform our mind and brains through repeated practice. That's where the power of meditation comes in.

At the beginning of the twenty-first century, Richard Davidson, a professor of psychology at the University of Wisconsin, and his team measured the brains of expert meditators—Buddhist monks and other longtime practitioners—and found something unusual: the meditators shared a rare and distinctive brain wave—a high-frequency gamma wave—thought to be indicative of neuroplasticity, high-level information processing, and learning, like the eureka moment of a flash of insight. This brain wave is something seldom seen on a normal EEG. It turns out that these meditators were able to generate minutes-long trains of this high-frequency gamma pattern. "The high-amplitude gamma activity found in some of these practitioners are, to our knowledge, the highest reported in the literature in a nonpathological context."[5] More remarkable was that meditators could turn it on or off at will. With the publication of this discovery in the *Proceedings of the National Academy of Sciences,* meditation went from a marginal research field in neuroscience to front and center, as one of the best evidence-based paradigms for the cultivation of neuroplasticity and learning.

Remarkably, we now have an understanding that attention training through meditation is like a secret ingredient or gateway that can empower our minds to consciously sculpt our brains according to our needs and our potentials. This is largely because of another key aspect of neuroplasticity: *it occurs preferentially in the field of attention.* What this means is that a meditation practice (like mindfulness) that trains us to control our attention, expand its capacity and flexibility, and sustain it for longer periods is like having our hand on the gearshift or joystick that allows us to consciously guide our brains' moment-to-moment plasticity and long-term capabilities.

We can use this type of attention control to consistently focus on the qualities that boundless leadership comprises, gradually installing and establishing them as traits through repeated focus and exercise. At the same time, we can shift attention away from the obstacles we've learned impair our basic capacities and competencies—things like negativity bias, distraction, fatigue, and attachment to outcome. Mind training through meditation allows us to use neuroplasticity to consciously sculpt how our brains work, building the best qualities of leadership into our minds and lives.

This powerful new science clears the way for us to explore the timeless art of contemplative practices that enable us to unlearn the habits and instincts of stress that lock us into our self-limiting survival mode of being and leading and empower us to access and develop our boundless innate potential for thriving sustainably as leaders, organizations, and societies. Before we explore those practices and their real-world application, we must dispel some of the myths surrounding today's popular forms of meditation and yoga.

A great deal has been written and said in recent decades about mindfulness but from the standpoint of the time-tested tradition it comes from—the teachings of the Buddha contained in the Pali

Canon—the current and popular definition of mindfulness as "paying attention to what's happening in the present moment, without judgment" amounts to less than 5 percent of the traditional ancient methodology that modern science is proving to be so effective for retraining the human mind/brain for flourishing.

Paying attention to what we're experiencing in the here and now without preconceived bias is only the first step on the path of training the mind. It allows us to shift out of our default survival mode of mindlessly, compulsively chasing short-term gain and avoiding short-term loss without noticing our negativity bias toward scarcity thinking and worst-case fears. But once we've shifted out of our mindless default, we've hardly even begun the journey of exposing and dismantling our stress-reactive habits of thinking, feeling, and acting. That journey requires our practice to move beyond simply paying attention to making clearer assessments and judgments that guide better decisions about how to conduct our thinking, feeling, and acting. The full journey of attention training only begins with simple mindfulness. From there it moves to three other practices that allow us to stop reactive habits of mind, unlearn biased perception, and discern and choose the boundless path of thriving. Through these practices, mindfulness leads directly to insight—a highly discerning clarity that builds the deep self-awareness that supports our lifelong learning and transformation. In other words, this rigorous and complete practice of mindfulness forms the foundation for overcoming cognitive stress and developing the boundless leadership discipline of mind. Mindful attention training is a practice that focuses especially on turning stress-prone habits of thought and perception into the qualities of presence, balance, unbiased awareness, and discernment that make up the discipline of mind.

Beyond even this expanded practice of mindfulness, we must move on to training wise compassion. Here too we must dispel a range of myths about compassion that derive from our modern culture of survival and from misunderstanding increasingly popular contemplative practices like loving-kindness and self-compassion.

While most of us were raised on the myths that social emotions like empathy and compassion are sentimental weaknesses that only lead to ineffectiveness and burnout, over fifty years of evolutionary biology and current neuroscience have completely debunked and reversed these modern myths. It turns out that stress emotions like fear, anger, envy, greed, pride, and shame in fact erode peak performance and well-being, while positive social emotions like empathy and compassion unleash peak performance and promote optimal health and well-being. What's more, compassion practice is not a sentimental matter of self-soothing or self-indulgence. Insight-guided heart-based meditation practices in fact empower us to transform these stress-reactive emotions like fear, anger, and shame, along with our inner critic, into the positive social emotional qualities of empathy, resilience, engagement, and inspiration. These qualities in turn are what support us in building the competency for compassion that gives rise to the trait of authentic engagement.

In other words, training in wise compassion is the contemplative training that enables us to unlearn and reverse the emotional factors of stress and trauma and tap into our boundless potential to connect with ourselves and others in more equitable, engaging, and empowering ways. In short, the four progressive practices of compassion training we teach in boundless leadership—equal empathy, self-compassion, wise give-and-take, and mentor emulation—are the essential practices that lay the foundation for the boundless leadership discipline of heart.

Finally, despite the common Cartesian mindset built into modern science and culture since the Enlightenment, we are not disembodied intellects who must or can rise above our human emotions and bodies. Not only has the new science shown us that we think and communicate more clearly when our hearts are feeling safe and open, it has also shown that our minds, hearts, and brains are in fact fully interconnected with our living breathing bodies. This interconnection is not only constant and complete, with every moment of mind/brain activity impacting every organ and cell in our bodies, it's also a two-way street, with every organ and cell, every movement and breath, impacting all levels of our mind and brain.

There are modern myths we must debunk to understand the role of our bodies in leadership and life. First of all, we inherit the myth of Social Darwinism, that our bodies evolved for combat and that brute physical strength is what promotes resistance to stress, physical power, and positive energy. This myth has led to a view of physical exercise as building muscle mass, brute strength, endurance, and power, and requiring a teeth-clenching grit and self-destructive drive. The fact is that this mainstream approach to physical training has not only clear, short-term benefits but insidious, long-term costs. For one, driving our minds and bodies not only makes us prone to physical wear and tear, often leading to injury, it also requires us to tap into the mindset, emotions, energy, and chemistry of stress, reinforcing the death grip stress has on our minds, hearts, and bodies. Even the runner's high that comes from pushing ourselves enough to induce a stress-driven flow state based on adrenaline, steroids, and endorphins is tainted by the energy and chemistry of stress, making us adrenaline junkies.

Is there a real alternative to staying in shape physically that helps eliminate the biology of stress and cultivate the clean energy and chemistry of thriving? The answer is decidedly yes. Through studies of embodied contemplative practices like positive imagery, empowering recitation, yoga breathing, and restorative movement, we've come to understand that many body-focused practices alter the stress-reactive balance of calm and arousal in fundamentally different ways that promote clean energy, where endorphins are mixed not with adrenaline and steroids but with social well-being transmitters like oxytocin, vasopressin, melatonin, and growth hormone.

Rather than brute force and short-term power at the cost of social well-being and connection, these practices promote mammalian flow states that support bodily flexibility, resilience, balance, and tone of the kind we see in expressive arts like poetry, theater, music, and dance. Not surprisingly, these embodied learning practices allow us to disarm the bodily guarding and posturing of unconscious stress activation and to gradually unlearn traumatic body memories along with the rigid reptilian body language of dominance versus submission. As these practices help heal visceral stress and unconscious trauma, they help us access the primal well-being network that supports mammalian flow states along with the qualities of body—boundless vision, empowering speech, natural flow, and fearless embodiment. These qualities in turn support the competency of fearlessness that builds the trait of embodied flow, laying the foundation of the boundless leadership discipline of body.

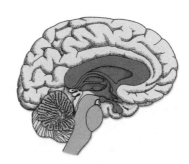

How the Trainings and Traits of Boundless Leadership Rewire the Brain

	STRUCTURE	MIND/BODY TRAINING	LEADERSHIP TRAIT
▦	neocortex	mindful attention	self-awareness
■	limbic brain	compassion	true engagement
▨	brain stem	vision and energy work	embodied flow

As we move through the parts of this book devoted specifically to the three disciplines of boundless leadership, we will return to refine and flesh out the why and how of the contemplative practices we offer. As you explore the practices that build the qualities that make for progress on the path of boundless leadership, we expect that you'll feel how each practice builds on the previous one and how each discipline forms the foundation for the next. At the same time, as you move through each set of practices, we will introduce you to the business application that will help you translate the inner progress you're making into changes to how you engage the daily challenges of work. Finally, as we come to the end of our journey together, we hope you'll sense how the new science and art of transformation we've explored can prepare you to optimize your way of being in mind, heart, and body, empowering you to show up at your best, to bring out the best in others, and to have a greater, more meaningful impact on your life and world than you ever dreamed possible. We'll close our journey together by helping you create a vision for yourself as a boundless leader, a plan for practice that will empower you to realize that vision, and a map of the transformation you intend to make in yourself, your organization, and the world we share.

Part Two

THE DISCIPLINE OF MIND

TRAIT OF SELF-AWARENESS

6 LEADERSHIP IS AN INSIDE JOB

You may have noticed that our culture doesn't seem to put much stock in the mind. We hear a lot about the brain, neural connections, and neuroplasticity—and these are all important—but people don't talk about the mind. Why is that?

As humans, we have a history of moving away from the less tangible parts of our being toward something that is more solid, quantifiable, graspable, of moving from our lived inner experience to our physical body, but the reality is that the subtle part of our nature—our intelligence or awareness—didn't develop by accident. Every one of our capacities evolved slowly over millions of years of natural selection. If mind doesn't matter, why would evolution wire it into us? What is the use of our minds, our subtle, internally experienced flow of lucid awareness or clarifying consciousness?

Where would we be if our decisions and actions were hardwired into our brains, not fluidly open to novel experience, fresh perspectives, and creative responses? The capacity to continuously see things clearly, to stay radically open to an ever-changing landscape, wade through an endless sea of new information, and be nimble enough in our outlook and planning to brainstorm innovative takes and ideas is the essence of our intelligence. If our minds were not so rewirable and free-flowing but nailed down to the fixity of particular software or hardware, how could they manage the flights of shifting and soaring that allow us to create, cope, and manifest our best self? Supremely agile or nimble leadership requires this lightness of higher awareness.

We increasingly think of mind as the forefront of learning and awareness—the purest form of human intelligence that is the most open and flexible. If you have full access to your nimblest, most malleable information processing bandwidth, you're going to be able to download and adapt to the ever-evolving complexity of the world over time. But having that access is not a given—like any muscle, the mental muscle of awareness needs regular exercise and use to develop and stay strong. This especially comes into play when we examine the first trait for the discipline of mind that empowers boundless leadership: self-awareness.

THE TRAIT OF SELF-AWARENESS

Self-awareness—the capacity of the human mind to free itself from its own bias and habits—is the highest type of awareness. This fully open scope is unlike a normal state where we're focused narrowly on one incident or challenge; it's like suddenly emerging from a long tunnel in the mountains and seeing a vast panorama. As with a panoramic point of view—like a 360 evaluation of someone's performance, especially when that someone is us—the most valuable bits of data are the ones that are often hidden in our blind spot. What's in our blind spot—all the background and context of our biased experience and habits—is what most limits the full openness and capacity of our awareness. This is why self-awareness, more than our usual outwardly focused awareness, lets us take in the gestalt, the whole environment including what is outside us and what is inside us, simultaneously with the biases we're unconsciously bringing to the situation, rendering our minds capable of self-monitoring and self-correcting.

These biases not only affect our day-to-day interactions, like prejudging what we think of a presentation based on who is giving it, but can undermine an entire career. One of Joe's clients was the CIO of a large investment company whose able CEO had a serious problem with alcohol that led to a pattern of sexual harassment of female employees. Joe's client tried to confront his colleague repeatedly with this problem and pattern, and urged him to get help. Unfortunately, the CEO had a mindset of impunity rooted in a deep sense of superiority and entitlement hidden in the blind spot of his self-awareness, making him unable to heed his colleague's advice in time to keep his position. Joe's client was elevated to CEO by the board, in large part because his disciplined practice of self-awareness was reflected in a comprehensive assessment by his peers and direct reports as well as by the search firm the board hired.

However gifted and capable we are, none of us can wish away the blinders placed on our awareness by the default limitations of our human minds and brains. Over time these blinders become the single most critical limits to our capacity to continually grow and excel as leaders. This is why we talk about exceptional leadership being an "inside job." The filter through which we process everything—our experiences, interactions, information—is *us*. If our filter isn't letting information in or is adding or distorting information, there is no way we're going to have a good assessment of the situation. It isn't just which proverbial lens we are looking through but how clean and intact it is that determines our clarity of awareness.

As leaders, our awareness—in general and as self-awareness in particular—is our most valuable instrument. If it's blocked by a bias or preconception or it's stuck in one mode, it's influencing the situation and we're not fully aware. We're not going to be able to see many angles or hear other points of view. If we want to arrive at our full potential in business or life, we must expand our awareness. One way to do this is to objectively look not just at the information we're taking in but at *how* we're taking it in, because if we don't check our biases, it's like we're putting the wrong starting point into our GPS, and we won't end up where we want to be, regardless of the intelligence we bring to bear on the matter. What makes boundless leadership different from conventional leadership is that it allows us to observe, check, and adjust what our minds are doing at any given moment. Being able to assess how we take information in, continually fine-tuning our instrument, requires developing what we call attentional flexibility or metacognition—that is, applying equal attention to what we're facing and to how our minds are operating.

METACOGNITION: THE CAPACITY FOR SELF-AWARENESS

The process of metacognition means stepping back and seeing not just what's in front of us but how we're engaging it—our mental state. This allows us to clean the lens of our awareness and reset and align our healthy attentions to better "see" and meet a situation.

If, for instance, we're going through a major personal or business transition, and our bias from early life or past adult experience predisposes us to be risk-averse, being highly self-aware of that bias and when it's affecting our judgment could make all the difference. One of Joe's clients who's an investor developed his self-awareness to understand that his conditioned fear of failure biases him to sell stocks prematurely when the market is volatile, causing him to leave the elusive profit on the table. But in one recent case, he was overwhelmed with personal setbacks and allowed his fear-based leanings to define his thinking, causing him to lose 80 percent of an upswing in the value of a trade. In his case, self-awareness was a skill he was developing, one that was still susceptible to being affected by day-to-day conditions. In times of overwhelm, his intention to compensate for his bias was not strong enough to keep him on point. With determination and consistent practice, eventually his self-awareness became more of a trait, unaffected by the prevailing winds.

This is but one example of how the essential mechanism of metacognitive self-awareness is flexibility—being able to widen our lens out and shift attention to the big picture, which may hold key data about our biased frame of reference or about other possibilities we've shortsightedly overlooked. If this particular client had been able to maintain his metacognitive view rather than take action from his narrowed and biased perspective, he would have secured greater profits. Another key dimension of metacognitive self-awareness is that it allows the mind to tolerate complexity, even the cognitive dissonance of holding seemingly opposing facts and variables within an expanded, inclusive awareness. This capacity allows us to get a much clearer view of things as they are while simultaneously expanding our perspective as new, even contradictory evidence appears.

To use a tech analogy, think of metacognition as a system that supports optimal data gathering. If you're trying to make the clearest decisions, you absolutely want clean data; you don't want it to be narrowed, skewed, or biased by a preconception about the data you're going to get or what it means. Beyond that, you want to be sure you're getting the full benefit of the largest possible scope of the data—that you're able to receive as large a quantity of data as possible—that is, big data. The logic is the same if you're a scientist seeking findings that are significant and reliable. You want to gather the results of an experiment as objectively and as comprehensively as possible.

What may be surprising is that it's possible for us as leaders and as humans, given the right principles and practices, to push the limits of our natural intelligence, our mind's capacity for observing the world and our place in it, so that we can understand things more cleanly and systematically than we normally might. As boundless leaders, metacognition allows us to push our capacity for self-awareness much further, so we're reaching the full scope of what is happening in any given situation—with fewer or even no unseen biases or limitations.

When we reach a point of self-awareness, we can take the next step. We don't just gather clean data; we objectively analyze it and act upon it. When we change the quality of our input and the way we process information, not only does our perspective expand and change, but we see more clearly and completely what can be changed in our organization or in any given situation. Metacognitive awareness or open awareness practice creates that capacity to accept what is and to be with it, without bias or reactivity. It allows us to hold the complexity of what we've learned, becoming fully creative in how we interpret and act upon it.

From a business perspective there is a clear connection between the strength of our metacognition, power of our self-awareness, quality of the decisions we make, and impact of our planning and execution. In fact, the most meaningful leverage that comes from greater awareness is not taking in cleaner, bigger data, but making a cleaner, clearer, more encompassing assessment, and hence better decisions and implementations. Whenever we make a decision, we implicitly assume a host of assessments, but we've been taught to think of our decisions as based on external information, objective data, and real-world inputs. As boundless leaders, we work to shift that process inward, using mindful insight to reveal, check, and adjust those implicit assessments from the inside out.

Think about how common it is for businesses to be in the midst of a go/no-go decision like invest or pass, release or postpone, or commit to one platform over another. Those discussions, based on the same facts and analyses can still generate vehement disagreements. The disparity is not in what the data suggests but rather in the more personal and conditioned value system that underlies the conversation. From our experience, the majority of the friction, healthy or not, that builds consensus among a group is sourced from one person's unspoken bias to minimize risk versus another's desire to maximize opportunity. It is easy to see that if our preferences were not implicit, unconscious biases but within our scope of self-awareness and explicitly articulated, better decisions could be made faster.

That's where the "inside job" of leadership comes in. The assessments that matter most aren't our explicit assessments of external data somebody else gives us but the implicit assessments of internal data we process (often unconsciously) within ourselves. This first leverage is the fundamental shift from conventional leadership to boundless leadership.

NEGATIVITY BIAS REDUX

The biggest obstacle and key limitation to self-awareness is our negativity bias—our instinctive tendency to cling to the worst-case scenario or grasp at short-term gain in situations of uncertainty, challenge, and stress. It's an evolutionary default state. For survival reasons, we are five to ten times more concerned with the negative than with the positive, and we stay that way unless we learn to flick that switch.

We evolved our negativity bias for good reason. Those of our ancestors who worried more were likelier to survive. But now that we've eliminated most of the dangers we evolved to survive, that bias becomes one of the greatest obstacles to making accurate assessments and feeling appropriately positive in our work and lives. When we're not self-aware, we're not able to self-correct for our negativity bias and unconsciously close ourselves off to what's good in ourselves, other people, and the situations we face.

The good news is that we have the basic flexibility to bring awareness and balance to our minds and lives here and now. We all have the natural ability to override our biases and to make the appropriate shifts at all levels of our being—mind, heart, and body.

The hitch here is that we must intentionally learn to notice our default negativity settings and disarm our survival mode before we can shift into what we call thriving mode. We must consciously learn to clear our awareness and be comfortable in our vulnerability if we're going to open our minds, hearts, and bodies to becoming self-aware, compassionate, boundless leaders. This is why a critical aspect of being a boundless leader (or an able leader of any kind) is agility of mind or attentional flexibility.

THE POWER OF ATTENTION

Through our understanding of neuroplasticity we've come to recognize how the mind and the brain develop through use and how the repeated focus of attention stimulates the growth of states and traits within our mind and nervous system. When we reflect on this powerful new science, we see that attention may be the most critical part of the apparatus of our minds *and* our brains.

This is where the training of attention—the many practices we share in this book—becomes so important, because the only way we can shift out of our default settings and their negativity bias toward greater self-awareness is by conscious control of attention. Remember, our negativity bias comes standard; if our attention muscles are weak, our minds and brains get stuck expecting worst cases or assuming a scarcity of goods. Unless we consciously train our attention and direct it to self-awareness, our minds automatically take the good for granted, gloss over it, and fail to dwell long enough on the positive to let it register and install. The most critical part of the power of training attention and developing clarity is to boost our natural capacity to notice our mind at work and use self-awareness to help it work better. And the most critical piece of self-correction is to expose and reverse our negativity bias by practicing shifting our attention from worst-case fears and scarcity thinking to a robust capacity to register the good in the world around us and in ourselves. That basic ability to shift attention from survival biases to thriving optimism and open-mindedness is what empowers our minds to recognize, own, and access the boundless untapped potential in ourselves and others. This is one of the reasons mindful attention training is the basic practice we recommend for the discipline of mind. Even your first small steps in training attention will help you recognize when you're stuck in the negative and get unstuck from it so that you can shift your mind to the positive. The more you train, the more you'll incrementally shift the balance.

On the one hand, this is as simple as the "objects are closer than they appear" warning on many side-view mirrors; there is a bias, adjust. Yet it's one of the most obstinate habits of mind. If our clients are describing a negative experience, they use terms of always and forever, as if this unwanted outcome were inevitable, just a question of time. If they are conveying a positive outcome, they mitigate and lessen its value with thoughts like "I got lucky" or "I should've done better" or "I'm not sure I can do it again." This is not a question of confidence or humility; it's a core issue about overcoming our ingrained habits of negativity, so we can lead from the place of what is possible rather than what could possibly go wrong.

We've all heard that one of the critical aspects of being a good leader, never mind a boundless leader, is agility of mind. But the agility it takes to change our thinking given new external data doesn't hold a candle to the agility we gain by becoming more self-aware. If you're not self-aware, you're not able to self-correct. Picture the people around a conference table at a meeting. Each sees their own agenda—What about the budget? Why won't they see my idea? When can I go to lunch?—and often discussions run parallel instead of toward a decision or a conclusion. Being able to shift perspective and see the whole is attentional flexibility in action. But we won't be able to shift as long as we stay unwittingly stuck in our biased agenda and point of view. The capacity to shift adroitly is most important not in terms of shifting our strategy or execution but in terms of shifting who we really are—that is, when it comes to our short- and long-term development as leaders. If we can watch how we're able to develop awareness over time we're able to direct our attention toward those qualities that are going to empower us to be more effective as leaders or humans. This conscious self-regulation is about being able to direct ourselves like the conductor of an orchestra toward the qualities that bring out the best in us and in everyone around us. It is akin to the work Carol Dweck popularized around growth versus fixed mindsets. Without self-awareness to notice and adjust the factory settings that no longer serve us, we will be incapable of performing necessary upgrades and adapting to the conditions at hand, rendering not only our mindsets but our capacity for growth and improvement limited and fixed.

Once we approach the conversation about mind in terms of our and others' human development, the next big theme to consider, especially as leaders, is the impact of the fact that our minds can be trained and our brains can be sculpted. As we've discussed, neuroplasticity and the importance of this research to leaders show that where we put our attention drives the engine of plasticity and neural change.

This is because the mind isn't a solid thing that is living or sitting somewhere but a dynamic, fluid energy and information musculature that can grow and develop special abilities if we attend to and repeatedly practice them, like the muscle training that athletes and musicians rely on through attention and repetition to perfect their performance. It is the same focused creation of new neural pathways that can affect who we are and how we show up on a consistent basis. This understanding of the plasticity of the mind and our capacity to train the qualities we want and need is the bottom line when it comes to the discipline of mind. We may be familiar with certain states of mind or habits—reacting, thinking, feeling, responding—but the mind itself as a pure natural capacity and our highest intelligence can take many forms. The quality of mind, especially when consciously guided and shaped by trained attention, is the cutting edge of our evolution as human beings and the gateway to accessing and embodying boundless leadership.

The good news is that when it comes to attention, we can develop the metacognitive awareness and self-awareness we need by cultivating our mind's natural capacity for clarity in the here and now. That's why, in boundless leadership, we cultivate clarity as the core competency in the discipline of mind.

7 MAKING BETTER DECISIONS

The Synergy of Self-Awareness and Clarity

If you think about it, a business's success can be defined as the net of all its good decisions—the more good decisions we make, the more successful we are. The implication is plain: the more we can improve our capacity to make sound judgments and good decisions, the better we'll do as leaders, and not incidentally, as human beings. But what makes for more accurate judgments and better decisions?

Inside of decision-making, the competency that is crucial is clarity of mind. We define clarity as the capacity to see things precisely as they are, not filtered through distorting lenses of clinging to what we want, avoiding what we fear, mistaking our preconceptions for reality, or not paying attention in the here and now. However simple the term sounds, clarity of mind is difficult to reach and sustain because we frequently encounter the following five obstacles:

1 Negativity bias
2 Distraction
3 Fatigue
4 Misperception
5 Attachment to outcome

THE STICKINESS OF NEGATIVITY BIAS

When it comes to obstacles to clarity, it's important to talk not only about the habituation of the mind to go toward the negative, but to understand how sticky that negativity is. When presented with a choice, positivity slips but negativity sticks. Our instinctive tendency is to cling to the worst-case scenario or grasp at short-term gain in situations of uncertainty, challenge, and stress as opposed to the (often equally or more likely) best-case scenario.

DISTRACTION

The second obstacle to clarity, distraction, is defined as "something that prevents someone from giving full attention to something else." With the advent of the Internet and the many devices that deliver it to us and connect us with each other, that "something else" has increased exponentially over the past few decades. Attention is task dependent but myriad studies, especially those by marketing companies and web architects, have shown a continuing decrease in the amount of time we can focus on a single thing. Our ability to pay attention is diminishing and constantly challenged by everything from unfiltered data to beeps when spam email arrives. If distracted drivers can't see the road ahead of them, neither can distracted leaders.

To give you a sense of how this issue is escalating, early studies demonstrated that ten years ago the average adult could fully focus on one task for about twelve seconds, but by 2018 the average adult's focus was down to eight seconds. In contrast with this, many reports cite the average length of concentration on one detail by a goldfish as nine seconds! This is a vivid illustration of how dangerously low our ability to focus has deteriorated in relation to how distracted we are. One of the beautiful things about the boundless leadership practices is how they help us restore and enhance our ability to focus—they're the opposite of distraction.

FATIGUE

The third obstacle to clarity is fatigue—foggy, slow, clouded attention that is neither clear nor incisive or precise. We know when we're tired, our minds tend to get drowsy and dull, so fatigue, especially cumulative or chronic fatigue, frequently gets in the way of clarity. This is why getting tired has such a negative effect on our ability to make accurate judgments and good decisions. Studies of professionals in decision-making roles like doctors, judges, and pilots[6] show that the efficiency and accuracy of decisions are adversely impacted by fatigue. Similarly, the collateral cost of fatigue on clarity is that when we're tired and prone to mistakes, we may instinctively avoid making decisions, especially weighty or complex ones.

Fatigue also diminishes our ability to self-regulate, to see the big picture, be aware, and wisely manage our moods or motivations, even when others are impacted by our decisions. Think about it: we know how hard it is to resist that cookie when we're tired. As for the impact on others, Jonathan Levav, a professor of business at Columbia University, and his colleagues studied a group of judges and the outcomes of their rulings in relation to when they'd had a break. It turns out that "you are anywhere between two and six times as likely to be released if you're one of the first three prisoners considered versus the last three prisoners considered."[7] At the beginning of their shift, judges are more inclined toward a favorable decision up to 65 percent of the time, but as more cases are presented and the shift continues, that percentage decreases to almost zero. Two takeaways: (1) fatigue is a major obstacle to clear thinking so prioritize rest and self-care, and (2) if you ever have to appear in court, try to arrange to go first.

MISPERCEPTION

The fourth obstacle to clarity is misperception—our inability to see things correctly and for what they truly are or our misunderstanding of what is going on in a given situation. It starts when we make assumptions and interpretations. We reify these as truths or facts. This is the most insidious, and most difficult, impediment.

Misperception comes in all sizes and shapes, but one of the most perilous manifestations is fueled by our deep-seated need to focus on validating our thinking—positive or negative—rather than being open to discovering something new. This becomes especially disempowering when we accept someone else's comments or actions about a situation or ourselves as an objective reflection of our performance, devoid of their biases, prejudices, or state of mind. This was made especially clear while working with one of our client organizations. On a Monday morning Elazar met with the company's CEO for a coaching session before hearing a presentation from the senior vice president. Elazar noticed the CEO's focus wasn't on the business at hand but rather his troubled marriage and impending divorce—the issue consumed his psyche and emotional outlook. The afternoon coaching session included a call with the senior vice president that focused on the presentation she'd made to the CEO earlier in the day. She and Elazar had spent several sessions preparing for it, covering content, delivery, and especially the negative impact of her low self-esteem. "It was the worst presentation I ever made," she reported with disappointment and shame. "I should have worked on it more over the weekend. I shouldn't have slacked off." From Elazar's balcony view of the full situation, he knew clearly that the cause of the poor reception was fundamentally the mindset of the CEO and not the content or delivery of the material. Despite progress over the previous months to enhance her self-esteem, the SVP's unspoken expectation that she could never match the CEO's energy or intelligence stood no chance of countering his foul mood, and so the SVP misperceived herself as the source of the issue, incorrectly reaffirming her sense of inadequacy. Misperception of a situation can not only lead us to a bad decision but can often reinforce a core negative belief about who we are.

Misperception of a situation is bad enough, but it can get worse. We are all vulnerable to conditioned biases about people with different backgrounds or experience—differences in race, gender, class, or culture—or about anybody who has a different style of communication or self-expression. When we interact with others, we can become more focused on who we think they are than on who they truly are or what they're saying. This is one of the fundamental pitfalls of leadership: jumping to preconceived judgments of others without all the data. This misperceiving is one of the most toxic things you can do. As a leader your job must include growth, not only of revenues and profits, but of people and possibilities. A fixed view of who people are or what a particular gender, race, or age group can accomplish not only stunts growth but eats away at the fabric of trust, hope, and inspiration that are key for decent leadership, never mind boundless leadership. To be clear, we are not suggesting that you ignore underperformance or lower your standards of excellence but rather to perceive reality clearly as it is and not taint it with what you expect or want it to be.

Misperception is damaging in its impact and far-reaching in its consequences, yet it's so difficult to overcome because it's insidious— often we don't know we're blinded by bias and preconceived notions of what is or is not, what should and shouldn't be. While decisiveness is often valued in leaders, conviction can work against us as well as for us. Misperception is the converse of clear thinking and will definitely not help you in becoming a respected or strong leader. Ray Dalio, the founder of Bridgewater Associates, the largest hedge fund company in the world, has spoken in many interviews about how his success is a direct result of his meditative practice, because in his practice he can create a separation between what he would like to happen versus what is actually happening—misperception versus correct perception. When a leader constantly works to check and correct misperception, they're able to bring deep and continuous clarity to the process of making decisions.

ATTACHMENT TO OUTCOME

We become so attached to the outcome, so focused on the results we want and how we think things should be, that we can't see things as they are, making us unable to think or see our real options clearly. Often, our expectations of a desired outcome become so fixed we are unable to communicate and connect with people who are affecting our expectations, and we become removed from the truth and clarity we need to make good decisions. Although such rigid insistence on getting what we want is often vaunted as a key trait of leadership, the facts show that it can be a huge liability, which is why it's the final obstacle to clarity.

The negative impact of our attachment to outcome on decision-making has been quantified in research done by the Department of Organisational Behaviour at INSEAD and the Management Department at the Wharton School of the University of Pennsylvania. They studied two groups: one comprised of people who were taught a mindfulness meditation practice involving focusing on the sensation of breath and the other (control) group instructed to think of whatever came to mind. The researchers presented all the test subjects with a decision-making problem, asking them to imagine they ran a printing company and had bought a printing press for $200,000. What if, a week later, their competitor went out of business, and they could acquire their press that was more technologically advanced, faster, and better than theirs for only $10,000? However, they could not sell their current press. Would they purchase it? What the researchers were looking at is something called "sunk cost" bias, meaning that when we make an investment, when we have a fixed attachment to an outcome, we start thinking differently and don't see the facts as they are. In the group that did not meditate, 44 percent of them said they would buy the cheaper newer press, but the majority said they would not. Among the group of meditators, 78 percent said they would buy the better press—that's almost double the odds of making the better business decision! What happened? Attachment to the desired outcome fueled a bias that kept people from seeing and assessing the facts around a key decision clearly. Specifically, among the non-meditators, their bias to protect the investment they already made in an expensive press and dismiss new information put them at a disadvantage with the meditating subjects who were able to have a clearer understanding of how their emotions affected their decisions, due to the practice of open awareness meditation.

WAYS OF TRANSFORMATION

If you're able to confront and work through even one or two of these obstacles enough to diminish them, you'll feel the impact of increased clarity on your leadership. However, there's no reason to believe you cannot diminish or even eradicate all five. This may seem a superhuman feat, but a regular practice of training attention can empower you to consciously regulate and shape your qualities of mind, heart, and body. This is not only possible but predictable! In doing so you can spark a significant transformation in your leadership and decision-making within and beyond business.

This transformation is exactly what a client named Jocelyn experienced. When she started working with us, she had one foot out the door of her company. The new CEO had a different style of management and sprinkled in her own team of senior managers with a strong sense of favoritism toward them. The need for Jocelyn to "get out and save her soul" as she put it was juxtaposed against her expected windfall in assets from the company's exit strategy that was about eighteen months away. The most difficult part for Jocelyn was working with her colleague, "Nick the nemesis" as she referred to him, the CEO's obvious confidant. Nick was comfortable being aggressive, taking credit, shifting blame, and undermining Jocelyn. This was especially painful as he wasn't especially competent and had recently received a share of Jocelyn's responsibilities. Nonetheless, Jocelyn was intent on using the experience with the CEO and Nick as an opportunity for personal growth and took her boundless leadership training to heart. Her biggest effort was directed toward overcoming misperception and attachment to outcome. Through greater clarity and self-awareness, she was able to see more clearly what she was doing to deepen the rift and solidify the "nemesis versus angel" lens through which she saw the situation. She worked on her intentions (something we will further illuminate in the application of C.A.T. at the end of chapter 13) and was able to release the dominant intention of "protecting herself from the enemy" that defined their interactions.

Over time, Jocelyn was able to better see the stress and pressures Nick was under and even how his lack of competence was tormenting him, especially as the go-to manager of their demanding CEO. Jocelyn loosened her attachment to the conditioned need to receive only praise and to achieve a tremendous amount by a certain age. Instead, she realized that she could own her process, her integrity, and how she showed up for herself and others; being outcome-focused had undermined that. She was able to replace her survival-based intention of "us versus them" with a more growth-oriented one of being of service in her interactions with Nick. Not only did this shift in approach help Jocelyn "save her soul" without leaving the company, it had a positive effect on Nick as his style did not endear him to anyone else either. In time, Nick became one of Jocelyn's strongest allies.

THE FOUR QUALITIES OF MIND

Jocelyn's experience in the account above is neither unique nor exceptional; it's a dependable outcome of developing the four key qualities of mind that overcome the five obstacles and contribute to growing the competency of clarity and thus the trait of self-awareness:

1 Presence: the capacity to feel connected and attuned to one's body and lived experience of self and world in the moment, here and now

2 Balance: the capacity to maintain an equilibrium in which we respond (rather than react) to the full range of pleasant, unpleasant, and neutral experience

3 Unbiased awareness: the capacity to bring a clear, open awareness to every aspect of our experience in the moment, without our instinctive biases of clinging to what seems desirable, aversion toward what seems threatening, and inattention to what seems neutral

4   Discernment: the capacity to engage unbiased awareness to perceive more freshly and clearly the reality of our experience and the nature of our motivation in any given moment.

We will explore each quality in depth as we further investigate the discipline of mind.

8 MAKING THE SHIFT FROM STRESS-DRIVEN SURVIVAL TO THRIVING IN CLARITY AND SELF-AWARENESS

Once we realize the enormous benefits of training in clarity and self-awareness, and we take in the empowering new science that shows how our minds, brains, and bodies have a natural capacity for overcoming default blocks and limitations and developing our full potential, the next question is: How does this work? *How do we understand and foster that transformation?*

First, take a step back. We've talked about the connection between the competency of clarity and the trait of self-awareness, but what exactly is their relationship? Psychologists often describe the process of mind/body learning in terms of the interplay of states and traits. We enter a specific state of mind, brain, or body based on a range of specific factors or conditions. For example, when we first learn to ride a bike, we might start by watching others, then get a feel for the bike by sitting on the seat and balancing with our legs. Whether we learn with training wheels or a steadying grown-up hand, we then try to get the feel of how to balance while gliding or even pedaling. Eventually, we get into the zone—a state of mental presence and physical balance that allows us to stay steady as we pedal, steer, and ride. That zone is what we call a mind/body state—a moment-to-moment experience of a specific competence or capacity we didn't know we had until we accessed it through learning.

The next big stage in the process of learned change is repetition. If we practice entering that state repeatedly and often enough—getting on the bike frequently—our minds, brains, and bodies take hold of that state and "install it" as a stable trait—a condition wherein the competence or capacity we learned is now there by default, so we can access it naturally, with minimal thought or effort. In the case of a bicycle, we can ride without thinking about riding.

The relationship between clarity and self-awareness is the interplay between a moment-to-moment mind/body state and a newly installed mind/body *trait*. Developing clarity in any one moment is like standing on a threshold that can lead to a new way of being based in the trait of self-awareness. And when self-awareness becomes second nature—a lasting trait—clarity becomes readily and naturally accessible to us on a moment-to-moment basis.

It all sounds so easy, so where do you start? The plain fact is that despite our natural capacity for change and our vast potential for vital capacities like clarity and self-awareness, most of us start by constantly bumping up against the obstacles to clarity. This is no accident but a humbling reality built into the human condition. Clarity and self-awareness are the outcomes we seek in the discipline of mind. Because they don't come easily, they need to be learned, practiced, and installed in much the same way as riding a bicycle. To understand why and how we need to work the discipline of mind, we must step back even further and take the longest possible view of our nature.

SURVIVAL AND SOCIAL MODES

We've seen how evolution equipped our ancestors' and our human brains with basic operating modes for the two key conditions we routinely encountered in the wild. To prepare us to combat imminent physical threats, we evolved a survival mode that keeps our minds, brains, and bodies locked into the self-protective states of stress and trauma. On the other hand, to prime us to take full advantage of conditions of safety and abundance, conditions we eventually learned to create via social cooperation, we evolved a thriving mode that primes our minds, brains, and bodies for social engagement, social learning, and cooperation. For better or worse, these two modes are as incompatible as forward and reverse in a car's transmission.

In the context of boundless leadership, it comes as no surprise that these two evolutionary modes support radically different applications of attention. The survival mode locks our minds and brains into a search-and-find application wherein our attention is inevitably projected outside ourselves—either scanning with hypervigilance or fixated in tunnel vision—onto anything we experience as potentially life-threatening or lifesaving. Once we're in this mode—which is our reptilian evolutionary default—it doesn't matter whether our attention is scanning like a wide-angle lens or narrowly focused like a telephoto. In both cases, attention in this mode is highly filtered and polarized by biases and externally fixated. In other words, it's as far as possible from clarity and self-awareness.

In contrast, attention in thriving mode functions more in a learn-and-choose application that embraces our outer and inner worlds equally, openly exploring and selectively savoring whatever we see as enriching or beneficial. In this mode—which requires our conscious assent and intent—it doesn't matter whether our attention is inclusive like a wide-angle lens or focused like a telephoto, in both cases it tends to be at once radically open, nimbly flexible, and equally focused on both the inner and outer worlds. In other words, our attention is naturally supportive of both unbiased clarity and complete self-awareness.

What this evolutionary backstory tells us is that clarity and self-awareness are not new skills we can learn in our default mind/body state like we might learn baking, statistics, or golf. They are what some researchers call state-specific capacities—that is, capacities more easily accessed and mastered in a mind/body state outside our default survival mode. This helps explain the stubborn nature of the obstacles to clarity, which in one way or another are all rooted in the survival-driven biology of stress and trauma. It demonstrates why training our mind in clarity and self-awareness is not a trivial challenge. Because it requires us to take on a much greater challenge: shifting out of our default survival mode driven by the fossil fuel of stress and trauma into our thriving mode, sustained by the green energy of safe connection and social engagement. This is why understanding how to develop clarity and self-awareness requires us to understand the basic science of stress and stress reduction. Fortunately, decades of research have elucidated the general facts we must grasp to know how to start working on training clarity and self-awareness.

FOUNDATIONS OF TRAINING

To begin with, we need to review the basic findings of stress research we covered in part 1. Those findings start with the understanding that the majority of harm done by external stressors is also—in a negative sense—an inside job. Over 80 percent of the impact stress has on our minds, brains, and bodies depends on the habitual ways we interpret and react to external challenges we experience as stressful. As we said in chapter 2, the model we adopted for boundless leadership, based on the work of Sheldon Cohen,[8] views our stress-reactive habits as part of a cycle of stress and trauma that has four main phases. These involve a chicken-and-egg cycle of mutually reinforcing habits at different levels of our mind, brain, body, and ultimately life. To refresh your memory, they are as follows:

1 Cognitive appraisal
2 Emotional reaction
3 Visceral reflex
4 Cumulative impact

Perceptual stress habits are those habits of worst-case thinking or imagination that overestimate how threatening a stressor is and simultaneously underestimate our capacity to effectively cope with it.

Emotional stress habits are distressing feelings and emotional memories of fear, anger, isolation, and shame that make us feel socially overwhelmed or isolated, aggressive, defensive, helpless, or powerless.

Visceral stress habits are the instinctive reflexes to fight, fly, faint, or freeze that grip our body when we sense ourselves in imminent danger of either social or physical harm.

Lifestyle stress habits are day-to-day embodied ways of being, acting, living, and relating that over time add to our feeling burdened, overwhelmed, unsafe, and burned out, as if we're merely surviving from crisis to crisis, trauma to trauma.

We also used our favorite illustration of this cycle: overreacting to a deadline imposed by your boss or board. How often and how quickly do you react to a deadline with a worst-case scenario with thoughts like *That's insane, I'll never make that. They are trying to ruin me. I know I'll be fired. Without this job I'll run through my savings and then what will happen to me and to my family? I might as well die.* Locked in such a reactive cycle of escalating negativity, a deadline becomes a death threat, and we have the emotional, visceral, and behavioral damage to prove it.

On the other hand, in the bullish culture of modern leadership, the stress may come from a stress-reactive attachment to outcome based on scarcity thinking. You may have heard yourself say things like, "If we don't jump on this opportunity, it will pass or our competitors will, so it's all hands-on-deck, drop everything else, full speed ahead. I don't care what it costs. There are no excuses. I won't take no for an answer because failure is not an option." However essential this drive or frenzy seems to be in your work life, make no mistake that it's sending an alarm that locks your mind, heart, and body into survival mode—giving your system the message that your life and safety are at risk and hang in the balance. When our stress-reactive habits are activated by threat perception or scarcity thinking, our attention is locked in its search-and-find application, activating one or more of the obstacles to clarity and blocking our ability to access or train self-awareness, rendering us unable to fully meet the challenge at hand.

How can we stop or reverse the cycle of stress and trauma? The good news is we can slowly but systematically expose and unlearn the habits of stress that lock us into survival mode. By consciously exercising our capacity for positive neuroplasticity, we can shift our default mind/body state away from the self-protective biology of stress and trauma toward the socially engaged biology of thriving. This deep transformation helps support incremental shifts in our attention, activating the learn-and-choose application that empowers us to access and grow alternative habits of thriving, namely, the qualities that support and sustain the mind's competency for clarity and our trait of self-awareness. This need for deep transformation helps explain why, when it comes to the discipline of mind, the rubber meets the road in the practice of attention training.

DEVELOPING AND TRAINING ATTENTION

To train our attention and develop the discipline of mind we must shift out of stress-reactive survival mode into well-being and thriving. To do this, we recommend the contemplative practice of mindfulness. The popular notion of mindfulness gaining ground in recent decades suggests that it simply involves paying attention without judgment to our experience in the present moment. However, the actual practice of mindfulness is more ambitious and complex. It is about learning to pay conscious attention to our experience in the here and now, but in a specific way—without stress-related bias or reactivity—and only as a starting point. In boundless leadership we think of mindfulness practice as training all the attentional muscles that support the discipline of mind, the discipline that gives us the strength we need to start shifting our default state of consciousness from stress-driven self-enclosure to boundless clarity and self-awareness. And to access and strengthen our clarity and self-awareness, mindful attention training builds our mental muscles through four key steps we introduced in chapter 2—body mindfulness, nonreactive mindfulness, mindful awareness, and mindful insight—each of which helps us counter one of the phases of stress and develop one of four qualities that support clarity and self-awareness.

How does this work? To begin with, in body mindfulness we learn to pay attention in a centered and intentional way, overcoming distraction by consciously focusing and refocusing on our breathing body. This practice makes us more able to catch and break perceptual stress habits and to cultivate genuine presence.

In nonreactive mindfulness, we move on to train attention on our implicit bias and emotional reactivity—including negativity bias and attachment to outcome—by focusing on how we feel and react to our body's natural sensitivity to pleasant, unpleasant, or neutral sensations. This practice makes us more able to calm and break emotional stress reactions and to cultivate equanimity or balance.

After developing these two narrowly focused lenses of attention, we open the scope of our training to two wide-angle lenses. In the third form of mindfulness practice we train a transparent, spacious attention, exposing and correcting our unconscious misperceptions by focusing and refocusing on an unusual state of radically open awareness. This practice eventually helps us grow more able to calm and release the visceral stress reflexes that anchor implicit bias and to cultivate a relaxed and radically open quality of mind we call unbiased awareness.

Finally, by focusing on examining the day-to-day workings of our mind and life by practicing mindful insight directed at everything that passes through open awareness, we gain the power to unlearn stress-driven lifestyles and cultivate healthy discernment as a quality of being and leading. This capacity to change the course of our lives empowers us to shift away from the dirty energy of stress and toward the clean energy of well-being, overcoming fatigue and feeding our natural capacity for flow.

These four practices comprise the basic training we need to transform our minds from self-protective and stuck in survival mode to socially engaged and nimble in thriving mode. In particular, we see how each practice of mindfulness helps counteract one of the four factors of stress that drive the five obstacles to clarity, while simultaneously cultivating one of the four qualities of mind—presence, balance, unbiased awareness, and discernment—that support our moment-to-moment competency for clarity, which eventually consolidates the powerful leadership trait of self-awareness.

9 PRESENCE

The Brain Is a Social Organ

After exploring the obstacles to clarity and self-awareness and the negative impact of the innate setting of survival mode, we can investigate the qualities that cultivate the competency and traits of a boundless leader's mind, starting with presence. Presence is what sustains the transparent openness and flexibility of attention that yields optimal clarity and self-awareness. Presence means showing up fully conscious of where we are here and now, not where we were or where we might be someday.

As leaders and particularly as people in business, we tend to think of presence as power, confidence, charisma, strength, and maybe even forcefulness, but that is only one facet of presence—a more guarded, fearful, or forced presence with all the energy focused outward. Presence from a boundless leadership perspective is sourced from within, coming from a place of deep connection to self, making it simultaneously more open and aware in a holistic way. This engaged and embodied inner presence is becoming an increasingly crucial factor in leadership as the complexity and speed of the outer environment reaches a point of overload.

Outwardly focused, stress-driven presence leads to a distraction from the inner world—ours and those of others—which leaves us in a superficial and disconnected mode where we're communicating with each other without being fully aware. In this mode, we often mindlessly repeat what we said, check our phones, or show other signs of inattention. It makes the people around us feel they're not important or connected to us, and this perpetual distraction made worse by constant multitasking continues to become normalized in our work environments. How often have you found yourself in a meeting with most of your attention focused on something else? The skin-deep, stressed brand of presence—trying to show how busy or indispensable we are without really showing up—is a lack of true presence. Often how those around us experience that mode of being is "This is not a friendly or productive environment," or "I don't feel safe or valued around this person because I clearly don't matter."

That old model of presence—reflecting a surface power play of dominance or compliance—clearly has the impact of evoking a partial presence in others that shows up in the annual Gallup studies on employee engagement.[9] In most of those studies, engagement repeatedly tops out at around a third of employees with fully two-thirds remaining unengaged to some degree, because who would want to be part of a system where they are not seen as real human beings who matter?

Ironically, conventional leadership presence comes from a deep inner place of fear, shame, or anger, leading to a need to cover up and protect. People can instantly tell the difference between forced or shame-based presence versus sincere, connected presence. There's nothing more powerful than when someone is ready, willing, and able to connect with us in a genuine manner. That sincere presence opens up the other person or the group and creates a resonance based on consistent cues of safety, acceptance, and connection.

The benefit of true presence isn't just its impact on others. By being able to focus on the here and now, not only are we able to bring our full capacities to bear, but those capacities can operate at higher levels. Imagine preparing for a crucial presentation. We create the content and flow and consider responses to objections and questions that might arise. That is helpful. Yet, how often, despite adequate preparation, do we leave a meeting feeling we should have answered a question differently or were blindsided by a situation we did not anticipate and could not adjust to? Many times the perfect award-winning response comes to us easily, but after the fact.

We've also experienced the opposite: the most insightful combination of words, delivered in the most appropriate tone and body language. The difference? Presence. Genuine presence gives us the ability to read the room and to adjust in real time, effortlessly. It is not based on our ability to anticipate and prepare but to process an array of information and access our inner knowing to respond most skillfully.

Beyond being more effective, real presence can be more natural and satisfying than forced presence, which involves work. To be fully present in mind and body and have the people around us sense that presence may require intention at first, but eventually it becomes a new normal and can feel more effortless. And if we're feeling more easefully and naturally present, this has an inevitable impact on those around us as well. Even a message of presence like, "I'm glad we're together for this meeting" can fundamentally shift the tone of the meeting.

Although in business, we tend not to call people out for distraction, being present ourselves and giving others permission to show up fully can have a radical impact. A parenting analogy comes to mind here. Lack of presence never works with kids. If you're checked out, the children in your care will notice and often exploit it or check out too. When you're present yourself, it's much easier to coax them to drop the distraction and connect with you.

Our capacity to connect with each other depends on creating an environment of safety that leads to engagement. Neuroscientists are learning that the brain is a social organ. What that means is that we did not evolve to compete with other humans but to link up in cooperative bonds and groups. While competition is part of human life, it still takes place within social contexts that assume a deeper cooperation—whether sports, politics, or even war. Contrary to the modern view of humans as individuals first, our brains are not at their best when we feel isolated and alone, but when we feel safely connected and socially engaged with a team, group, or community. In *The Polyvagal Theory: Neurophysiological Foundations of Emotions, Attachment, Communication, and Self-Regulation* neuroscientist Stephen W. Porges describes this overly self-interested and competitive style as reptilian, because it tends to be driven by the primal self-protective part of our brain we share with reptiles and all vertebrates—that is, by the antisocial imperatives of survival, fear, and control.

Reptilian-style leadership comes from a primitive system of social dominance, behavior in which threats of physical or social violence are used to intimidate, shame, and control others, such as those explicitly used by the military and the police. In business this usually shows up in the stereotype of bosses puffing themselves up by barking orders or growling threats, while "their" people cringe or react to please them without question or challenge. We know now that an organization run in this way is clunky and uninspiring compared to what Porges calls mammalian behavior—the way of being we cultivate in boundless leadership—everyone working and playing together, each individual bringing their best to the table and truly elevating the whole.

PRESENCE AND CLARITY

When it comes to how presence affects clarity, remember that clarity is the highest capacity of our new brain and the result of the primal, self-protective parts of our brain feeling safe enough to let the newer, more sociable parts of our brain lead. It's where our attention is most nimble and our consciousness is the most expansive, hence where we have the most flexible, fine-tuned engagement. But being in mammalian mode requires much more than just an absence of imminent danger. If we're not getting and giving messages of safety and connection, our nervous systems are not fully in mammalian mode but in a more frazzled, fractured, and self-limiting rut. Without a regular diet of safety cues, our brains default into survival mode, which involves fragmenting and internal blocking of our capacity for attention, clarity, and awareness.

Even when our minds seem highly active—referencing the past, busily interpreting the present, and projecting into the future—we are typically harboring an underlying fear of exclusion or disconnection, as in an anxiety daydream or mental horror movie. The first practice of mindful attention training—bringing the mind repeatedly to attend to the breath—helps us connect to the visceral reality of our breathing body right here and now. This deceptively simple exercise not only grounds our higher brain in our immediate embodied presence, it simultaneously offers consistent and vital cues of safety and connection to our bodies and lives—sending the message that all is well.

Most of the messages we receive when we pay attention to our bodies here and now are reassuring, in contrast with the messages we receive when our mind is on autopilot, operating in survival mode, and tainted by negativity bias. As you'll see, this practice of tuning in to and repeatedly breathing in the good news of being alive and well in the here and now will, over time, allow you to ground your mind and brain in reassurance, creating clarity, openness, and engagement as you'll be truly present.

In business dealings or in any relationship for that matter, the leverage for positive connection and impact is in this moment—one moment of presence at a time. More often than not, there is little or nothing we can do about the past. And the more we're preoccupied with the future, the less we're prepared to do anything meaningful about it because we're not fully showing up in the present. That's why the primary activity of the discipline of mind is training our attention to let go of the past and future, of all the challenging desires and fears we have about the world, and to reach into the most basic facts of our lives here and now by shifting our attention repeatedly away from all those abstractions back to the ground zero of our living, breathing body, here and now.

Try it.

Practice

LEVERAGE IS IN THIS MOMENT— BODY MINDFULNESS MEDITATION

1   Settle into a comfortable sitting or lying posture on a chair, cushion, yoga mat, or bed.
2   Turn your attention to the place in your body where you most sense your breathing.
3   When you get distracted or dull, keep patiently returning to where you sense the breath.
4   Focused on the breath, practice feeling present here and now.
5   Continue this practice for as long as you can without stress or fatigue—say, five to twenty minutes.
6   Return to the practice, ideally at a regular time and place, three to seven days a week.
7   Tune in to this practice for brief presence pauses when distracted or dull in daily life.

10 BALANCE

Developing True Confidence

Presence is related to balance in boundless leadership. The second quality in the discipline of mind, balance is a key factor supporting the competence of clarity. It involves an ongoing process and continuous challenge for leaders who want to stay connected to their strength, since it entails getting back on track when distracted, diverted, pumped up, or knocked down. Getting centered must be followed by *staying* centered, and becoming present and balanced over time requires the capacity to keep our center of gravity somewhere in the middle ground. But balance is not about a rigid, frozen, or blandly moderate stance. To the contrary, balance refers to the agility, nimbleness, or grace that allows us to catch ourselves when external or internal forces push us from one extreme to the other, allowing us to return to a more fluid, centered responsiveness that we think of as equanimity.

We all tend to speak about balance in our lives—being overwhelmed with work or not having time for family or ourselves—but here we're talking about balancing our state of mind. One day we close a big deal and get positive feedback, the next we find out part of our business took a big hit or our team or clients are justifiably upset. How do we avoid getting carried away by and attached to the highs or deflated and caught up in the lows? To stay in clarity, we must expose and remove the blinders of our default survival biases—exaggerating the negative on the one hand and clinging to the positive on the other—to avoid getting caught in extreme binary thinking and reactive emotions.

In fact, staying in clarity requires us to expose and remove even the insidious bias that subtle nuances don't matter—since they're neither black nor white—so we can clearly appreciate the shades of gray that may be the most significant features or context for what's going on in a leadership situation.

From a scientific perspective, our nervous systems evolved in part as a contrast enhancer to help us survive. Our minds are wired by default to enhance contrast and respond quickly: *Predator or friend? Poison or dinner? Danger or safety?* The binary and reactive logic of our nervous systems may be good for quick reflexes in life-or-death situations, but in most circumstances, it keeps us bouncing back and forth, making it hard to stay poised, mentally nimble, thoughtful, and nonreactive. Even when we're not constantly on the rebound, the polarizing nature of our survival mode typically blinds us to the nuances that, in our everyday civilized life, usually make all the difference.

When we work with clients, one of the metaphors we find helpful is the idea of riding a horse. When you're riding comfortably on your horse, you're telling the horse where to go, you're centered, you're balanced. When something knocks you off the horse and you've fallen, the horse drags you—you're no longer in control. Balance within the context of boundless leadership gives you that ability to stay in the saddle, rather than be at the mercy of the prevailing forces. We look for that sense of being centered, being balanced in that moment in time, otherwise we'll either not have an impact or we'll have the wrong impact.

There is a counterpart to this in the mindfulness and contemplative traditions where mind is described like the rider and the breath or the energy in the nervous system like the horse. Either way, the idea is that you need to stay connected to your animal, to the source of energy inside your body and your nervous system, to stay poised and modulated so that you don't get thrown by circumstance, and if you are, so that you can return to center quickly.

Apply this to the workplace. Imagine you rehearse a presentation with a colleague before you meet with your team and higher-ups. Your colleague supports your conclusion, affirms the facts, and tells you you're going to be great. However, in the formal presentation, not only does your colleague not support you, they challenge your process. Part of you wonders, *Why are they doing that? Didn't they agree with me earlier when our boss wasn't here?* You're thrown. If you stay off balance you might think, *Why are they sabotaging me? Should I be aggressive about it? Should I call them on it?* If you expend your energy wondering, *Why is this happening?* you'll lose control. There could be myriad reasons for their behavior, but the point is to redirect that energy back to what you came to do. Stay the course. Through balance you'll be better able to marshal your resources to address the situation in the present and not lose any power through dispersed energy.

Returning to the neuroscientific perspective, think about this in terms of the autonomic nervous system, the system that drives reactivity. It could be fight or flight if we feel alarmed or it could be faint or freeze if we feel more threatened and shut down. Those two parts of our system, which are based in the older, reptilian part of our brain, are designed to be extreme and rigid, not nimble. We're not reptiles, we're mammals, so we have newer wiring that's specifically designed to help modulate and calm the nervous system and give us greater control, to balance the older, extreme reactions so that we can navigate the world in a social, connected (as opposed to reactive) and constructive way.

That capacity to keep fine control over our nervous system is something that can be trained. Anyone who has mastered something—artists, athletes, leaders, healers—has an inner confidence and centering that is quietly calming the system and drawing on the energies that are needed in the doses that are required to not let circumstances drive them. You have probably seen this in leaders you admire—they are neither pushed into aggression nor flustered by challenges. Instead, they stay centered in their response and bring the appropriate energy to each situation. In most cases, this confidence didn't come without training. Yet, you can see the seeds of the capacity in most people. Even leaders who easily get distracted and overwhelmed can often override their mind's habit to scramble and fret when faced with a serious situation, so they can focus more fully on the critical issue.

The practice that cultivates this balance is what we call nonreactive mindfulness. It helps us go to the root of the reactivity in our system, our gut feelings that lurk below the surface yet, in a bottom-up process, trigger reactive emotions that push us into compulsive actions. These emotions range from getting irritable or angry when we're feeling sick and tired to getting obsessive and clingy when we are attracted to something that evokes excitement and desire. In a third, less obvious, case of reactivity, we are typically triggered into disconnecting or glossing over the subtle shades of gray between the polarized extremes, because a nervous system locked into survival mode acts as if we can't afford to pay attention to the neutral.

Nonreactive mindfulness practice was designed to help us face our sensitivities and not react to stimuli, instead bringing the mindful calming awareness we need to respond skillfully. If something is pleasant, we want to savor but not cling, not get too anxious. If something is unpleasant, we want to bear with or soothe the discomfort without aversion or anger. And we want to stay centered, balanced, and curious about the nuances in between—the majority of experiences that we have. When we're in the extreme places we lose valuable information that we need, and we lose the flexibility we need to be nimble and agile.

The following practice trains us to respond skillfully, going straight to the root of our reactivity rather than letting ourselves be gripped and pushed around by it before we're even aware. We've all had days when we woke up feeling unsafe, unwell, anxious, or unfulfilled but were so fixed on getting through our agenda that we only wound up facing our gut feelings later, after we'd gotten ourselves into trouble by blowing up, getting derailed by a compulsive craving, or just spacing out at crucial moments. We have evolved and been trained for the extreme—for flight or fight, friend or foe—but to find balance and support clarity, we must learn to loosen the tremendous grip of our survival mode and shift our sensitivity into the thriving mode of equanimity and balance.

Practice

LOOSENING THE HOLD OF THE EXTREME— NONREACTIVE MINDFULNESS

1   Settle into a comfortable sitting or lying posture on a chair, cushion, yoga mat, or bed.
2   Turn your attention to the place in your body where you most sense your breathing.
3   When you get distracted or dull, keep patiently returning to where you sense the breath.
4   Spread your awareness gradually throughout your whole breathing body.
5   Scan your whole body for areas of pleasant, unpleasant, and neutral sensations.
6   Release reactive clinging to pleasant, pushing away unpleasant, and ignoring the neutral.
7   Practice savoring the pleasant, soothing the unpleasant, and appreciating the neutral.
8   Return to the practice, ideally at a regular time and place, three to seven days a week.
9   Tune in to this practice to restore balance when you feel reactive in daily life.

11 UNBIASED AWARENESS

Escaping the Trap of Fixed Judgment

A leader's effectiveness will be diminished if they lack the capacity for unbiased awareness—the third quality of the discipline of mind that breeds clarity. Unbiased awareness is the ability to be present to reality as it is, free from preconceived ideas or programming, not swayed by polarizing positive or negative biases, attachment, or aversion, and not disconnected or distanced from the nuances and complexities of genuine experiences.

This leads to the question, How is unbiased awareness different from ordinary awareness? In ordinary awareness, we unconsciously filter our experience through implicit biases, innate and learned. We have a preconceived notion of how things should be—often based on wishful thinking or worst-case fears—and that notion becomes a filter that limits or removes the vital information we need, like the complex way people and things combine strengths and weaknesses, are constantly in flux, and are invariably relative and contextual. We see things in a biased way because we expect or desire a certain outcome, so we look for data that supports our point of view as opposed to seeing what is really going on and making our best decisions. In ordinary awareness we see things in a biased way because we hold negative views such as that people are limited or opportunities are scarce, and we only see those limits and downsides. These kinds of biases become ingrained in our biology and unconscious conditioning, so they can't be easily recognized or avoided. They're insidious, lurking like blinders or blind spots in our minds, and have a powerful effect on how we do business.

In our workshops and retreats we often ask participants to examine what they add to what they see or experience, to deconstruct the process to as fine a degree as possible. Often, their first insight is to remark on how ubiquitous their biases are. These include how often they have their minds made up *before* they have the interaction, how much of what they experienced was based on their previous encounter with an individual, and how their own moods, needs, and already-established agenda of what the exchange should be about impacted the encounter. Their second insight is usually the disheartening realization that they have the same level of negative bias toward themselves, which is often an unrelenting critical view of their inadequacies. The third insight is how ingrained and intertwined these biases are with their worldview. The plethora of hidden biases are evident even in the open and safe environment that we foster in these retreats, so imagine what is actually happening in the constantly shifting and frantic pace of business. Although unhelpful at best and toxic at worst, this tendency is not a result of being defective or doing something poorly but rather a function of how our minds work.

From a mind-science point of view, awareness is a raw and open capacity for processing new learning and information. Whenever we attach awareness to a specific judgment, assumption, or identity it limits the clarity and bandwidth of this capacity. This narrowing of our awareness is the result of how our minds work and how we learn from experience. We tend to hang on to old experiences and judgments and use them as a basis to predict or interpret what is happening in the present. While we think of this as a good thing, as a way of gaining knowledge and perspective, what we're doing at the same time is making ourselves less perceptive, narrowing our bandwidth, and building bias into our awareness. To learn without having our experience limit us, we must develop the capacity to constantly reassess and purge our preconceptions so we can start fresh in the present moment, seeing the whole and not merely the parts of the reality we expect.

Getting locked into our biased perception is an obvious obstacle when it comes to understanding, communicating, and negotiating with others. Often, when we try to communicate, we get lost in our story and can't relate when another person's story is different. This is how getting stuck in our biased consciousness makes it hard for us to understand, negotiate, compromise, and collaborate, showing another key benefit of expanding our awareness by exposing and breaking out of our ingrained biased frame of reference.

A host of different habit patterns block our awareness, including ones that come as evolutionary defaults—like our primal stress reflexes—and ones that have been set up by early learning. Both kinds of biases make it hard for us to be fully open to what is happening in the present. In fact, most of the time what we think of as perception or experience is largely (if not mostly) virtual, based on dredging up old memories to create an interpretation of what is happening and pasting them over what's really happening. As a result, we work with distorted, filtered information. If we don't have the capacity to see through this default habitual awareness and return to our primal, natural intelligence, we're going to be limited in terms of our ability to show up in the present moment fully aware, equipped with relevant experience, and open enough to continually learn. To tap into our primal capacity for unbiased awareness, we must be able to erase biases and start anew, receptive to a new person's point of view in a new situation and open to fresh data and ways of thinking, feeling, and acting.

Although this is true for us as human beings, as leaders there's another aspect to this quality that's key: the impact our awareness has on other individuals or on our team. When the person you're working with—colleague or report—does not feel you're open to their experience or seeing them for who they are but instead are prejudging them or treating them differently for reasons unrelated to the task at hand or their performance, it gives rise to a sense of bias or unfairness that can poison a negotiation, a project, or even an entire company. This is where biased awareness can lead to disengagement, gossip, and judgment among coworkers. All that trouble inexorably arises from a sense of people not feeling they are being heard and seen. As long as a leader lacks the capacity for unbiased awareness, they're going to be limited by their blind spots and manifesting the opposite of clarity.

This quality may feel challenging to us, because we tend to think of ourselves as open-minded and aware: *I don't have any biases.* The thing is it's not natural or neurologically possible for us *not* to have biases. Biases are key to how our brain develops, how our nervous system works, and how our mind grows. Whether we talk about default survival biases or the biases that come from early preverbal learning or adult social conditioning, these implicit settings help us speedily assess and respond to the complex challenges of our lives. If we didn't have these preconceived notions, navigating the everyday would be impossible.

At the same time, if we're unaware of these biases and not continually assessing, revising, or deleting them when incorrect, they become blind spots that lock us into a rigid, limited vision of ourselves and the world. Unless we are honest and do some real work, digging down to address our assumptions about who we think we are and our perceptions of others and ourselves in relation to them, we are not going to have that fully open mind or presence that allows us to take in people or new situations and ideas with clarity and unbiased awareness.

As we apply ourselves to becoming boundless leaders and to doing the work, we become aware of how much judgment we have in our minds toward others and ourselves. For instance, those of us who are systematically privileged as male leaders, especially white male leaders, have been trained to assume that we must know the answer and be in control. Yet there are times when we don't know or can't control what is happening, and as long as we're unable to expose and reject that bias, we may be unable to acknowledge the truth and listen to others' experience and ideas, especially when those others come from a systemically oppressed race or gender. That tendency can lead to us being dismissed as "out of it" or controlling, rather than opening an opportunity for deeper dialogue, engagement, and mutual trust. On the other hand, those of us who are systematically oppressed as female leaders, leaders of color, or both have typically had to work twice as hard to be recognized and heeded and often struggle with internalized biases that get in our way, especially with people from dominant groups in denial about their bias and privilege. In fact, we often see our biases reflected in the challenges coming from those we lead and those with different backgrounds and experiences. When we're able to stay open and aware, we are more able to recognize the blind spots that limit us. The reason it's so difficult to do is because we start out wholly or mostly unaware of the biases that cause our blind spots. How would we work with them?

You can think of the following practice as going up to the balcony to have a view of an entire theater—the audience and the stage. The mindfulness practice of open awareness meditation is one way to do this. It is a practice that lots of people find challenging yet indispensable. It's about going into the open and clear part of our mind where we can step back from what we're thinking, seeing, and feeling. Open awareness practice is a way to be bigger than our thoughts, experiences, and minds, as we access our natural capacity for metacognition, which is the capacity to take it all in and see the unfiltered version. From there we can recognize that we do have biases, we do have these instincts and preconceptions, and so we must be aware of them and not close our mind off. That's why open awareness, although a challenging practice, is a vital one.

Practice

THE VIEW FROM THE BALCONY— OPEN AWARENESS MEDITATION

1 Settle into a comfortable sitting or lying posture on a chair, cushion, yoga mat, or bed.
2 Turn your attention to the place in your body where you most sense your breathing.
3 When you get distracted or dull, keep patiently returning to where you sense the breath.

4 Once your mind settles, turn your attention to the awareness that's watching the body.

5 Move through the usual thoughts, feelings, and images to the clarity of awareness itself.

6 Practice resting in that awareness, letting go of habitual thoughts, feelings, and images.

7 Try to immerse and expand your mind in that clear, still, open awareness for five to fifteen minutes.

8 Return to the practice, ideally at a regular time and place, three to seven days a week.

9 Tune in to this practice to free and clear your mind of biases that block you in daily life.

12 DISCERNMENT

The Key to Incisive Decisions

Discernment—the fourth quality of mind—is what emerges when we make a point to attend to our experience from the vantage of unbiased awareness. In boundless leadership, our understanding of discernment differs dramatically from the conventional take. We see it as based not upon perspectives and judgments derived from past experience but rather on our ability to break free from the past and see things freshly as they are here and now. This clear discernment involves the ability to see the whole field—the panorama—to recognize what matters most within it, and to consider what happens when those elements are in conflict.

Unbiased awareness gives us the perspective to see things more clearly and fully—without judgment—as it allows us to collect more accurate and current information. However, it's discernment that gives us the ability to analyze and assess that information in light of our evolving needs and interests as well as within the larger context of our community, company, and ultimately a constantly changing world. As we seek the clarity to make more sound decisions, discernment comes early in the decision-making process, where we try to align our current assessment of the information at hand with our present intentions. Based on how our needs align with the facts on the ground, we're prepared to discern the best course of action here and now.

The contrast between our view of discernment and the more conventional definition is similar to the contrast we drew in chapter 9 between inner presence and outward presence. In the same way as conventional, outwardly focused presence lacks the connection to our own and others' internal reality, so conventional experience-based discernment lacks the radical openness to the fluid reality of a situation and the evolving needs in the here and now. Discernment is typically seen as an intellectual calculation, but if it doesn't include discerning in a global way—stepping back and looking freshly at what's going on inside as well as outside us—then we're likely to miss the *most* important variable in that calculation: the assumptions we're starting from that bias, limit, and skew our ability to see clearly and determine what the best course of action is for individuals and the collective in the here and now. When it comes to business, when we take ourselves out of the equation, we've lost leverage.

The power of fresh and full discernment adds the final quality we need—together with presence, balance, and unbiased awareness—to support the mind's competency of clarity. Unlike the more conventional business qualities we've all heard about like "command and control" and "focus on the bottom line," the boundless leadership qualities of clarity involve the conscious regulation of the inner and outer dimensions of reality and work together to sustain an ability to assess and shift the reality of what's going on within. *Am I present? Am I able to be centered or balanced, or am I living in the extreme? Can I clear my mind of bias and see what's going in inside me and in the world?* Even when we reach a place of true discernment of the outer situations we face, as boundless leaders we must continue to ask ourselves two questions: *What are our intentions? What are the best internal and external courses of action?*

The reason our focus in conventional forms of presence and discernment tends to be narrow and one-sidedly external is because our minds and bodies evolved a default survival mode and tend to get stuck there. If you think about it, if you're being charged by a saber-toothed tiger, you'll want to put your attention on the tiger and not stop to ponder your feelings, the feelings of others, or the nuances of the environment—you either protect yourself or die. However, this narrowing and externalization doesn't only operate when we're feeling threatened. It also limits our capacity when we're going in the survival mode of scarcity and going for something desirable, where we compulsively chase what we assume are rare opportunities—perhaps competing with other companies for a big contract or other candidates for a promotion. Whether we're feeling a sense of threat or scarcity, when our mind is in survival mode, we lose track of ourselves and the nuances of the real world we're doing business in—the contract or the promotion becomes the saber-toothed tiger if you will, and we lose sight of the panorama when it comes to the inner and outer landscape. We must remember that we are our own primary resource, and if we're trying to make judgments without understanding the prejudgments that are clouding our thinking, we're cutting off the greater part of our ability to see what's happening right then and there, in the present.

It's not our fault that our minds work this way! Both evolution and our life training assume and reinforce our default survival mode. That is the human root of most of our gnawing self-doubt and insecurity, not to mention our limited capacities for presence, balance, unbiased awareness, and discernment. To master the fine art of these qualities of mind and to access and develop our competence for clarity and install self-awareness as a new mind/body trait, we need to practice training our attention to empower our sense of safety, security, and connection. When the mind is still and present, when it's balanced, open, and pliable, we can notice things more precisely and truly deal with the particularities as we make assessments. *Am I seeing this clearly? Are my attentions aligned?*

The best and most efficient way we've found to achieve the shift to real discernment and clarity is through the practice of mindful insight. This last exercise of attention is an advanced application of the unbiased awareness we trained through the practice of open awareness—the view from the balcony. When we're in open awareness we're taking that step back, trying to unbias our minds and clean the lens of our awareness so we can examine data afresh—without preconceptions, theories, or past data points. That way we are able to face it without the filter of our past, our bad or good experiences, or our expectations. In the practice of mindful insight, once we have that clear open field or lens, we reengage. It is a fine-tuning of our lens, which we now focus on what is happening in our minds and in our world, allowing us to notice and observe with a greater degree of curiosity and openness. Think of it like the experience of looking at a friend's face as if seeing it for the first time.

If you cultivate this capacity to continuously see things afresh, you'll stop operating on autopilot, become better able to assess each situation, and make decisions that meet your real aims and needs.

Practice

LIKE THE VERY FIRST TIME—MINDFUL INSIGHT

1   Settle into a comfortable sitting or lying posture on a chair, cushion, yoga mat, or bed.
2   Turn your attention to the place in your body where you most sense your breathing.
3   When you get distracted or dull, keep patiently returning to where you sense the breath.
4   Once your mind settles, turn your attention to the awareness that's watching the body.
5   Move through the usual thoughts, feelings, and images to the clarity of awareness itself.
6   Make that open awareness a workspace to reassess habits of mind, speech, and action.
7   Discerning which habits limit you and which habits empower you, let go of the former and develop the latter.
8   Return to the practice, ideally at a regular time and place, three to seven days a week.
9   Tune in to this practice to discern the most empowering course of action in daily life.

13 APPLICATION

Leveraging the Power of Intention

As you work with the discipline of mind within boundless leadership, you'll engage the practices, strengthen the qualities, and develop more clarity. One of the best ways you can bring this clarity into play is by better understanding your intentions. Conflicting intentions often lie at the root of our most ill-advised efforts. For instance, if someone criticizes us, we often feel the need to correct them. We may feel that we're being helpful by setting the record straight, but our critic feels we're being defensive and are not listening or taking responsibility. If we examine our intentions in a situation like this, we might notice that underlying our conscious intention to correct an error there is a deeper, unconscious intention to punish our critic for embarrassing, diminishing, or challenging us. When conflicting intentions motivate our actions and reactions, they create a dissonance that detracts from our effectiveness. Metaphorically, it's as if we're facing in one direction while our bodies are moving in another. In other words, intention has its own physics: if you try to satisfy conflicting needs simultaneously, then like an object impacted by a variety of forces, the result of your actions will be diminished to the degree that your intentions are scattering rather than aligning your aim.

On the other hand, when we bring clarity to the workings of our minds, we are able to refine our complex set of intentions and can consciously choose the intention that best aligns with our individual and organizational interest. When we can choose our lead intention and redirect our conflicting intentions accordingly, the impact and benefit of our decisions and actions are increased.

There's a second reason it's important to clarify our intentions: they launch or initiate our actions. If our intention at the beginning of an action is a few degrees off, by the time the action is completed we're going to be exponentially further from where we intended to be. If you're aware of your intentions and make a small adjustment in the beginning, then your completed action will be more in line with your desired outcome.

For example, when our meditation practice has become a more stabilized and organic process, we are able to be still and deepen awareness. So much so that we might notice a tickle in our throat and then focus on and calm that tickle before it becomes an involuntary cough. Think of noticing that tickle as the first intention of an action; if you could leverage your awareness at that point, you could change the trajectory and avoid an outcome before it became inevitable.

THE CHAIN OF AWARENESS

To better understand the process of clarifying our intentions, you can examine where your current level of clarity falls in the chain of awareness, which is composed of the following five successive steps:

1 Stimulus: A mosquito lands on your arm.
2 Recognition: You notice the mosquito on your arm.
3 Intention: You want to stop the mosquito from biting you.
4 Consideration: Kill it? Flick it? Spray it? Ignore it?
5 Action: Take action based on your choice.

The chain of awareness usually plays out in a moment, but each step occurs sequentially. Consider what this process feels like depending on where you direct your awareness in the chain. What if you had no awareness until after you took action at the fifth step? We've all experienced this: *I can't believe I said that. I can't believe I did that.* When your awareness is at the end of the chain, you're in a trance—not only are you not aware, you're not even awake.

What if your awareness occurs directly before taking the action, between steps 4 and 5 in the chain? This is reactivity, not intentional action. You're aware of the action before you take it, but you did not choose the action, you just did it.

However, if awareness happens *before* consideration (step 4), you're being mindful: *I have options. I could be aggressive or conciliatory. I have many things I can do before I take action.* That's a better place to be.

What is even better is having awareness as the intention arises, during step 3, before your field of consideration is narrowed. You decide who you want to be in the next moment, what part of yourself you want to show up. That is consciously setting an intention. And if you're aware at that level, you can direct your action and change the outcome of an event exponentially. That's having complete mindful awareness.

You might be able to have awareness even at the moment the stimulus occurs before step 2. In that case, we refer to your level of awareness as pure presence. A mosquito landed on your arm and you're present, aware of the sensation of a bug about to bite. *No problem. I'm here, I'm present.*

Finally, sometimes the depth and stability of our awareness are such that it seems we anticipate what's coming; we have an awareness that's present even before the stimulus occurs—that's being prescient. All of us have experienced every stage on the chain of awareness from trance to prescience.

Once you know that the further down the chain you place your awareness the more limited your options are, you can decide from which leverage point you want to manage the outcome of your actions. Where do you want your awareness to be as a leader of yourself and others? Which "you" do you want to have show up when you bring full clarity and self-awareness into play?

C.A.T.

Once you understand the sequence in the chain and have linked clarity and self-awareness with your intentions, you can work with intention skillfully. Most of our actions are influenced by competing intentions that we're not always aware of, so you may find yourself challenged or confused when making decisions. For example, you may become excited about a new routine and then procrastinate or lose interest quickly. Sometimes you'll self-sabotage or find yourself indecisive or even stymied by a simple or familiar task. When you encounter any of these types of resistance, chances are you're dealing with conflicting intentions of which you're unaware. This is why our application of C.A.T. is so effective. Here's the process:

Clarify intentions
Align intentions
Take action

When we clarify our intentions, we become aware of the whole array of them at play in a specific situation, not just the obvious ones. This allows us to consciously align with the most appropriate intention. Here's how the process works:

Clarify Intentions

List all the intentions you have for a particular decision, meeting, or course of action. The first few are usually accessible and close to the surface:

I want to have this meeting because ...
I want the result of this decision to be ...
I want the outcome of this conversation to be ...

Then you want to look below the surface and ask yourself the following:

What are some of my partially hidden intentions?

What are the intentions arising from my attitudes and views?

What intentions might be based on the implicit assumptions I make about me and others?

If I were to be completely honest, eschewing my current mood or my history with this group or individual, what other intentions do I have?

Add your answers to the list. It is critical to resist any shame that may come up about your more personal or primal intentions like wanting to get credit for your work, highlighting a colleague's shortcomings, or covering up a mistake. Then, go deeper and ask these questions:

What are the intentions shaped by my conditioning—my early emotional experience or my adult social and cultural conditioning?

Which of my core beliefs and needs are informing my intentions?

Is there a historical need emerging in this situation?

Beliefs such as our need for approval, safety, and acknowledgement from the people we're interacting with, supporting, or supported by as well as those unmet needs from our primary caregivers, will likely foster our subconscious intentions to satisfy those needs through the current situation.

For example, you may have intentions for a meeting with your manager that actually reflect your need for approval from your father. Or there may be an unconscious intention that relates to an implicit racial or gender bias—you feel a need to please or appease a person of different race or gender. When we clarify our intentions, we can see how things from our personal life are connected with and seep into our work. That is why you want to push and identify the intentions that arise, even if they don't seem to make sense. Again, there's no need for shame or judgment, so list as many intentions as you can and go as deep as you can. Remember, whether you list them or not, those intentions are affecting your impact, so you'll benefit from bringing them to your awareness and addressing them appropriately.

By doing this you can have a better idea of how you want to work with your intentions. It's a layered process:

1   Intentions that are on the surface: the ones we recognize and easily acknowledge
2   Intentions that are just below the surface: attitudes and assumptions that affect our thinking
3   Intentions that are deep, even buried: beliefs and worldviews that were conditioned during childhood

When it comes to the last two types of intentions, it's vital to ask what parts of your past may be skewing your consideration of the present situation. By analyzing your intentions, you'll foster clarity of what is almost always a more complicated set of needs than you might expect.

To help you access these three levels of intentions, you can group them into intentions you might have for the following:

1   Yourself
2   Others: employer, family, or team
3   The whole: business, community, or world

Although a more detailed exploration of your intentions will serve you, we've observed while working with our clients over the years that almost all intentions fall into two categories:

1   Those designed to protect you and keep you safe
2   Those that help you grow and expand

We all have both sets. If you're brutally honest and identify your full list of intentions from both perspectives, you'll be better able to clarify the emotional forces resulting from your competing intentions.

Once you've clarified five to nine intentions—move to the next step.

Align Intentions

Begin to align your intentions by asking questions like this:

> Out of all these intentions, which one do I want to dedicate
> my energy to the most?
> Which one is the primary intention?

Then explore the other intentions by asking the following:

> Is this intention relevant to this situation?
> Is this intention supportive of my primary intention?
> Is this intention about something different in my life?

In the end, you'll place each intention into one of three categories:

1   It supports my primary intention as is.
2   It is a relevant intention for this situation but needs an
    adjustment to fully support the primary intention.
3   It is not an intention that needs to be dealt with in this
    particular situation. In other words, if it's not best suited
    for the situation to which you're applying C.A.T., you can
    remove the intention and deal with it separately.

Take Action

Once you've gotten rid of the extraneous actions and have clarity, consider your next step:

> I have a few intentions that are aligned pretty well.
> What action should I take?

By clarifying and aligning intentions, you're essentially walking
into a dark room and turning on a light. Once you illuminate the entire
room, it's easy to see where you are and what actions to take. What
could have been difficult is now quite easy because you've mitigated or
eliminated any conflicts in your intentions within your conscious and
subconscious mind. Without the conflicts, your lens is not obscured

by ambiguity, ambivalence, and confusion and the next right action is more readily visible.

Let's apply this to a somewhat common event, such as an important meeting—in this case, pitching a large account. As you make your list you might uncover the following intentions:

Do well at the pitch to land the new account.
Show my boss I deserve the promotion under discussion.
Convince my subordinates that I am worthy of the respect
    they are holding back.
Prove to my father I deserve the approval that has eluded me.
Quell my inner critic's focus on my inadequacy.

Once you've clarified all the intentions at play, choose the lead intention and align the rest by choosing one of the three categories mentioned earlier:

1   Keep the intention exactly as it is.
2   Keep the intention but make a slight adjustment.
3   Recognize the importance of the intention but
    acknowledge it's better served by addressing it separately.

In this case, doing well in the presentation to win the account is the lead intention. Showing your boss you're worthy of the promotion under review is a clear and legitimate intention for the meeting and you would keep it as is (category 1). Convincing your subordinates that you're worthy of their approval might be a reasonable intention for the meeting, yet it is dependent on their assessment of you and will likely undermine your effectiveness as you subtly check in throughout the presentation to see if they approve. This, then, would be put in category 2, and you might shift the intention to *I want to model giving a great presentation for my team*, moving the center of power toward you and inspiring you to perform at your best, which would engender the team's respect. Securing your father's approval based on your performance, as well as your inner critic's, is a fool's errand for this presentation and falls into category 3. Understandably, it's one of the more driving needs most of us have, and we should appreciate and skillfully satisfy it, but using this pitch meeting as a way to satisfy external and internal critics will not have much value.

When we don't align our complex intentions, our energy is dispersed and usually at cross purposes with our primary intention. For example, the desire to do well becomes overwhelming as we've allowed so much to ride on it, inflating it into a do-or-die performance. This added pressure and stress will intensify the default-mode network and negativity bias it stimulates, creating a strong drag on our ability to be our best. In fact, the added stress may cause us to be impatient with our team members and show irritability and anger due to their imperfect execution, further eroding any respect they have for us. By aligning the intentions, we direct our energy toward the most important intention for this particular event and align, adjust, or drop the ones that weaken the trajectory of that primary intention. In this case, when we understand that winning the account is our main priority, we can unburden ourselves of the added needs to please others and shift our focus back to the matter at hand and better access the best we have to offer.

Aligning your intention with your action is crucial since even small shifts can have large consequences. For instance, one of our clients received an unfair evaluation. Before her meeting to give her feedback, we went through her intentions. The primary intention was wanting to tell her manager that she felt she'd been unfairly treated. Other intentions included protesting the manager's inaccurate conclusions, wanting to advance her career, and a desire to be reengaged with management's inner circle. As we continued our discussion, she wanted to change one word in her lead intention: she no longer wanted to *tell* her manager how she felt, but for her manager to *know* how she felt. This effortlessly shifted our client's anger-fueled energy to one of openness and clarity, creating an environment more conducive to being heard than one where accusations and defensive responses flew back and forth. After the meeting, our client reported a powerful outcome: "It was the first time my manager saw me." Having clarified her intentions, our client was able to check her alignment with her real aims and make a small shift that changed her approach and likely the outcome.

C.A.T. is a useful application that leverages clear thinking, allowing you to examine and resolve your conflicting needs and motivations and act in a more focused and impactful manner. This application can be used to improve our response to many different situations—everyday activities, critical decisions, conflict, procrastination, and even self-sabotage. One client used it to better deliver negative information to an aggressive, intimidating CEO, while successfully keeping the discussion focused on solutions rather than the usual blame and attack. Another client who had neglected her self-care during her ascent at a Fortune 50 company decided she wanted to lose weight for her health, career, and her children's sake, yet she continued to self-sabotage until she applied C.A.T. to her competing intentions. When she thoroughly examined her intentions, she realized that she'd internalized some worst-case moments from her past where she felt she was an object of prey in her slimmer body, an implicit memory that was fueling her self-sabotage.

A third client, by more fully understanding the forces behind seemingly conflicting intentions, used C.A.T. to unravel how her desire to provide for her family and longing to have more meaning in her work need not be mutually exclusive. Other clients have used C.A.T. to better see and address the fear of failure that underlies most indecision and procrastination or the self-critical intentions that contribute to self-sabotage as well as to conflicts between how they feel they should portray themselves as opposed to who they really are or want to be.

That is the power of C.A.T.!

REVIEW

We began by exploring how and why we need to develop clarity and self-awareness if we want to break out of the limits that our survival-driven way of being and leading places on our attention and our mental capacity.

We defined clarity as the competency or moment-to-moment state of radical openness and lucidity of mind and self-awareness as the new trait of embodying clarity about our inner and outer lives as a stable, abiding way of being.

We learned that the obstacles to clarity and self-awareness are rooted in the survival mode we inherit as our default way of being, specifically in the four phases of the cycle of stress and trauma that maintain that survival mode. This brought us to the practices we need to train our minds—the four forms of mindful attention training that allow us to counter the four phases of stress, while cultivating the four qualities of mind that support the development of clarity and self-awareness.

We explored these key qualities of mind—presence, balance, unbiased awareness, and discernment—and how they are accessed and developed by the four forms of mindfulness—mindfulness of the breathing body, nonreactive mindfulness, mindful awareness, and mindful insight.

We described the application of clarifying and aligning intentions that leverages the greater clarity of mind to better understand the forces that shape our actions, so we can positively impact those we lead as boundless leaders.

Part Three

THE DISCIPLINE OF HEART
TRAIT OF AUTHENTIC ENGAGEMENT

14 CREATING THE CONDITIONS FOR OTHERS TO BE THEIR BEST

The discipline of mind, with its underlying trait of self-awareness nurtured through the competency of clarity, helps you align your intentions so that as a leader you can be your best. Building on this, the discipline of heart is about how you as a leader can inspire *others* to be *their* best, to access their potential and bring it into their lives and work. The trait of authentic engagement and the competency of compassion that nurtures it come together to prepare you to lead from a place of caring connection.

As you develop this discipline of heart, you'll also develop a deeper understanding of our total interdependence with others locally and globally. As leaders, and as humans in general, we are wired by nature and trained by our culture to hold on to a sense of our fundamental separateness, yet current science, combined with the ever-increasing connectivity of our lives today, is inexorably challenging that mistaken view. Not only has the new science shown that our ingrained sense of separateness is misleading, but the mounting complexity and interdependence of our world means that this misperception blocks our ability to understand others and meet the real challenges we face. Whether we question how we constantly influence one another for good or ill or take a systemic view of how business works in the digital age, seeing ourselves as independent from others sets us up for a rude awakening.

Our rising interdependence is such that experiencing ourselves as separate from those we lead or the context in which we live and work is not so different from our right ear feeling completely disconnected from our left toe. From a broader, big-picture perspective, we are all part of one infinitely complex living system, and what happens to one part or what is needed from the other part will inevitably affect the whole. Thus, we lead from a place of compassion, because it manifests the reality of how interdependent we truly are. With that understanding we can effect change more easily, which is why it's genuinely good business!

A MATTER OF COLLECTIVE EFFORT

Thinking about this trait of authentic engagement and its core competency of compassion in action, Elazar is reminded of how he's always been moved by Rwanda's President Paul Kagame, who helped liberate his country from vast and devastating genocide. As a leader, Kagame chose compassion and altruism as the way forward, pursuing reconciliation and forgiveness, rather than vengeance and punishment. When Elazar asked him why as a victor he chose this less traditional path, Kagame offered a more calculated answer than expected. He said that punishing the rebels would have drained his country of much needed resources at a critical time, while reintegrating them through healing and compassion could energize Rwanda to become a thriving nation.

Kagame's situation was extraordinary in many ways, but it overlaps with the average conditions of business and everyday life more than you might think. While conventional leadership views and approaches success as almost exclusively a matter of individual effort or qualities, the simple fact is that no individual is smart, able, or strong enough to succeed as a leader without the support of multiple social systems—families, schools, teams, corporations, nations, cultures. As a corollary to the old hyperindividualist view, the culture of modern business sees the collective productivity of a company as almost exclusively reflecting the capacity of its stars—the handful of individuals who are singled out and groomed for privilege and power as leaders. In both cases, the modern culture of individual success is a troubling myth based on an evolutionary blind spot and egregious accounting error. Success for humans—whether measured as an accumulation of wealth, power, market share, influence, social impact, or even happiness—by nature and necessity always was and will be a matter of collective effort.

Any story or measure of success that neglects the engagement and productivity of all the individuals who contribute to that collective effort is inevitably partial, shortsighted, inefficient, and inaccurate. When we add the mistaken science that led to conventional approaches to leadership—the myth that stress drives performance—to this equation, we arrive at the self-limiting strategy that seeks to propel individual engagement and collective productivity with the threat of exclusion and fear of failure. Whether this strategy leads you to threaten or diminish yourself through a harsh inner critic or to threaten or diminish your team with public shaming or firing, it violates the tone and environment of safe connection our hearts and brains need to engage with and inspire others.

With a greater understanding of interdependence and the compassion to authentically engage others comes leadership based on the power of positivity. This type of leadership builds on a foundation of safety rather than undermining confidence and trust with negativity. Motivating and encouraging others begin with creating an environment of mutual understanding and care, rather than trying to manipulate by injecting fear and humiliation into every situation.

The greatest challenge of leading with compassion is that, at the end of the day, we can't give others what we don't have in ourselves. The foundation of the discipline of heart is to develop the competency of compassion and the trait of authentic engagement within our hearts (and minds) so that we can model them for others. In the end, this discipline is about our ability as leaders to face and overcome our common demons—implicit biases, reactive emotions, and worst-case beliefs—rather than defining and basing our relationships upon another person's behavior. As that ability grows, we tap our emotional resources and expand our leadership capacity, putting us well on our path to boundless leadership and truly inspiring others to join us.

To cultivate this capacity for authentic engagement rooted in compassion, you must clear the biases and reactions that block authentic engagement with others and then turn your inner critic into a coach to build the qualities you need to show up with compassion for yourself and everyone you work with. The fundamental shift you'll be making through this discipline of heart is one from a default fear-based setting of social survival to an emotional thriving mode of social safety and connection. This fundamental shift in your emotional life will support you in developing the qualities you need to be at your best with others and to help them reach and maintain *their* best as individuals and team players.

The practical application at the end of the discipline of heart is the ability to take empowered responsibility. Once the grip of the inner critic is loosened, once you nurture and listen to the inner coach within yourself, you'll have the ability to tap into the positive emotional qualities that empower you to take responsibility for your leadership without the usual negativity of shame and blame. As you do this and model it for others, it will become a positive contagion, sending a ripple effect through any organization, eventually shifting every member from the shame-based place of finding fault to a proactive place of being engaged in finding solutions.

THE FOUR QUALITIES OF HEART

When we lead with heart, we begin modeling what others can have as well, emanating reassurance and safety that bring out the best in others. Like the discipline of mind there are four qualities within the discipline of heart that support the competency of compassion and ultimately the trait of authentic engagement:

1 Empathy: an accurate understanding and appropriate concern for the inner lives of others
2 Resilience: the capacity to disengage from stress-reactive emotions and shift back through acceptance to positive social emotions like care

3   Engagement: the ability to establish and sustain an authentic, positive social bond based on empathic concern and responsiveness

4   Inspiration: the capacity to tap and harness the uplifting power of positive social emotions like compassion and altruism and to model and spark that for others

We'll take a deep dive into these qualities, but before we do, we'll explore the competency of compassion and the boundless leadership trait of authentic engagement.

15 THE INTERPLAY OF COMPASSION AND AUTHENTIC ENGAGEMENT

The Real Strength of Leadership

The first step in the discipline of heart is to develop the competency of compassion, which is the source of the trait of authentic engagement—the trait governing the social-emotional dimension of engaging and working with others. Authentic engagement is a relational state of mind wherein we're genuinely connecting to other people with care and where we engage others with an open heart and mind.

Compassion underlies the development of authentic engagement, but how does it work? *Compassion* is a word that gets used a lot, but what is it *really*? Think of compassion as the active consequence of an upgrade to empathy. Empathy involves realistic, unbiased understanding and *felt* acceptance of what's going on inside another person's mind and body—it's a basic connection to the lived reality of another human being: *I know how you're feeling, and I care. I feel for you.* Compassion is the next step in the process of engagement. It's not just understanding how a person feels, not just having a sense of that feeling and caring about the person's experience as something that matters; it's the component of responding intentionally and actively based on understanding and empathic concern. The compassionate mind/body state begins with the authentic intention to engage and/or respond in whatever way might help relieve another person's suffering. The embodied intention, response, and action of compassion can take myriad forms, from expressing our concern in our facial and body language to offering our help, and culminating with stepping in on behalf of someone.

It makes sense that compassion is so important in boundless leadership, especially for building authentic engagement, because we cannot be authentically engaged with another person if we don't know and care how they're feeling, if we're unaware of or lack a meaningful link to their mind/body state. How can we connect positively with another human being if we have no idea how they feel? Or if we know how they feel but ignore or dismiss their inner experience as if it doesn't matter? A merely functional engagement with others, even if it's not negative but simply neutral, will usually be experienced by others as uncaring or inauthentic on a human level. Consequently, only a genuine caring engagement has the power to bring us together in mutual understanding and genuine teamwork.

We've seen that with our clients, leading with compassion is not an easy leap, because it's in direct opposition to the flawed traditional leadership approach that expects humans to check their emotions at the door. Yet the unanimous response after leaning into compassion rather than skipping over another's need has been a resounding "Wow!" This is the case, even if the person you're connecting with from a place of shared humanity and compassion is not aware that you're doing so. One example among many is when Elazar was working with his client Chris on his first major presentation to the finance committee since being hired by a new company. Having reviewed the strong presentation, Elazar was unclear as to why there was a palpable negative energy emanating from Chris regarding the upcoming meeting.

Chris explained, "The chairman of the finance committee was vehemently against me being hired." Although the underlying anger was understandable, after working with Elazar, Chris agreed to visualize the chairperson not as an enemy who was opposing him, but as another human seeking happiness who sometimes got lost and confused in its pursuit—no different from Chris's bouts of confusion. Having flipped the perspective away from defending his stance in an us-versus-them view to one of care and compassion toward an interdependent whole prior to the meeting, Chris emerged victorious from the presentation having obtained agreement on his recommendation and feeling he and the chairperson shared a meaningful and unexpected rapport. Why is compassion such a powerful game changer?

TRANSFORMATIVE COMPASSION

Authentic compassion involves overcoming the key weaknesses in our emotional systems, the internal construct we call the traumatic self-habit. This often implicit intuitive sense of our vulnerability to other humans may be front and center or hidden in our hearts, but it is universal, given our primal experiences of infancy and childhood—how vulnerable, powerless, and dependent we were on the empathy and care of others.

That traumatic habit of self is reflected in our shared human social insecurity: *What if you don't like me? What if you want to get rid of me? Who will care about me?* The traumatic self-habit, or "self-state" as psychologists call it, is typically the root of our emotional worst-case fears and commonly anchors our negatively biased and insecure inner narrative of being exposed or rejected as not good enough. This traumatic self-state is especially strong when it reflects adverse experiences of abandonment, neglect, or abuse, but it is invariably present in everyone since we have all been so exquisitely vulnerable in our lives that inevitable moments of inattention, misattunement, or exclusion spark traumatic experiences of life-or-death panic.

As leaders, we encounter intense social pressure because the future and well-being of many people and often the systems that support them depend on us. Being human, at some point this pressure will trigger us into our worst-case emotional state, making our interactions in the present highly stressful. That stress may not register in our minds at first but instead come in under the radar by triggering emotional and visceral stress reactions in our hearts and bodies. We might become unexpectedly anxious or restless in an interaction that would normally be comfortable, or perhaps feel dry-mouthed, overheated, or chilled during a presentation. Once triggered, our traumatic self-state may expose us to the second-guessing of our inner critic. This can reveal emotional insecurities like doubting if others respect or like us, or even evoking mistrust about the sincerity of our colleagues' comments. Under such intensified social stress, we might become disproportionately hurt or angry, fighting a deep inner sense of rejection or shame. Or we might react with a primal urge to blame or attack others whom we fear may judge or exclude us.

Those emotional reactivities will arise if we haven't worked through our traumatic self-state, recognized the worst-case social emotional traumas in our past, and learned what present-day challenges trigger and hijack us with disruptive stress reactivity. This is why cultivating compassion is not solely a matter of trying to be nice or caring but requires the sustained application of self-awareness enhanced by heart practices (like those of empathy and resilience we will explore in chapters 18 and 19, respectively).

The discipline of heart empowers us to be more authentically concerned for all those we meet as well as readily inclined to actively help. As our practice develops the qualities that support compassion— unbiased empathy, resilience, engagement, and inspiration—you will become able to authentically engage not only with family, friends, and close colleagues but also with neutral and challenging people in ever-widening circles of care. You'll see that compassion can be cultivated in both dimensions: the horizontal, as we expand the circle of people we feel compassion for, and the vertical, as we understand someone else's needs are important to them and might be more important than ours are to us and thus important enough that we are moved to support them without any agenda whatsoever.

BENEFITS OF COMPASSION

Given the work involved in developing this broader, intentional compassion, it's vital we grasp the benefits of living and leading authentically with care. Why should we bother to become more compassionate?

Think about human or mammalian life. Where does it begin? With a caring adult empathically connected and compassionately responsive to a vulnerable newborn. That's the strong force necessary for our survival that defines our entire social ecosystem, wherein we live and learn connected to each other physically, intuitively, and emotionally. If we're building a team or a company or any larger social system, it makes sense that the underlying force nurtures the ecosystem through care and compassion. You can see the impact of this force in the growing cadre of companies that have mitigated (if not replaced) competitiveness with collaboration as the culture or gestalt of the organization. On a quantitative basis, compassion is seen as the driving force in the companies that practiced "conscious capitalism," which Raj Sisodia and his colleagues studied, showing that these companies beat the S&P 500 index by a factor of 10.5 over a five-year period.[10] But mostly, you can *feel* the difference when you enter a room infused with care and consideration rather than power plays and posturing or when you're focused on how you can include someone in your concerns rather than scanning for their microaggressions of excluding you.

If we understand that functioning as a team or as a business relies upon our ability to work together, to help one another, to support one another, and maybe even to challenge one another in a constructive way, then we understand that compassion is the tool for that interdependence. If I'm feeling what it's like for me to be in an interaction and what it's like for you to be in the same interaction, and I care about both of us, then we're emotionally protected from the interaction devolving into a self-protective, fear-based, worst-case scenario.

In business we are often in a situation of negotiating or overcoming conflict with another individual or group. Even with colleagues, these situations can be based on a win/lose paradigm where we must get the upper hand to achieve our best outcome. We had a client who was preparing for such a meeting. Melissa had worked as a consultant for five months and was hoping to receive an offer for full employment. Although she and the company had the same interest, Melissa believed the delays and deflections around her hire were signs that the offer, if any, would be below her expectations. In addition, the CEO had proven himself to be cunning and hard to pin down in conversations. As the meeting approached, Melissa felt she needed to take an aggressive stance and delineate what was and was not acceptable in job title, responsibilities, and compensation. However, because her other options were limited, she was concerned she might be boxed into a corner and have to walk away from the offer. Through our coaching, she came to understand how this fear-based approach would likely create a cycle where each party would need to protect their stance from the other. She reframed the meeting and approached the conversation from a place of deeper understanding that the position would only work for her if it worked for the CEO as well. With this amended mindset, rather than launching with an explanation of her needs, she decided to genuinely understand the CEO's views and needs—those articulated and the ones in the spaces between words. On this mutual ground they shaped a position that was ultimately better than the one Melissa had sought.

Compassion is especially important when situations are difficult. As the saying goes, "Trouble shared is trouble halved." When things get contentious in business, or in a meeting, or even in a conversation—with our boss, direct report, or anyone—it's important to bring compassion into the interaction and protect the participants' nervous systems from being thrown into reactivity. If we don't, things may escalate in a negative way, and we can lose the capacities for mutual understanding and constructive dialogue we need to resolve any conflict. Compassion helps protect our minds and our relationships from difficulty and harm because it empowers us to do difficult things more effectively by staying connected through that difficulty. This can even be experienced in a moment when anxiety and fear are coloring our emotions as we engage the muscle of compassion to connect us to others authentically, flipping our state of mind to a calmer more connected one.

Compassion also brings out our potential. Its value isn't limited to concern for a few trusted people. It's not about being nicer or kinder than others. To be human, we must all have a basic competence for compassion. Think of it like a mental or emotional muscle: like any physical muscle, compassion can be exercised, developed, and cultivated. That's where the training comes in. As we do this, we develop the trait of authentic engagement—the foundation for the social-emotional qualities of boundless leadership.

TRAIT OF AUTHENTIC ENGAGEMENT

By developing and installing compassionate states into our hearts and minds, we arrive at a lasting trait we call authentic engagement. Authentic engagement allows us to expand instead of contract, to reach out to others rather than walling ourselves in. It empowers us to lead naturally from a place of genuine care, from a deep interdependence, and to foster an environment of safe connection and mutual positivity. There's an openness and acceptance to authentic engagement, but it's also proactive and responsive.

We seldom encounter such a positive or expansive view of engagement in conventional business situations. Instead we're trained to think in far narrower, self-interested ways, as a matter of individual carrots and sticks—we learn to rely on financial incentives or promotions as carrots, and threats of failure or exclusion as sticks, creating a mind state of scarcity that makes authentic engagement appear foolish.

Early in Elazar's career when he was at American Express, the company had a recruiting video that proudly announced, "It's a jungle out there! And we're looking for the fittest who can survive in a dog-eat-dog world." The engagement they were fostering was highly stress-driven and competitive, based on narrow and shortsighted self-interest. That's what leadership believed made a company strong. Recently, we've come to see that companies fostering engagement based on collaboration and inclusion over aggression and domination end up being more successful, in terms of employee satisfaction as well as financial gain.

This new paradigm in business resonates with the revolutionary shifts in contemporary science. A new consensus in biology and neuroscience is powerfully supporting a new direction in views of engagement and styles of leadership. When Joe was a medical student in the 1980s, he was told, "Park your empathy at the door, otherwise you're going to burn out." This modern myth was based on the same ethos Elazar found at American Express. In both cases the idea was that only the steeliest, most unfeeling and aloof of physicians or executives would have what it takes to survive the jungle of medicine or the C-suite. In medicine and business, this dominant myth arose from a now-discredited interpretation of Darwin's evolutionary theory known as Social Darwinism, or Neo-Darwinism—survival of the fittest—that defined "fittest" as a matter of cutthroat aggression, competitiveness, or brute force. Over the latter half of the last century, new research[11] by biologists like Theodosius Dobzhansky and Edward O. Wilson spurred a return to Darwin's core view of natural selection, which was closer to "the survival of the most cooperative." This research was based on a growing recognition of social evolution—the vital importance of animals helping each other—and emerged not only from studies of social animals like mammals but also of different species coexisting, cooperating, and coevolving for mutual benefit. A classic example is the remora fish, which evolved to adhere by suction to the backs of whales, turtles, sharks, or rays, and lives by consuming the waste of their host, while cleaning parasites and dead cells off their host's skin.

With that new science came a clearer understanding of how we as mammals survived: by trading our predatory features for those that allowed us to understand one another, learn together, and work cooperatively. Consider us human beings: We're the most highly evolved weaklings. We have no fangs and no claws, and we are thin-skinned and not terribly fast. Clearly, we're not here to be fierce predators or brute defenders. The fact that we're so sensitive to one another, and that we can be expressive and share our inner states, dreams, and emotions, is how we're designed to gain a selective advantage: we become more adaptive and powerful by linking up in ever-larger groups. Scientists began to recognize why such physically vulnerable creatures could adapt and cooperate most efficiently and end up endangering our historic predators rather than the other way around. This fundamental shift in biology dovetailed with the emergence of systems theory and ecological views of nature as well as the new quantum physics, which sees matter more as a cohesive wave or energy field than an array of separate atoms.

THE BRAIN IS A SOCIAL ORGAN

How does the old view that the best leadership is the most competitive and aggressive, that the best leaders have powerfully driven egos, square with the new science of cooperation and compassion?

Not at all.

A similar shift has been underway in neuroscience for the past fifty years. The brain is now seen as a social organ, no longer a competitive one. We understand that it's not just the emotional brain that works best in social mode but the thinking brain as well. Even the reptilian brain thrives in social mode! We're learning that we, as mammals, evolved to have our brains connect with each other, communicating and cooperating in a positive social environment of safe and authentic engagement. When we're in a relationship of teamwork, creativity, and innovation, we accomplish more and are better able to sustain our performance with ease and true contentment and support our team, organization, and community. That's why altruism and solidarity are vital to the new boundless leadership of authentic engagement.

If our brains perform best when we're feeling safe and connected with people, the safer and more connected we are, the more we can reach our potential. This activates the newer parts of our brains—the cerebral neocortex—but it also engages us with our emotional and reptilian brains because we're no longer there to fight or flee, faint or freeze but to learn, grow, and play together.

This history of mammalian evolution explains why, in boundless leadership, the discipline of heart is about authentic engagement. As leaders, we can't bring out the best in a human being if that human being doesn't feel safe and connected with us and with the people around them. The old ideal of the leader as a "lone ranger," who pushed his people to "tough it out," has conclusively been shown to be totally scientifically off base. For example, when we consider what happens to orphans who develop in severe deprivation of physical tenderness, nurturing interaction, and loving play, it turns out that, far from being stronger, they wind up with cognitive and emotional disabilities because their brains don't have the fuel to develop fully or properly.[12]

If you want to bring out the best in a team, a unit, a company, or any collection of human beings, you must be connective and able to engage, and it must come from an authentic place, not a strategy. In part 1 we explored the difference between awareness that's directed outward (the more stress-driven awareness that most people think of as being attentive or "on") and the self-awareness that empowers the mind in boundless leadership (awareness that is constantly tuning in to ourselves) and the same holds true in engagement or social emotional skills. A leader might have charisma or a narcissistic ability to project themselves as powerful or magnetic, but that's not boundless or authentic engagement. Overpowering people emotionally or socially and getting them to comply will not lead them, their team, or company to performing at their best. One of the most important aspects of leadership, especially boundless leadership, is inspiring others. And you cannot inspire or motivate anyone by instilling fear or shame.

FINDING THE "AUTHENTIC" IN AUTHENTIC ENGAGEMENT

A colleague of Joe's, neuroscientist Stephen Porges, the world's leading expert on the autonomic nervous system, shared how he had been asked to consult with a large organization to explain how understanding our mammalian nervous systems might inform business or leadership. Stephen wound up drawing a distinction between mammalian-style leadership and reptilian-style leadership. In mammalian leadership—which derives from the brain stem, which is the deepest part of our brain, right up to the highest regions of neocortex—we feel safe, socially connected, and engaged. Our brain and whole being are open to bonding, connecting, communing, and sharing. That's a different mind/brain state from when our nervous system is feeling predatory, preyed upon, or in scarcity-scavenger mode, or when it gets locked into a primal survival mode that's reptilian and antisocial.

We can expand upon this to recognize the distinction between old conventional leadership, where people inflate themselves and their power to coldly manipulate others, and boundless leadership, where people open and expand their hearts to reach out to others and invite them into mutual connection and sharing. This understanding is one of the key forces powering the organizational shift from a compliance-based HR department to chief people officers focused on human potential.

This distinction is crucial because if we want to inspire mammalian trust and connection in others, we must live and model it ourselves. That's the "authentic" in authentic engagement, the trait inside the discipline of heart that drives boundless leadership. It is about becoming a mammalian-style leader, who calms fears rather than fueling them. What grows this mammalian trait of authentic engagement is the heart-expanding competency of compassion. Since compassion is not only the wellspring of authentic engagement but also the emotional source of all genuine individual and collective success, we should explore its psychology and maturest expression: altruism.

16 THE PSYCHOLOGY OF COMPASSION AND ALTRUISM

The Secret of Success

Now that we've come to understand the new science of compassion, we can appreciate the psychology underlying this core competency. We've said that developing compassion allows us to build authentic engagement, but the question remains, How do we train and expand our natural potential? As we know, compassion is not about being nice or pleasing others—it's about relating with accurate empathy, concern, and skill to the reality of other people's lived experience, a vital step toward social cooperation that explains the powerful win-win biology and psychology of positive emotions evident in the new fields of affective neuroscience and positive psychology.

Consider the shifts in what we believe about positive emotions. In our older view of humanity, based on our misguided faith in the "survival of the fittest," we were taught to see negative emotions as somehow protective and generative. This misguided history is expressed in the celebration of stress-reactive emotions like greed, pride, envy, and rage, as summarized in the famous mantra from the movie *Wall Street*: "Greed is good." This speaks to a psychology that goes back to the beginnings of modern economics wherein key thinkers from Thomas Hobbes and Adam Smith to Thomas Malthus and Herbert Spencer assumed human nature is primarily competitive, aggressive, and self-interested and that social and economic progress can only be made by harnessing these antisocial forces. As our understanding of human nature and evolution has progressed, we've come to know that the emotional energies and attitudes that most empower us as mammals, and that help us succeed as human individuals and communities, are not primal self-protective forces but positive social emotions. This is a novel and difficult concept to embrace as the ingrained belief that equates force with strength and eliciting fear with power lingers for many executives.

The new science of emotions shows that most of the emotions that have been associated with good business, such as arrogance, aggression, impatience, hunger, and ambition, are limiting not only to our potential for teamwork but to individual performance as well. When it comes to our emotional energies, they are the equivalent of fossil fuels or "dirty" energy sources as opposed to clean renewable ones. The primal asocial emotions are dirty energy because they are tainted with the old survival drives of stress and trauma. They may motivate us but in a way that is simultaneously engaging the self-protectiveness, reactivity, tunnel vision, scarcity psychology, and negativity bias of a threatened animal. This activation of primal survival systems is not only limiting but exorbitantly energy consuming. It imposes needless limits on our mental, emotional, and physical performance, while subjecting our minds, hearts, and bodies to the inexorable cost of biological wear and tear, not dissimilar to the pollution created by fossil fuel.

Positive emotions have the opposite effect on our systems. They provide clean energy that empowers us to act and be with others in a constructive way as they sustainably fuel our ability to feel well, be satisfied and happy, and ultimately perform at our best. Specifically, positive social emotions like love and compassion are now known to be key drivers of well-being, meaning, and purpose. The most extensive longitudinal study of human development ever done was conducted at Harvard Medical School and followed a large cohort of undergraduates over eighty-five years, comparing them to a financially and socially less privileged cohort of similar age and gender from South Boston. The findings revolutionized modern views of mental health and led to the development of the young field of positive psychology in the 1980s and '90s. The study showed that, under both conditions of privilege and adversity, the presence of loving, caring relationships is what makes the crucial difference in the development of happy lives, success, health, contentment, and well-being.[13]

When we combine this new positive psychology with what we're learning in neuroscience, we find how powerfully these positive emotions like love, care, joy, and equanimity affect us, fundamentally improving the overall capacity of our brain function at all levels. In effect, positive emotions serve as internal messages setting a tone of overall safety, connection, and well-being that impacts our brain along with our minds, hearts, and bodies for the better. By helping to modulate the autonomic nervous system that regulates levels of calm and arousal, they provide the energy our brains need to function optimally while not wasting any on needless defenses.

In essence, these positive social emotions have an optimizing effect on our primal reptilian brains. Metaphorically speaking, social emotions stroke our inner reptile, turning it into a happy, friendly creature. That's because even at the reptilian level of the brain stem, we mammals evolved neural structures and networks (the brain stem social engagement system as well as the new "cuddle and play" hormones, oxytocin and vasopressin, respectively) to calm self-protective stress reflexes and supply the clean energy that fuels compassion.

In addition to tuning our mind/brain to its full capacity for social engagement, including cognitive, creative, and analytical work, the other thing positive emotions do is expand our scope of awareness and engagement. Whereas negative emotions are tunneling, "I'm afraid of that" or "I want this thing and nothing else," positive emotions are expansive. They tend to open and turn our minds toward the world, making us more interested in and receptive to others. What's more, when we're bringing positive energy to a conversation, a meeting, or any situation, it helps foster social connection, engagement, and influence. As a result, our horizons expand and our capacity for leadership grows boundless.

NEUROSCIENCE OF EMPATHY AND COMPASSION

Compassion is wired into us at birth, but it's not the only preset that comes standard. If you look at the emotional brain, it's designed as a contrast enhancer. It's designed to run in one of two modes and decides which mode it's supposed to be in based on how it filters information. We've been discussing the mode of social engagement that helped us survive by empathically bonding with others, but there's another side to the coin. A stress-reactive mode evolved to kick in when we weren't with kin or when we were together in a dangerous situation like confronting a predator.

Often, when we experience a relationship or social setting as threatening, our worst fears and reactive emotions get the better of us. Unfortunately, when this happens, not only are emotions like fear, anger, and shame released, but our positive emotional capacity for empathy, compassion, and engagement is also halted. This is called the reactive or traumatic mode of our emotional brain.

In addition to being wired to work as a binary processor, like a transmission that can only run in forward *or* reverse, our emotional brain is also wired into an early warning system. It's initiated by mirror neurons—neurons in the perceptual regions of our cortex that continually scan visual input about other people's facial expressions and body language. These neurons are linked to filters in the emotional brain including the alarm bell called the amygdala and the emotional memory bank called the hippocampus. These filters compare that scanned input about other people with our emotional memories to try to match what we see with what we felt in the past, so that we can better identify the emotional states of those around us.

There's a major glitch in this system: It processes information about our social environment through two circuits. The quicker of these does not pass through the conscious regions of the cortex or even the emotional memory banks but goes directly to the amygdala, the early warning alarm that is biased toward the negative, toward recognizing risk. We've all experienced this when we're walking alone at night, "sense" someone following us, and become alarmed or when we meet someone who makes us uncomfortable for no reason we can name. The opposite happens as well when we're looking at someone across a crowded room, and they notice us and become alert. In these instances our brains are gathering and scanning subliminal input to decide what this means: *Safety or danger? Friend or foe? Innocent or predator?*

In these instances, the alarm bell in the amygdala rings as it begins assessing the situation for anything that might be negative or threatening. It remembers all the worst things that ever happened to us and stores them in a database of harms, dangers, and worst cases. And if there's anything that remotely matches this stored information, the amygdala sets off the alarm bell: *This person is a threat!*

This unconscious mirroring and interpreting happen automatically and usually before we're aware of it. It's filtered through the lens of all the emotional experiences we've had in childhood and adult life. This is a distorted lens because in childhood our lives depended entirely on the people around us—whether they were kind or harsh, attentive or negligent—creating a distorted sense of our vulnerability and powerlessness. The moment we receive subliminal messages or cues of distress from others—maybe somebody's upset at a meeting or a colleague is cranky or harsh—we can be triggered into a state of anxiety, reactivity, or irritability. We're wired to respond to these subliminal messages without any awareness or quality control. And when we do that, our traumatic childhood memories of vulnerability often flood in and trigger stress emotions and reactions that shut off our capacities for empathy, compassion, and authentic engagement. In some cases, this may only involve a modicum of distress and some visceral stress reactions like heart palpitations or butterflies in the stomach. In others, the messages may trigger a full-blown panic attack, overwhelming our nervous system with signals to fight or flee. This self-protective wiring is far older than human evolution.

The good news is there is another mode of our emotional brain, the one that kicks in when we feel safe and connected. And that's the ideal mode when we're working together to create a situation where we want to communicate and collaborate. We do this by using the other part of our emotional brain, the hippocampus, to give context and send messages to ourselves like, *I'm safe in the world. I'm not a kid anymore. I don't need to feel powerless. I don't need to overreact. What's happening here is not that I'm in danger but that somebody's having a bad day.* Even assuming we're facing a difficult situation, and the people around us are upset, what's needed is not fear and reactivity, fight or flight but rather the social mammalian capacities of empathy and compassion to best deal with this situation.

Understanding the two modes of our emotional brain is key to the discipline of heart, helping us to learn to shift out of the default mode of stress-reactive emotions and into the mode of empathy and the positive social emotion of compassion. Once we learn to monitor our reactions to others and make the shift to positive emotions rapidly and effectively, the path toward developing our social emotions is revealed and becomes a superhighway to the most powerful of those emotions—altruism and inspiration—elevating our leadership to its apex.

THE CALCULUS OF ALTRUISM

We define altruism as being attentive to how we might benefit or impact others instead of how we might benefit ourselves. It's a word that can be seen as rarefied and exceptional, signifying an emotion only a saintly, selfless person could be capable of. Yet altruism is neither exotic nor otherworldly, but part of our real lives. When you get up and give an older person on the bus your seat, you're being altruistic by considering the other person's comfort or discomfort above yours in that moment. When you allocate precious time to help a colleague, you're being altruistic. Altruism is basic to the positive give-and-take that allows us to be a team player and caretaker. It's fundamental to leadership because as leaders we've got to think about the big picture and how our actions impact and benefit our team, the company, and even the world. Think about building or running a company where everyone is at odds, focused only on their narrow self-interest. It's unsustainable.

The thing about altruism is that it's a way of adapting to the truth that our well-being isn't dependent solely on our individual actions; our lives are all infinitely interdependent upon the actions and reactions of the people around us, rippling throughout our days and maybe even backward and forward through generations. In today's digital marketplace and global economy, we're seeing how totally our lives and livelihoods depend upon the actions of others around the world and can impact their fate. The altruistic mindset is a maturing of our awareness of what the real conditions of our well-being, happiness, and success are. We're so interconnected with all those around us that our thriving depends on *their* thriving. This can be illustrated by the familiar analogy of hell being a circle of people with short arms and long spoons trying to feed themselves, while heaven is this same circle of people feeding each other. If we are serious about our well-being, we must find that capacity within our nature that empowers us to think about others as much as or more than we think about ourselves.

Once we recognize that the number of people our well-being depends on is exponentially greater than the individual we call "I," we realize that thinking in an objective, big-picture way about our success, well-being, or happiness means thinking exponentially more about others than ourselves. That equation is the calculus of altruism.

Although a vital emotion for a leader, altruism can be difficult to access, especially when so many of us have been trained in a highly competitive ecosystem. It's easier to think about ourselves, family, and loved ones than a stranger on the other side of the planet. Still, we can't ignore our ingrained and highly evolved social capacities, and altruism is the purest of them.

As you'll see in the chapters that follow, we can sculpt our minds and rewire our nervous systems for altruism through the compassion training practice of emulating altruist mentors and heroes. By aligning ourselves with these role models and harnessing our inspiration to emulate their way of being, our clean energy of compassion and altruism can become a driver of authentic engagement and boundless leadership.

EVOLUTION OF COMPASSION: UPGRADES ARE POSSIBLE

Emulating and aligning ourselves with our enlightened leaders are more than an act of admiration, they are important aspect of developing our competency of compassion and the trait of authentic engagement. To understand this, look again at the evolutionary logic of mammalian life. We all know the cliché, "Two heads are better than one, ten friends better than none." Sensitive, emotionally connected, and responsive animals can enhance their survivability by creating a safe field or setting of cooperation. Within a certain realm of being bonded with others, we become safer and more powerful because we're coordinated.

If you think about our evolutionary transition from reptiles, when we became mammals about seventy million years ago, it didn't seem clear how nature got away with that experiment. After all, our reptile ancestors laid thousands of eggs and most of those, within hours, would hatch, and the young would slither away, ready to survive. On the other hand, mammal mothers bear very few young in the womb, and they emerge completely helpless and requiring extensive care for months or years. You'd think having large numbers of instantly survivable offspring would be an evolutionary advantage over a few extremely vulnerable offspring, but surprisingly it turns out that the mammal experiment seems to have worked better. After all, we're the ones making all the other forms of life on the planet extinct, not vice versa.

This is because we're specially evolved to be sociable and teachable. We learn updated survival information from our parents, and all the time we spend being helpless and impressionable in their care allows us to download current or local information that's not in our genes but can help us adapt to new environments and learn in ways that expand that range of adaptability. In contrast, our reptilian ancestors are restricted to genetic programs that are fixed, rigid, and limited.

Our interdependent social natures allow us to have a capacity for connectivity that supports extended group learning throughout the life span, the biological basis of what we call culture. We are the result of countless incremental upgrades wherein increasingly large brains allowed our ancestors to learn over increasing time spans and cooperate in increasingly larger groups. Over the course of our ancestry as mammals, we've become highly skilled cooperators and social learners. That's why understanding the evolutionary background of compassion—the emotional basis for our highly cooperative form of life—is vital.

There's a fly in the evolutionary ointment, however: evolution didn't fully prepare us to cooperate in the exponentially larger groups that the development of civilization has made possible. Our nervous systems evolved to bond intensely with the first people we encounter, usually our parents—that's imprinting. That capacity conditions our social and emotional brains, so that we have a special feeling of connectedness to the people we're closest to, making it easier to connect with those who seem like us, whether they are or not.

Because our emotional brain tends to group and sort people into "like us" and "not like us," we're always deducing who's going to help us, who's going to make us feel safe and happy, who's unsafe and may hurt us, and who seems neutral and doesn't fit into either category. Because of this, we engage others unconsciously by grabbing hold of the friendly, glossing over the neutral, and pushing away the challengers. Because our brains are wired this way, if we're going to build compassion, we must engage authentically with people in all three groups, not just the easy ones. That's where our work and lives will increasingly stretch us because our ability to lead depends on how authentically we can connect with colleagues in increasingly diverse workplaces and with people in different sectors and parts of the world in our interconnected age, not to mention those for whom we've developed some implicit prejudice. If we want to bring the best tool for the job, to engage the strong force of compassion and altruism with all these different people, we must upgrade our default wiring and break through our implicit biases and reactive emotions that make our relationships stressful in different ways.

We do this with something called equal empathy practice, which develops our capacity to understand every person near and far, bypassing the distorting filters or knee-jerk reactivity programmed into our emotional brains. Once we expose and disarm our biases and reactions, we expand our empathic awareness and learn how to understand more and different kinds of people, in larger and larger groups.

This practice involves taking advantage of another aspect of our nervous systems that is vital, and that is the emotional malleability we have, based on neuroplasticity and genetic fluidity. This emotional malleability is basic to all mammals, as evidenced by how our fellow mammals often naturally adopt and rear orphaned mammals, sometimes of a completely different species. This capacity is what allows us to be socially malleable, to learn to include more people in wider circles of care. As part of this malleability, we have the capacity to revise our childhood biases and emotional scripts about friend and foe so that we can open our hearts and expand our awareness, adopting one individual or group at a time. Given that basic work of clearing our blocks to equal empathy, we become ready to open ourselves, to get to know others realistically, and to build trust with them.

That's the good news. Although we have obstacles to realizing our potential for compassion and altruism, we also have a deeper capacity and malleability for expanding or upgrading our earlier programming and bringing our emotional brain to the broader capacity of our conscious, primate brain.

SCIENCE OF COMPASSION TRAINING

We now know human beings have evolved to develop the capacity for universal compassion and can overcome the obstacles of survival-based implicit bias and emotional reactivity. It's important to further train our capacity to overcome those obstacles and exercise the mental muscles we need. Beyond equal empathy, what do we mean by compassion training? How does it work? What's the evidence that our brains have the capacity to shift out of stress-reactive emotional mode and into proactive empathy and compassion?

In the past few decades, new research on how compassion training impacts us has begun to clarify the neuroscience behind how our emotional brains shift gears from the reactive mode of stress emotions to the proactive mode of compassion and engagement. Starting in 2008 and continuing through the past decade, dramatic findings coming from a number of labs around the world have shed light on the neuroscience of compassion. Most of these studies involve training undergraduates—novices in compassion—in five to seven sessions that teach the basic insights and skills of compassion.[14] The initial studies were done using images of faces in distress, which our brains are geared to read and respond to with social contagion—the survival tendency to unconsciously feel what those around us seem to feel—as our mirror neuron early-warning system evokes adverse emotional memories stored in the amygdala, triggering emotional and visceral stress reactivity.

As we would expect, before compassion training, the brains of the novice subjects displayed considerable reactivity in the amygdala. After training, something quite remarkable was discovered. There was much less amygdala activity and connectivity between the amygdala and higher brain regions that interpret the upset. Instead of the stress response system being triggered through social contagion, the social well-being system kicked in. Researchers knew this because they saw more activity in regions of the emotional brain that prepare us to respond socially, and this was linked with activation in the higher brain region that plans and executes action and with the emotional reward system in the emotional and reptilian brain that registers satisfaction and well-being. In contrast to the painful stress activation before the training, after the training, participants' brains showed the same proactive engagement that gets stimulated when we love anything—whether it's our favorite coffee or a dear friend—and move to approach it—a powerful satisfaction instead of fear and avoidance. Essentially, the emotional brains of those trained in compassion had undergone a powerful shift from reactive mode ("Get me out of here!") to a proactive, authentic engagement mode, wherein they felt safely connected, caring, and ready to respond to the distress of others.

As a psychotherapist, Joe hears a constant refrain from business leaders: "Whether it's in the boardroom or the bedroom, difficult emotional interactions are the biggest stress in our lives." These recent studies of compassion training show that we can learn to shift out of the emotional brain mode that reacts, enhances, and overreacts to those difficulties and into the mode that securely accepts, leans into, and responds skillfully to them. This can make a huge difference in our ability to perform well in difficult situations and be boundless leaders and also help to reduce our stress level and make it easier for us to stay positive and enjoy being of help or service to others. That's why the science of compassion training is indispensable in terms of understanding our potential to be boundless leaders.

As you'll see later in the discipline of heart, the most powerful way to prepare our minds and nervous systems to step into a boundless level of leadership is by identifying mentors—people who embody compassionate and altruistic qualities—and aligning our sense of ourselves with their way of being. It's important to choose well, because some compassion is inauthentic and we need to know the difference.

17 DEBUNKING THE STEREOTYPES

Authentic and Inauthentic Compassion

We've looked at empathy, compassion, and altruism from the neuro-psychological and social-emotional perspectives as connective states of mind that bond us with others in open, accepting, and proactive responsiveness. We've also looked at them in terms of recent research on how collaboration and cooperation allow companies to succeed not just from a human resource perspective but financially as well. What remains for us is to challenge the cultural stereotypes of compassion that make it hard to connect our sentimental view with the new science and practice.

Informed by an outdated view of human life as a competition between self-interested individuals, we've learned to be skeptical if not cynical about compassion. Compassion often figures in our modern worldview as a moralistic injunction or self-indulgent sentiment, which is at best saccharine and ineffectual and at worst self-defeating or self-injurious. This disparaging take leads us to identify compassion as a sentimental form of moralism and caretaking, which do not qualify as authentic types of compassion but are instead immature or misguided caricatures of care. The table below highlights the four criteria of authentic compassion and the four masks of inauthentic compassion:

AUTHENTIC COMPASSION	INAUTHENTIC COMPASSION
Objective understanding: Understanding based on correct information about the mind/body state of another or oneself	Sympathetic distress: The wish for others not to suffer based on projecting one's personal needs, rather than an accurate read of how *they* are suffering
Equanimous concern: Concern for the suffering of all people *including oneself*	Codependency: The wish to protect the people we are attached to, to protect our relationship or avoid conflict
Authentic responsiveness: A genuine concern to relieve suffering rather than a personal self-interest to please others	Caretaking: Gestures of care motivated by a personal need to see oneself and be seen by others in positive way
Effectiveness: Wise and skillful action that relieves suffering, whether kind and caring or tough and fierce	Bypassing: A fantasy of the power of our caregiving rather than the reality of effectively relieving suffering

How do we know when compassion is real and when it's not? Behind the masks of inauthentic compassion there's usually something else at play—like pity, self-importance, or righteousness. We might catch ourselves slipping into a rescue fantasy, like when you're feeling badly for someone but that feeling is tangled up in a wish to show how important you are, how well you're doing. Whatever it may be, within inauthentic compassion there is some distinction or distance between you and the object of that compassion, rather than a deeper, more genuine human connection. We often sense this when we express concern for someone in a difficult situation—a serious illness or financial setback—which we can't or don't want to identify with and would rather push away.

Authentic compassion is a centered response that avoids the extremes and where you authentically feel for the other but remain a separate person. You're not narrowly self-focused and bypassing the reality of the other's predicament, but neither are you sentimentally overidentified or attached to them or the appearance of being nice. You understand and feel for them and naturally respond with care: "I see you're struggling. I know what that's like, I've been there. How can we help you?" Then you review potential solutions and take the appropriate action. It's this realistic empathy, the genuine and active care for another human who could be you but isn't, that tells you your intention to help is authentic.

GIVERS, MATCHERS, AND TAKERS

How does unmasking inauthentic compassion apply to leadership? We can see the nature of compassion from within the context of business with a study that speaks to this so well.[15]

Adam Grant, the youngest tenured professor at the Wharton School of the University of Pennsylvania wrote a book called *Give and Take* wherein he analyzed data about salespeople and their easily quantifiable performance. His research spanned different industries, qualifying the salespeople as to whether their habitual style of selling made them givers, matchers, or takers. Givers are people who aren't focused on what they're receiving; they're willing to give freely and openly. Matchers are willing to give but expect something in return. Takers are solely focused on receiving, with no real interest in giving.

Grant's analysis revealed a number of surprising findings. First of all, the worst performers when it came to sales were in the givers group. A conventional approach to business would affirm this as an expected outcome and the mindset of those who believe "It's a dog-eat-dog world. Don't let yourself be taken advantage of." But as Grant examined the data, he found that the *top* performers were also in the givers group. *The best salespeople were givers, and the worst were givers too.* He dissected the data further to see if he could distinguish the two types of givers. It turned out that givers who performed best overall were those who were authentically giving; the group that did the worst were the ones who we interpret as inauthentically giving. They performed more poorly than the takers.

What does this show us about inauthenticity? There's a clear correlation between the masks of compassion like sentimental concern and codependency. In other words, "I don't want to do this favor for you, but I don't want to be somebody who isn't seen as a giver" or "I don't know how to face conflicts of interest, they make me nervous, so it's easier for me to help reflexively than to think through what's most helpful." The problem is that over time, such inauthentic givers burn out; they are unable to perform well because they don't know how to face conflicts and set skillful boundaries.

Having the presence of mind to delineate boundaries reflects a key criterion of authentic compassion: effectiveness. Joe advises his clients to notice whether they're being codependent by asking themselves, "Do I feel I'm obligated? I *have* to be nice *or else* . . .?" If the answer is yes, you can rest assured you're in the terrain of codependency wherein seemingly compassionate actions arise from a sense of life-or-death, do-or-die pressure. It's as if you're assuming a relationship is so brittle that admitting you can't help will break it. In that case, you're operating in survival mode—your awareness and heart are shut down. You're not sensing what the other person needs and wants because you're preoccupied with your need to protect the relationship. All too often, codependent caregivers end up pushing help on people who don't want it or aren't ready to receive it because of their pressure to be perceived as helpful.

In the discipline of mind, when we talk about self-awareness, we ask ourselves, "Am I doing this because I feel I should or am I doing this because I want to?" If we've developed self-awareness, we can tell these apart. The same applies to compassion: if we feel we *should* do it, it's likely inauthentic, but if it's what we want to do and it feels good, it's likely authentic and grounded in the four qualities of heart—empathy, resilience, engagement, and inspiration. As you might expect, these qualities are supported by the four dimensions of compassion. Objective understanding supports the quality of empathy. Equanimous concern supports the quality of resilience. Authentic responsiveness supports the quality of engagement. Effectiveness and skill reflect the quality of inspiration.

18 EMPATHY

Widening and Deepening
the Circle of Trust

Our first quality of heart is one we have touched on already: the power of empathy. Empathy is the core of compassion and essential for connection. It's something many people talk about but most don't find easy to define. We understand empathy as having two primary aspects: understanding and concern. The first is the ability to accurately recognize what's going on inside another person's mind and how that person is feeling. Neuroscientists call this capacity "cognitive empathy" or "theory of mind." After we recognize what someone is feeling, the second aspect is having a felt sense and authentic concern for them.

Empathy is not about judging or reacting to people's feelings. Instead, it acknowledges what is going on inside another human being—regardless if it's a feeling we have or might have had—allowing the other person to experience being known and seen. It's important to note that empathy is not just about individuals; it also allows us to know more about what's happening in the complex social world around us. Without empathy, there is no way for us to discern what's happening inside the minds and bodies of the people we live and work with. Imagine going into a negotiation with a colleague or a competitor without having any awareness of their motivation, concerns, needs, and interests.

Recently, there's been a substantial amount of research into the neuroscience of empathy.[16] Specifically, exploration of the differences between genuine and inauthentic empathy and compassion. If you look at the basic capacity we humans have as part of our social evolution, we see that it was necessary to have a constant intuitive read on what other people were feeling. This need applies to all mammals: if I'm a deer and a member of our herd twitches at the approach of a lion, my survival may depend on my having an immediate sense of and response to my herd member, since I'll need to run just as they will. Unfortunately, that survival wiring may wreak havoc on a team in a work situation. If we become alarmed every time one of our team members is having a bad day, we risk spending much of our time needlessly stressed and reactive instead of productive.

You may recall that as humans we've developed a capacity to read other people's body language using our mirror neurons. We constantly scan the faces and movements of those around us, and our response is processed by our emotional brain, which calls up memories of how we felt when *our* face made that expression or *our* body moved in that manner. This pattern-recognition system operates under the radar of consciousness and can prompt a "gut" reaction to others that we don't intend or of which we're not fully aware. When we're not making a mindful effort to understand other people and our reactions, our biased sense and reaction will often not be real, accurate empathy but instead the reflex response we call sympathy.

If we're not mindful of how our brains unconsciously read others, this reflex of sympathy can lead to all kinds of troublesome interactions: *If you're afraid, I'm afraid. If you're angry, I'm angry.* As we saw in chapter 16, some psychologists call this social contagion—the tendency to mirror the mood state we see others expressing, whether in the flesh or even virtually via the media or teleconferencing. Imagine a team leader walking into a meeting in a horrible mood. Within minutes, everyone in the room is likely to be in a funk too. The opposite can also happen with social contagion—the leader can enter exuding benevolence, and the team can feel better. Part of the vital role of empathy is developing our natural ability to do a reality check when our emotional brain is bouncing off other people like a Ping-Pong ball in unconscious social contagion or reflexive sympathy rather than connecting with them in *an accurate, impartial, and effective way.*

What are the need and benefit of real empathy? In a typical business environment, there's often an expectation about what we *should* be feeling, our reflexive sense of someone who is anxious or upset may be tainted by a negative bias and aversive reaction to their state of mind. The other person in that interaction may be dealing with something serious and will likely end up feeling worse since they're not being seen or heard. While the conventional wisdom in business and leadership may be to override the distress of our team, insisting they stay "on task," the emotional physics in the room likely involves making the distressed member feel worse rather than better and possibly triggering others to feel the same. Instead of pushing our team to stay on task, we've pushed them into a zone of distress and reactivity, which can spark defensive behavior, disengagement, or passive-aggressive responses—all counterproductive to the original efficiency and effectiveness desired.

We would never dream of applying that same bias or reaction to our customers. On the contrary, we would consider it an essential business practice to know what the customer feels and wants. However, our greatest assets, even before customers, are our colleagues and staff. If as a leader we don't meet them with empathy and care, if we feel it's enough to "manage" them or their feeling state, we're going to lose their engagement and motivation, and there's no way our team or company is going to succeed optimally. We may accomplish things, but it will be at the cost of undermining trust, collaboration, satisfaction, and creativity. That is why empathy is a key quality for boundless leadership.

Given the imprecision of language and lively debate in the scientific literature surrounding the term *empathy*, it's vital that our definition is precise. Researchers have tried various ways to distinguish the "noise" of implicit bias and reactivity from the "signal" of accurate information about other people's embodied minds. Some have called the noisy unconscious reaction to others "empathy," and distinguished it from the clean signal, which they call "theory of mind," "cognitive empathy," or "compassion."[17] We have chosen to call the noisy mode of reactivity "sympathy" or, when it involves negative reactivity, "sympathetic distress." And we've reserved the term *empathy* for the capacity to receive a clean signal from others.

In addition, we include the emotional response of authentic care and concern as a component of empathy, although some researchers define this as part of compassion. We align this caring responsiveness and concern with the capacity for emotional resilience (the second and next quality we train to help develop compassion). We define the active components of compassion—the intention to help and its expression in caring words or actions—as forms of authentic compassion. These we align respectively with the qualities of engagement and inspiration.

Given these distinctions, the good news about empathy and the other qualities that contribute to compassion that runs contrary to the conventional wisdom of twentieth-century science and business is that they can all be easily taught and learned. We know from extensive research[18] on the neuroscience of emotion—a.k.a. affective neuroscience—that these are natural qualities of the mammalian brain, based on repeated practice and the biology of learning/neuroplasticity, and so subject to cultivation.

How do we cultivate or train in empathy for boundless leadership?

Normally, empathy is spotty, based on whether our constitution or past experience enables us to identify with what another person is feeling. Fortunately, as most of us know from life experience, we can learn to become more accurately and broadly empathic. Therapists, nurses, teachers, coaches, and caretakers of all kinds must learn how to feel for people who might have different experiences from theirs. As leaders, the same holds true. We can't afford to settle for limiting our ability to empathize with people who are like us. We must empathize accurately and authentically with everyone. This means debiasing our heart—acknowledging and working through the natural emotional preconceptions that come from our childhood and our social conditioning—and then learning to refine and expand our innate capacity for unbiased empathy. This is a capacity wherein our empathy grows to an exceptional quality and degree, touching all the people we engage with in the course of our work and operating objectively, fairly, and impartially. This refined, expanded empathy involves not just debiasing but opening our heart to others, regardless of how "different" they feel to us.

One way to nurture equal empathy and widen our circle of trust is through the practice of equalizing self and other. This method of recognizing and reflecting on the kindness in all living beings may be the best equalizer because contemplating that quality helps open our hearts and minds to those we see as neutral and those we see as threats and naturally kindles the empathy and human kindness we normally reserve for family and friends.

EQUAL EMPATHY

The practice of equal empathy involves the following steps:

- Invoking a quiet state of mindful awareness
- Inviting the images of three people—one easy to love, one a neutral acquaintance, and one you find a bit difficult
- Observing your warmth, biases, or any negative feelings that arise
- Revisiting your three people one at a time as you release your bias and reactive emotions of clinging, indifference, or aversion

As you practice empathy, notice the biased perceptions and feelings of clinging, mistrust, and aversion clouding your mind and gripping your heart as you turn attention to these people. Try to question your biases by recalling how friends may hurt you or become enemies; neutral people are everywhere and indispensable to your life; and critics or adversaries can become allies or serve as great teachers. Try to bring an impartial element to correct these biases by reflecting that all people and all living beings are more alike than different. You may want to remind yourself, "Just like me this person wants to feel connected, be happy."

Purify your care for your loved one by letting go, and feel the love enhanced; build awareness and empathy for your acquaintance, and feel the expansion of your humanity and connectedness; bear with or even accept the challenging other, and feel the relief and confidence that brings for you both. Once you've successfully developed equal empathy for those you find easy, extend your practice to those you find more difficult.

When you've successfully developed equal empathy for multiple individuals, you move to groups you identify with, groups you find neutral, and groups you experience as "other." You may want to deepen equal empathy for all three kinds of individuals or groups by reciting phrases of loving-kindness toward each being or group, close, neutral, and far. For example, "May you be happy. May you be well, safe, and healthy. May you have joy. May you have peace."

We have a strong self-interest in learning to view others as being in any way like us or related to us. This offers an alternative to leading and living from feeling mistrustful and threatened, as we often do. The art of equalizing self and other is designed to help us break down the prison of harmful habits like practicing vigilance to make sure we are not being excluded, clinging to others as the silver bullet that will save us, and feeling antipathy toward the other as the enemy blocking us from our goal one brick at a time. By bringing an unbiased mindfulness and awareness to our perception and responses to all, whether they be bosses, peers, or reports, familiar or unfamiliar, on our team or rivals, we become better, fairer, more prepared leaders responding wisely and skillfully to challenges, wherever and however they occur.

The skill of equal empathy is like social-emotional kung fu that helps us build immunity to the stress and distress of others, rather than be triggered back into stress by difficult interactions. It serves as the first step in disarming and healing difficult relationships—whether with a challenging boss or employee or a diverse team or organization.

Practice

FRIEND OR FOE?
EQUALIZING SELF AND OTHER

1 Settle into a comfortable sitting or lying posture on a chair, cushion, yoga mat, or bed.

2 Center your attention on the place in your body where you most sense your breathing.

3 Once your mind settles, shift your attention to clear the workspace of open awareness.

4 Into that space, invite the image of a loved one, acquaintance, and challenging other.

5 Focus on each, noticing any biases and feelings of attachment, inattention, and aversion.

6 Practice trying to counter your biases so you can see and feel their equal humanity.

7 Return to the practice, ideally at a regular time and place, three to seven days a week.

8 Tune in to this practice to clear the biases and reactions that block empathy in daily life.

19 RESILIENCE

Transforming Our Inner Demons

Within the discipline of heart, resilience is the quality that allows us to release and bounce back from an insult, injury, or loss. It is a determining factor of our leadership capacity, consistency, and flexibility. In business, we're besieged by obstacles, setbacks, and disappointments, often from many sources. At some point, we're going to receive not just criticism but a big hit. Resilience provides the ability to rebound from setbacks, great and small. The alacrity with which we do this is a determining factor in our leadership capacity; the faster we can bounce back, the more consistently effective we'll be.

Conventional wisdom in business confuses resilience with grit, or hard-core toughing it out, but it's more than that. Resilience involves an element of letting go rather than gripping tighter and is a quality that draws on agility, equilibrium, and balance, rather than stubbornness and rigidity. When Elazar works with clients, he often asks, "Are you on your horse or are you off your horse?" Being a boundless leader is about your ability to stay fluidly in the saddle through all the ups, downs, and turns, rather than clamping down so hard you get thrown. Resilience involves learning to accept and adapt, whatever comes. You may get jostled around, but you are less prone to getting knocked off. Grit on the other hand involves trying so hard to control the flow of events that you're prone to getting knocked off or even dragged. Rigid tenacity isn't the answer.

Joe agrees that the idea of grit or toughing it out is the opposite of resilience. The essence of resilience is the ability to acknowledge and adjust to what went wrong, rather than clinging to it. The challenge is that most of us are not good at letting go. This isn't just because our culture has a one-sided preference for taking control rather than releasing it. It's because grabbing hold in moments of uncertainty or loss has been wired into our nature through evolution—it's a tendency reflected in our default negativity bias. When we feel threatened or attacked—be it by a saber-toothed tiger or a judgmental colleague—we dig in and hold on for dear life. Our instinct runs counter to what best serves us in the moment, because once we are triggered into social-emotional survival mode, we block the qualities we must use to sustain equanimity and navigate the challenge: empathy, resilience, engagement, and inspiration.

This predicament is rooted in our emotional negativity bias—our dependency in early childhood, when we relied entirely upon the love and protection of others. We endured some pretty rough emotional moments. Mom left the room, and we felt like she'd never come back. Her absence felt like the end of our safety and connection: *I'm going to starve and die.* And because of our negativity bias, we tend to hold on to such inevitable, worst-case moments, including stress emotions like shame and panic: *Oh, how horrible it feels to be abandoned by Mom* or *Maybe she doesn't love me, maybe I'm no good.* You can imagine that it's hard for us as infants or kids to let go of those emotions and bounce back when our caregivers are our entire support system.

That early life trauma is often reenacted in our emotional brains and bodies when we're dealing with social obstacles and confrontations: *That person doesn't like me, or they would have never excluded me from the conversation* or *Can you believe how unfairly they treat me?* These perceived social attacks or microaggressions trigger our deeper emotional wounds—the traumatic self-state or our wounded child, if you will. Given our negativity bias to hold on to the worst, our identity all too often sticks at *What if I'm not lovable?* or *What if I'm not good enough?* It's extremely hard for us to let this go and requires dedicated and ongoing boundless leadership practice. It takes understanding that our worst emotional memories are not the reality of what's happening now. Most of the time, the other person isn't trying to make you feel worthless or panicked—they simply disagree or are disappointed and wrapped up in their own stuff.

Learning how to release the momentary disconnect or distress and return to a positive emotional state defines the quality of resilience. This requires a fundamental self-acceptance or security, which is key to our human development. For example, as a kid when we feel connected to our caregivers, we receive the message that we're unconditionally important to them, and it makes us feel like, *I can be here. I'm safe and I'm connected*. But when there are disruptions or disappointments, which there invariably are, we develop a sense of insecurity.

These two parts of our emotional nature—threatened and safe—are constantly bouncing back and forth. It's important for us to know where we are on the spectrum and be able to shift, to let go of the worst case—*I'm not safe or connected*—and to build self-acceptance, self-care, and self-compassion. Tapping into these capacities builds resilience. It prepares us to face, soothe, and heal the emotional wounds that block our resilience, even though those wounds may be bound up in painful feelings of shame and beliefs like *I'm no good*. Understanding this vulnerable emotional landscape and having the care and skill to soothe and move through it are indispensable to trusting that we're okay. These capacities for self-acceptance and self-compassion allow us to stop our worst-case thinking and feeling and to reengage from a proactive place from which we can attain the best present outcome.

Take, for example, one of Joe's clients. The CEO of a billion-dollar public company, he needed help responding to board concerns about his tension and reactivity to critical feedback impacting his health, leadership of senior managers, and the entire business. By developing a practice of mindful self-awareness, the CEO learned to observe the way childhood insecurities drove him to seek praise rather than truth, as well as how negative information triggered his harsh inner critic, making him feel inadequate and overwhelmed. Practicing self-compassion freed him from his obsession with praise, making him resilient in the face of criticism and changing his leadership style in ways that not only reassured the board but led to him steering a major shift in company culture and branding toward wellness.

FRAMEWORKS FOR SELF-COMPASSION

The capacity for self-compassion can be practiced in many ways. The two frameworks we've found most effective are as follows:

- Mindful self-compassion
- The R.A.I.N. of self-compassion

As you'll see, both of these share elements but mindful self-compassion is more focused on emotional nurturance and well-being, whereas the R.A.I.N. of self-compassion involves a deeper encounter with and investigation of the cognitive and perceptual assessments that maintain our traumatic self-state.

In both of these frameworks we set the stage by grounding our minds with body mindfulness and mindful sensitivity and then clearing our minds with mindful awareness. We then turn our mindful awareness to our hearts and minds. This creates the workspace for our compassion training, which allows us to unlearn what we must and to relearn what we need, gaining access to our innate perceptiveness, flexibility, and objectivity. From there we can either work with what emerges when we open up our minds or intentionally use the space to process experiences and interactions that have been challenging.

Beginning with mindful self-compassion, the first step is to face what hurts rather than run or react, to be with what feeling is happening in this moment—rejection, hurt, anxiety, disconnection, or whatever it may be. This initiates our process of our conscious engagement with our experience, as opposed to normal life where we commonly live with all this hurt buried or bypassed, ignoring it until it erupts as an acute upset. Unfortunately, we often understand our hurt in an isolated and even shame-based way, assuming that it's bad to feel what we feel and that we're the only one who feels this. Our sense of shame or isolation is a large part of what makes our traumatic self-state so buried, its emotional and visceral experiences so distressing. The harsh, unhelpful voice of our inner critic says things like, "Why are you feeling that way? You should get over it. Grit your teeth, get tough, and push through, so and so never feels like this." Blaming ourselves for feeling shame and for having an inner critic only fuels the fire of self-inflicted suffering.

The second step in the practice of mindful self-compassion is to soothe our hurt with nonshaming acceptance, embracing suffering as part of our common humanity. We remind ourselves that our suffering is normal, part of being human. The hurt we feel is what makes us human, part of how everyone feels beneath the surface. Because we seldom talk openly about our fears, wounds, and hurts, we tend to carry a deep sense of shame or isolation: *It's only me who feels this way while everybody else seems fine.* Once we acknowledge and connect in a truly accepting and caring way with how we hurt, we can engage with kindness to deshame and destigmatize what we feel.

As our mindful self-compassion practice progresses, we see our subjective self is relieved of the pervasive self-critical feelings of shame or isolation surrounding distress. We can genuinely ask ourselves, "What is it that I need? What can I do that will be helpful?" We learn to listen deeply and respond with real care. We can be truly heard and seen by ourselves and committing to taking better care of our emotional needs. This healing attention begins to register with our traumatic self-state, embracing and integrating it as a valued part of our whole, healthy self. This healing internal experience prepares us to stay attuned to our felt sense of self and to make every effort to show it the acceptance and nurturance it needs.

Compare this to R.A.I.N. The practice contained in the acronym R.A.I.N. was devised by Michele McDonald, one of the first American mindfulness teachers. Essentially three of the four elements are identical and only the third element of R.A.I.N. is new or at least more explicit. This is the element of investigating our minds to reach the root of our social suffering. Here's how it works:

Recognize: We begin with a mindful recognition or mindful presence with whatever is hurting.

Acknowledge: We acknowledge and accept our hurts without shame or blame to break out of a trance of insecurity, isolation, of unworthiness.

Investigate: Investigation of our hurts adds a cognitive dimension of self-compassion, which is important as it allows for correcting, unlearning, and relearning the intuitive (mis-) assessments we made as small children about who we are and what the world is, writing a disempowering victim or entitlement narrative of ourselves as helpless and powerless.

Nurture: When we nurture or "nonidentify," we engage the combined work of nurturing our hurts emotionally. We no longer implicitly or explicitly identify with false negative assessments and beliefs about ourselves and the world.

In R.A.I.N. we apply an investigative mind that traces the different modes of stress reactivity to their common root: the underlying traumatic habit of self. In the process we may notice a primal fear of abandonment underlying clinging, a shame-bound self-enclosure that makes us ignore others, and a sense of inadequacy causing us to feel hurt and reactive toward others. We try to approach this vulnerable self-state with unconditional acceptance and care, letting it relax the grip on our heart and mind. The objective is to recognize and accept the old wounds that underlie our most vulnerable sense of self and investigate the worst-case beliefs we hold that anchor our traumatic state. R.A.I.N. practice allows us to return to and access the positive sense of ourselves as worthwhile, loving, caring beings and feel safely open and embodied in our hearts and in our interactions with others. As we absorb the nurturance and nonidentification, we may experience relief, freedom, and lightness, which open up a new understanding of ourselves.

By empowering us to develop emotional insight and care for ours and others' post-traumatic emotions and beliefs, the practice of self-compassion can allow us to heal and unlearn the self-states that anchor our social survival mode and reactivity. Given this capacity, we can maintain and install the prosocial mode of safe connection that evokes positive social emotions from tolerance and acceptance to love, compassion, gratitude, and altruism. What this looks like for leaders is a sense of genuine equanimity and magnanimity that allow us to rise above the fray of moment-to-moment distress or upset. This is how self-compassion training promotes resilience—empowering us to bounce back quickly from bodily fight-flight-faint-freeze reactions and stay continuously engaged in social embodiment and responsiveness.

Practice

TAMING SHAME—SELF-COMPASSION

1 Settle into a comfortable sitting or lying posture on a chair, cushion, yoga mat, or bed.
2 Center your attention on the place in your body where you most sense your breathing.
3 Once your mind settles, shift your attention to clear the workspace of open awareness.
4 Into that space, invite the present or remembered experience that most distresses you.
5 Try to meet the felt sense of that experience with fully present caring awareness.
6 Practice accepting it without shame or blame as part of our common humanity.
7 Try to heal the hurt and correct the shame-based belief that bind traumatic self-states.
8 Return to the practice, ideally at a regular time and place, three to seven days a week.
9 Tune in to this practice to soothe/correct the hurt/views that block resilience in daily life.

20 ENGAGEMENT

Tuning In to the Strong
Force of Emotions

The third quality of the discipline of heart is engagement, the interactive dynamic connection with another person based on a shared sense of mutual safety, empathy, and positivity. Typically, we are most engaged with individuals or groups with whom we feel an instinctive empathy, moderately engaged with those we experience as neutral, and least engaged with those we find challenging.

As we saw with empathy, this sorting by implicit bias reflects a social survival instinct and leads to the formation of cliques and the phenomenon of watercooler conversations where people self-sort into categories and engage accordingly. The challenge here is that our real need to engage fully with all the people we work with, especially as leaders, runs contrary to how our emotional brains have been designed by evolution and programmed by childhood. Since our brains evolved to act as contrast enhancers, distinguishing people who feel safe from those who feel dangerous and glossing over the silent majority in the middle, they tend to limit our bandwidth and block our full innate potential for positive engagement. The biggest problem is our negativity bias, which predisposes us to give in to suspicion, doubt, or fear in our relationships, even with those we consider close. This limits our ability to open our minds and hearts to be present with other people in a playful, cooperative, creative way and contributes to critically low engagement in the workplace.

According to the Gallup Poll,[19] which looks at this across industries and cultures, the level of engagement that reflects resonance inside a business has hovered around 30 percent for decades. The majority of employees have traditionally struggled with that sense of not feeling ready to show up, especially to show up with their best. While these numbers have been on the rise over the past five years, the bump seems to be driven by a minority of newer organizations that have consciously made a shift in leadership style and corporate culture toward the mammalian mode of emphasizing safety, connection, and positive human development. Why is this still so hard for mainstream leaders and businesses?

Our take is that it requires a conscious decision and intentional practice to override conventional business and leadership cultures that reinforce our limiting survival instincts. We sometimes say that we're living with an evolutionary hangover—our brains, bodies, and minds are wired for primitive survival. And what that means is unconsciously, when we're not paying attention, we drift back into a negative mode—self-protective, self-ruminative, or self-enclosed—and that's not a place where we can feel connected to other people. We've all had moments when we get stuck in worst-case feelings such as, *I don't know if they like me* or *I think management is on course to destroy the business* or *The presentation is going to fail.* Even when we're not especially insecure our default state is to straddle the fence between self-protection and inclusion, leaning (thanks to our default biases) toward the closed, self-protective side. To be engaged and experience resonance, we must be in what is an equally natural but statistically unusual state of mind—feeling a fundamental sense of security that empowers us to lean toward being open to all those around us and the world at large. This unusual state is a sign of optimal health, a fundamental sense of safety and connection that activates our capacity to be engaged with others of all kinds—unguarded, interested, curious, and playful. In the workplace that means fostering collaboration and creativity, both of which are crucial to a thriving business.

We can see why overcoming negativity bias to foster broader and more positive engagement is important when we examine this crucial sense of collaboration and creativity, since it is what most readily leads to a culture of innovation. The absence of this collaborative, creative sense can lead to disaster by preventing companies from evolving. Reduced teamwork and innovation are not the only costs, however; low engagement also launches a destructive cycle within an organization. Disengagement, especially extreme disengagement, is contagious. It can set off a chain reaction that motivates the best talent to leave and the mediocre to stay. This can escalate until management responds by analyzing the symptoms: Perhaps people aren't arriving on time, or they aren't following through on projects. Maybe they're taking dangerous shortcuts. But if only the symptoms are addressed by establishing consequences or demands for compliance, stress and disengagement are likely to increase. Disengagement can spiral in an organization when managers use the old business-as-usual strategies of driving engagement through imposing consequences and/or offering external incentives.

We must adopt the mammalian style of leadership that activates engagement, creating a strong force of resonance within a group. From the perspective of the human psyche, the natural thing to do is to cooperate and connect, but from the conventional business perspective, based on mistaken science and centuries of tradition, it's counterintuitive to say, "Since you're not giving what the company needs, I'm going to show more care because that will bring out your potential." Yet that's the essence of boundless leadership! If we're going to become boundless in how we lead we must turn it all upside down and return to the natural state of mind and heart.

That's how we mammals evolved. When we're engaged with authentic empathy, compassion, and care, we're at our best. The positive emotions we require are muscles we're born with that can be trained. While our self-interested modern culture teaches us to fear these emotions that may make us vulnerable or soft or that simply cannot be extended to more than a small circle of family, friends, and colleagues, current science has conclusively demonstrated otherwise. Anyone, regardless of temperament, personality, or level of emotional intelligence, can cultivate positive emotions that support a capacity for greater engagement. Decades of affective neuroscience and positive psychology have shown that the prosocial emotions of love, compassion, joy, and equanimity naturally promote the unfolding of our capacities for engagement and the widening of our circle of social effectiveness.

WISE GIVE-AND-TAKE

How do we continue to override our biases and cultivate the emotions that support engagement?

If we want a practice that helps build the quality of engagement, we must first unlearn ingrained attitudes toward self and others and upend expectations of the flow of give-and-take in our adult lives. While our inner child approaches our relationships with the naïve expectation of being able to take as much pleasure as possible while giving as little help and care as possible, our inner adult must learn a larger, more realistic view of the social world and reverse the direction of this flow by taking as much responsibility as possible and giving as much help and care as possible. This is especially true if we're looking to become boundless leaders. Rather than projecting our fears or frustrations onto others and holding on to unrealistic expectations generated by our traumatized inner child, we learn to care for ourselves and shift our capacities to improve our collective lives. By doing this we focus on what we can control and feel more empowered.

This is what the wise give-and-take practice helps us do. In essence we monitor the quality of an interaction to ensure that it's based on as much care as possible. Sustained by our oxygen masks of self-compassion we can be mindful of how we respond with care and monitor the level of our care. Traditionally, this practice is framed as a conscious reversal of childish self-indulgence, which seeks to get as much as possible and give as little as possible, into a mature engagement with life, which means taking as much care of and giving as much love to self and others as possible.

It is essential that we reframe "I" and "mine" around the new perspective of openness and the skills of compassion—the building blocks for our proactive, engaged social self. As in the natural process of parenthood, this shift happens organically, arriving at a more expansive and objective agency that embraces others as much as self. While the expansion of selfhood in the course of parenting is a natural process fueled by empathic openness and loving, compassionate care, the shift in wise give-and-take is a conscious extension of that process to our wider social lives. It amounts to adopting the whole of our team, company, and even all humanity as an extended family and choosing to relate to that family to the best of our ability as friend or relative. For this shift to be authentically engaged, we must exchange our myopic view of our lives, which is centered around self-interest, and replace it with an expanded one intimately involving the well-being of every individual in the web of life that is our world.

Wise give-and-take is a powerful practice for our everyday interactions. It serves to exercise and integrate our social emotions—equanimity, tolerance, acceptance, gratitude, love, and compassion—into a highly effective way of being in the world that galvanizes our altruistic resolve and embodies the spirit of enlightened altruism. By reversing attitudes toward self and others in the flow of wise give-and-take, we access an immense source of happiness derived from the appreciation that the less we need, the more we can give, and this is empowering.

Wise give-and-take starts with the practice of self-compassion. Breathing in our suffering with care and converting it into love. With that capacity of self-care as a home base, wise give-and-take extends that care to the world, shifting us into proactive mode and building bridges of empathy and compassion to one person and then one group at a time. This practice is gradual and progressive: you begin with yourself, move on to dear ones, extend it to strangers, and then offer it to challenging others until your circle of care includes all life. We rely on the application of mindful insight to stretch the limits of our capacity to feel wise compassion for others by taking our awareness of the suffering of others into our hearts and dissolving it into our healing insight and care so that we can give healthy love, human kindness, and radical acceptance to others who are close, neutral, or challenging to us.

The practice of wise give-and-take involves the following steps:

- Grounding your mind and body in mindfulness
- Inviting the image of another being who is close, neutral, or challenging to you.
- Taking in their distress with caring awareness and letting it touch your heart
- Maintaining self-awareness of how their distress might trigger you
- Soothing your heart until wise care and warmth naturally arise for them and their suffering
- As the wise care and warmth well up, sharing them with the other(s) by giving love

Remember that encountering a person or situation you find challenging may trigger your reactive self-state. If this happens, protect your nervous system and stabilize your practice by connecting the mental movement of taking in their distress with a mindful in-breath, linking the application of wise care with a pause before the out-breath, and joining the "giving" of love with the out-breath. This is called "mounting give-and-take on the breath." It harnesses the calming effect conscious breathing has on the autonomic nervous system to the work of transforming social stress into care.

Since our social stress reflects how the suffering of others can subliminally trigger our traumatic self-state, bringing equal caring attention to how we take others in and how we respond is the best protection during difficult interactions, for our minds and for our impact on others.

Once we practice this two-way caring attention through wise give-and-take, we not only grow our capacity to shift the quality of our experience and interactions toward authentic engagement but also apply that capacity under conditions of possible social stress in daily life. The practice for daily life within the quality of engagement is to monitor any social stress we experience and, when we notice a spike, to combine equal empathy for others and self-compassion for ourselves by shifting into wise give-and-take. If the stress seems high enough to be triggering, we can practice first taking in our distress, soothing it with wise care, then giving ourselves love and compassion. If the challenge still feels high, we can practice wise give-and-take mounted on the out- and in-breaths.

To use an automotive analogy, once we've disengaged the compulsive survival mode of childhood self-indulgence and reengaged the low-stress gear of positive social emotions like care and love, mindfulness of the in- and out-breath serve to lock in a social-emotional four-wheel drive that empowers us to negotiate the roughest interpersonal terrain with maximal human traction and minimal wear and tear on our body/mind. As we learn to take care of and give love to ourselves, we experience our stressed interactions with others who are close, neutral, or challenging to us as the interplay between *our* confused childhood mind and *their* confused childhood mind. From there we can naturally widen our circle of care and skill, engaging others and our larger world in a meaningful and effective way.

Practice

BUILDING OUR HEART MUSCLES— GIVING AND TAKING

1 Settle into a comfortable sitting or lying posture on a chair, cushion, yoga mat, or bed.

2 Center your attention on the place in your body where you most sense your breathing.

3 Once your mind settles, shift your attention to clear the workspace of open awareness.

4 Into that space, invite the image of a loved one, an acquaintance, and a challenging other.

5 One at a time, on the in-breath take the awareness of their suffering in with care.

6 Allow that awareness to touch and stir the warmth of human kindness in your heart.

7   On the out-breath, send that warmth out to them as love, friendship, or respect.

8   Practice extending wise give-and-take to others in widening circles of care.

9   Return to the practice, ideally at a regular time and place, three to seven days a week.

10   Tune in to this practice to engage others with genuine care and concern in daily life.

21 INSPIRATION

Encountering the Mentor Within

The final quality of the discipline of heart is inspiration, one of the key components because it provides the energy to fuel authentic engagement and the social-emotional skills of boundless leadership. We hear the word *inspiration* thrown around a lot, typically to suggest a quality of someone special, an aspect of personal charisma. Boundless leaders view inspiration in a different and specific way: as the social energy that fuels the expression of human altruism.

In terms of evolution, inspiration reflects the social high gear our nervous system can shift into when we're rising to the challenge of engaging with others in difficult or complicated contexts like helping, leading, supporting, or guiding them. It's a biological "second wind" or turbo boost that we're capable of as mammals that evolved to enable us to respond quickly and effectively to challenges facing our family or tribe in ways that galvanized solidarity, cohesion, and direction within the group. We see this distinctive social energy emerge as "team spirit" in the face of group challenges like team sports or first-response situations like hurricanes or medical emergencies, where leaders and other members of a team face a common task with a seemingly perfect balance of cohesion and specialization.

No leader can rationally argue that getting others to take a particular action is not a core function of leadership. However, perhaps as a vestige of the command-and-control culture, many leaders still believe that pushing behavior through motivation is no different than

151

pulling through inspiration, and with some leaders, it's considered better. In one client organization, the management team was deeply affected by negative comments on social media and company rating sites like Glassdoor. This created a radical assessment of the company's culture, protocols, and management style. In the final analysis, the underlying culprit was an implicit belief that management carried all the weight, and the rank and file were trying to get by with as little effort as possible, requiring a clear list of what was necessary for compliance and what the consequences for deviation were. After some authentic soul-searching and changes in a few key positions, the company shifted their goal to a greater sense of community, relying on inspiration for what might be achieved *together* rather than on a self-interested motivation based on fear of consequences for what could go wrong. There are too many variables to attribute a company's growth to a single change, but it's self-evident that the improvement in morale, collaboration, and innovation was directly tied to this shift.

Examples such as this show how leadership requires inspiration that is distinct from mere personal motivation. A leader who tries to inspire others from a fundamentally self-interested place will never have the same impact as one who is authentically engaged with their team and genuinely cares about the well-being and benefit of all. The confusion is common, but remember that personal motivation is all too often tainted by negative emotions like envy, greed, pride, or fear. These manifest as a self-interested strategy for motivating others, which is then driven or tainted by those negative energies: "Here are the consequences if you don't succeed," or "If you fail, the company will fail." But the energy of guilt or fear will never spark genuine inspiration.

Leading from inspiration is about tapping into positive social energy. If we're not in a positive part of our emotional spectrum, we're not going to become engaged in that high-gear way, and work process and culture are going to be less collaborative and more confrontational. There's a different quality to inspiration that is reflected in a wholly new mammalian chemistry, modulating the makeup of the reptilian brain with new mammalian transmitters like oxytocin (the cuddle hormone) and vasopressin (the play hormone). The distinction is especially clear in the chemistry of the play hormone, which is what socializes aggression and competition in team sports or rough-and-tumble play as kids. This is the quality that allows us to use our power but not in an ego-driven, antisocial way. Not out of fear, shame, hurt, or anger but out of fun, care, and concern for others—for the *team*. What we mean by altruism here is that mode that our nervous systems shift into when we're inspired and thinking about the other person or group rising to any challenge—play or work. This same evolutionary biology and neurochemistry is what energizes acts of spontaneous heroism.

In the discipline of mind we explored how boundless leadership starts with the ability to bring your best. In this discipline of heart, as a boundless leader, your primary job is to bring out the best in those around you, to help them access parts of themselves they didn't know existed. The ability to get them to go beyond what they thought, beyond what their previous limits and dreams may have been, is one of the deeply meaningful and powerful qualities of heart that make our leadership boundless. Inspiration simultaneously comes from and creates the conditions for genuine, shared positivity.

We're familiar with social contagion as a negative force. Because we're porous, social contagion leaves us open to being triggered into reactive emotional memories and states, but social contagion also works in a positive way when we "catch" the energy of inspiration from others in our group. If one person on our team is inspired, enthused, and positive, we tend to gravitate toward their energy. That's why people like spectator sports—even for the observer there's an infectious thrill in pushing limits as we resonate and connect with the players and fans.

We may think that an athlete has the power of inspiration or an exceptional leader has it, but we don't. The thing is, we do! We're all capable of more than we realize. We have a bigger "best" than what we're using.

We want to tap into the energy of real inspiration as leaders and set the best tone, but we also want others to be encouraged, positively motivated, and able to tap into theirs. It takes us back to that notion of heroism, of being an ordinary person in an extraordinary situation. We don't have to be special to inspire; we have to be in a *special place* within our nervous systems. The reality is we can train ourselves to keep returning to that positive social energy, even to use it as our default instead of the stress-charged energy of anger, shame, or fear.

As boundless leaders, we try to keep that flame of inspiration lit. Modeling inspiration is like lighting a candle and touching our flame to a few others' flames who then touch it to still others' flames, until the team, company, or community is illuminated by inspiration. It's a positive social contagion or influence and a way of leading without needing to impress or intimidate. One way to cultivate this energy of inspiration for ourselves and others is by drawing on people who have inspired *us*, the people who have lit *our* fire. We can do this by invoking and bonding with our mentors, with their exceptional ability, but more importantly, their exceptional presence, heart, and way of being.

MENTOR BONDING

The practice of invoking and emulating the mentors who inspire us offers a powerful way to tap and harness our potential for genuine inspiration. This mentoring practice involves the following steps:

- Grounding your mind and body in mindfulness
- Inviting the image of a mentor who inspires or empowers you
- Focusing on the qualities you want
- Disclosing all the personal limits and flaws you fear will keep you from accessing those qualities
- Rejoicing in your mentor's confidence that you can overcome them

- Seeing yourself taking in or accessing the way of being you admire
- Dedicating any inspiration or qualities you've accessed for the sake of all

The essence of this practice is exercising the power of positive imagery focused on overcoming our self-imposed blockages and simulating the mature, parenting qualities that support us in developing empowered roles and transformative lives. At the heart of the practice is the role-modeling relationship wherein the process of enlarging our habitual self and world is imaginatively simulated and rehearsed through the empowering influence of a mentor. Similar to a flight simulator and energized by an inspiring and caring role model, this practice empowers us to reenvision ourselves and the world in light of an ideal vision of life.

The practice relies on radical open awareness to deconstruct our traumatic sense of self and world and envision an encounter with a congenial role model who mirrors our ideal vision of that self and world. It rehearses appreciating, internalizing, and integrating the way of being we admire in mentors and models of wise compassion and altruism. Most important, in the selection of role models is a genuine sense of safety, admiration, hope, inspiration, even affection for a person who embodies qualities we wish to develop.

Mentors with whom we've had direct experience can elicit complex emotions. The intention here is to connect with the mentor's primary positive regard so that we can work through complex emotions and eventually accept the common humanity of the mentor and ourselves. The aim is not to deny one's experience but to intentionally harness the intersubjective power of the positive mentor bond as a crucible for insight, healing, and transformation.

As in the practice of mindfulness, the imagery we've explored begins by prompting us to envision our body in the lighter, clearer version called the breath body or body of light. What is new here is that this body helps make us receptive to the influence of an ideal role model, giving our sense of self the plasticity we need to absorb a more ideal outer role and inner way of being. This coarse and subtle self-imagery aims to expand our perception and emotional intelligence beyond reactive patterns. It also opens us to empowered self-images, positive emotions, and peak states of physical arousal and flow. Imagery and affirmation are contemplative power tools in part because they use ideal self-images within role-modeling bonds, but primarily because they prepare us to master the social-emotional and neurobiological art of transformation. When we envision a new self-image in this manner, the imagery prepares us not just for a new way of being in our social world but for new ways to live in our emotional body and nervous system.

As you begin this practice, don't doubt your ability to meditate with imagery! The trick is not to expect too much instantly but to work with whatever you can muster, trusting the process will bear fruit just like any new workout at the gym. At first you may need to be content with reading or listening to the scripts that guide imagery practice, as if they are poems or stories. The result you're seeking is that your imagery will grow as clear and real as normal perception, while retaining the transparency that comes from consciously creating and evoking a specific perception in the mind's eye. Eventually, this skill will help you alter the building blocks of perception, including your habitual sense of yourself and others. These shifts will open new doors in your awareness, experience, and response to the worlds around you and inside you.

The practice of emulating mentors of unwavering kindness, compassion, and altruism empowers us to speed the natural development of unconditional compassion. And based on that gradual process of self-transformation, an adaptive resilience state can eventually be installed as a stable, unchanging trait. This practice can serve us anytime during our everyday life. All it takes is to catch ourselves when we revert to overwhelm and trauma and to call to mind mentors who restore us to a sense of empowerment and inspiration.

Practice

WHO CAN YOU COUNT ON?—
MENTOR BONDING

1 Settle into a comfortable posture and envision your body as translucent and luminous.

2 Center your attention on the place in your body where you most sense your breathing.

3 Once your mind settles, shift your attention to clear the workspace of open awareness.

4 Into that space, invite the image of a mentor or role model who inspires and empowers you.

5 Focus on the qualities they model that you admire and want to develop yourself.

6 Share your strengths and challenges, then own the potential your mentor sees in you.

7 Ask for the guidance and ongoing support you need, then dedicate yourself to change.

8 Return to the practice, ideally at a regular time and place, three to seven days a week.

9 Tune in to this practice to tap into inspiration when you feel blocked in daily life.

22 APPLICATION

Empowered Responsibility:
Modeling the Problem-Solving Mind

Within the discipline of heart empowered responsibility is the practical application enabling us to break one of our most unproductive businesses habits: the reflex to find fault and place blame. This application helps us manifest an energy and tonality that engender participation and collaboration, take us to solutions efficiently, and deepen teamwork and trust. It allows us as leaders to have a positive impact in difficult situations, not only by solving tough business problems but by understanding and empowering the people we connect with.

Think of the anatomy of responsibility as a continuum rather than a single, static way of being. Our empowered ability to take responsibility is a manifestation of the level of safety and security we feel. The four levels of responsibility related to our sense of safety are as follows:

1 Taking no responsibility
2 Taking responsibility for our actions: requires a sense of basic social safety
3 Taking responsibility for our feelings and reactions: requires a level of psychological safety and self-acceptance
4 Taking responsibility for our intentions: requires a full confidence in oneself and comfort with vulnerability

Anatomy of Empowered Responsibility

Level of Safety	Minimal to None Feeling Unsafe	Basic Physical Safety with Others	Psychological Safety in Oneself	Full Confidence Safety with Self and Others
Level of Responsibility	Unable to Feel Responsibility	Accountable for Tasks	Emotionally Accountable	Empowered Responsibility
How We Show Up	Defending and Blaming	Responsibility for One's Actions	Responsibility for One's Reactions	Responsibility for One's Intentions

We've all experienced different levels of the empowered responsibility continuum. To use it as an application, we are suggesting that you become aware of where you are on the continuum and commit to moving to the next level. How might this be possible?

First, empowered responsibility is not about personal praise or blame but about understanding the dynamics of the situation. As we develop as boundless leaders, we are willing to say, "This is my part in this equation" as opposed to "I'm at fault" or "They're at fault." It's about the physics of how things play out; it's not personal. If it's raining, who is to blame? Is it the cloud's fault? The sun's? Is it the fault of the water that underwent condensation? Is it gravity's fault? Of course not. Rain is the result of a series of conditions coming together. Every circumstance works like that, including the complex social physics of teams of people collaborating within organizations and even larger organizational systems.

Most circumstances, even the simplest ones, are incredibly complex in terms of the number of conditions that had to conspire to create this particular outcome, this particular moment. When you break down any circumstance, you see that the conditions are almost infinite, so singling out any one individual or any one decision or action is ridiculously oversimplified. Because the conditions involved in any single decision or action are almost infinite, empowered responsibility also means trying to reach an unbiased understanding of all those key conditions that came together to create a particular situation. And since some conditions will be controllable, while others won't, empowered responsibility assumes the capacity to discern what we conceivably could change and what we must accept as is. Only when we are open to such a comprehensive, unbiased understanding can we arrive at the most elegant solution to any given problem.

Another dimension of empowered responsibility is recognizing that everything we do assumes the complex process of human motivation and behavior. It accepts an unbiased empathic awareness of the fact that the emotional conditioning and reactions of all the human beings involved at any point in the process are a necessary part of the equation. If something went wrong, did your team respond with anger?

Are we factoring in that a response of anger could escalate the situation, even though the people getting angry may have had nothing to do with the problem in the first place? Can we accept that there must be complex interpersonal dynamics involved in any particular outcome, positive or negative?

At its core, empowered responsibility is understanding that it's unhelpful to underestimate our role and contribution to the total equation. Especially as leaders we must be accountable for the subtle impact our intentions have on our behavior, as well as the behavior of others. This is where empowered responsibility assumes a deep level of comfort with our vulnerability and authenticity. Again, it's not about assuming the credit or blame. It's about having a clearer view. We must find a middle way—not minimizing our role but not exaggerating it either. Our humanity and leadership are part of all the circumstances that created any given situation, and we must clearly see our place in it.

The final dimension of empowered responsibility is that, like inspiration, it's contagious. When people are freed from the fear of exclusion, when nobody is blaming and nobody is shaming, when no one is attacking or feeling attacked, we're setting a tone wherein we're not afraid to be vulnerable and authentically engaged. When this happens, all involved will be inclined to come together to solve the problem or transform the situation. That's when our empowered responsibility serves to model the behavior we want in our team. That's when it turns into the positive energy of inspiration we want to participate in: *Let me feed that.* It's contagious once it's modeled, especially by the leader. Anybody can do it, and it will have an impact, but if a leader does it, that impact is almost immediate.

This was evident when Elazar was at a board meeting that became contentious. An error was pointed out that increased tensions even more. In the escalating tone of the meeting, Elazar noticed that something he had said was incorrect. By acknowledging his mistake without hesitation, he changed the tone of the meeting. Within minutes, while addressing a different point the chairperson mentioned, "If Elazar can admit his mistake, I guess I can too," reorienting the trajectory of the meeting.

Ultimately, with empowered responsibility we're creating an unbiased understanding of the complex causes and conditions—including all the individuals involved—that create any situation and approaching them with an energy and tonality that engender a sense of safety, engagement, authenticity, and collaboration. This takes us as directly as possible to a positive solution and deepens teamwork and trust. As leaders, it allows us to have an optimal impact, not just on the business problem at hand but on the people we're connecting with. When we can model empowered responsibility, we'll see radical results.

In essence, empowered responsibility sits at the crux of the discipline of heart. Not just as an application after the qualities have been developed but as a mindset that leverages those qualities to their fullest impact. Time and again, we've seen this with our clients. Whether it was a negative change to their power status, a continuously aggressive boss, a new colleague upending the status quo, an unfavorable reorganization, or a defiant and judgmental employee, at some point they had to address the question, "Why are they doing this to me, and what can I do about it?" In all cases the initial focus was on assessing what they needed to say/do to whom to effect the change they desired, usually to no avail. Only when they took responsibility for their role in the situation did things change.

Try walking through this transformation using the example of a conflict between you and your colleague or boss or the private equity team or anyone consistently rejecting your ideas, attacking you in the process, and threatening your psychological safety or even livelihood. Our conditioned inclination is to defend and directly or diplomatically fight back. Regardless of the method, this situation usually devolves into each side deepening their position and interpreting the data to support their viewpoint without any sustainable change in the situation. However, whenever a client pursued a counterintuitive path of paving their internal landscape first, change happened. Rather than seeing the other as the cause, they took responsibility for their own fears, indignation, and negative emotions that were triggered. They shifted focus away from changing the other person and used empathy to understand what pressures that individual may be addressing. Using self-compassion to reinforce their own resilience rather than allowing the inner critic to run amok, they were engaged from a place of inner strength and connected to the person they were in conflict with via a tone of authentic caring. Deepening their practice of compassion toward the other, they melted the false boundaries that separated them and better understood their interdependence. Invoking their mentor or their unconditioned intuition, they inspired the other to follow the path of clarity and authenticity and resolve the situation with care.

We all have experience with conflict, and by and large it plays out as a nuanced version of fight, flight, or freeze as we defend or amass a consensus that we are right, earnestly pursue other options, or inauthentically change our behavior, become passive-aggressive, or shut down and disengage. Yet, the discipline of heart is the martial arts maneuver that flips the situation from a Hobbesian-based approach to one that is aligned with the true nature of our human endowment, one that resolves the conflict through care and connection and uses compassion to move away from being downwind of a toxic breeze of aggression and separation to being upwind and directing the breezes of empathy and interconnectedness toward the situation.

Remember, empowered responsibility is not a preferred approach based on moral judgment or an admonishment we should all play nice. This approach consistently yields positive results even for an ever-widening circle of team members, fundamentally because it favors the clean energy that nourishes and inspires us and that we crave. Yet, this process can only begin when we *take* responsibility and *become* empowered to move from being stuck at the effect of circumstances and ignite positive change at their cause.

THE PATH TO EMPOWERED RESPONSIBILITY

We can't master the leadership application of empowered responsibility until we transform how we lead ourselves. Once we've worked with our inner critic and loosened its hold on us, we can turn it into an inner coach and heal the basic self-limiting drag of core shame and negative beliefs. We'll only enter the domain of empowered responsibility when we've moved away from the perfectionistic drive of self-critiquing or self-improvement toward a friendlier, human relationship with what we need to be when at our best.

As reasonable as the concept seems, we have a remarkably difficult time convincing our clients or groups of executives in workshops or retreats of the capacity of empowered responsibility. The first response tends to be, "The idea makes sense but not in my organization's culture. If your boss doesn't fire you, the other departments will eat you up and spit you out if you say, 'Yeah, I did that.'" Some respond with, "Nice idea, but you don't know my boss" or "The last time somebody took responsibility, you know what happened, right?" Still others share, "But my job is to fix things. I'm supposed to make problems go away, so how can I say, 'Hey, I caused that mess?'"

On the surface, there are many reasons to forsake taking responsibility, but experience has shown that empowered responsibility leads to solutions rather than keeping us mired in the problem. More importantly, when these capacities of accountability and vulnerability are skillfully engaged, they usually deepen the respect others have for us and the trust we engender, and they strengthen the psychological safety that allows the team to thrive. So what is the real obstacle? The key block to our even being willing to consider cultivating empowered responsibility is not outside us but within; it's our shame. If somebody is blamed, their shame is going to arise, and who wants to live with their shame? That feeling we may not belong or be accepted, seen, or valued is one of the most painful and terrifying of emotions. It's only natural that we don't want to feel it, because on the deepest psychic level, where none of us is a stranger to shame, this powerful aversive emotion feels like a social death threat.

In our experience, the real reason most of us are afraid to go down the path of empowered responsibility is because we're afraid of our deep-seated feelings of shame. In conventional business as usual, following a reptilian style of leadership, that hidden, buried shame is what is used to frighten, intimidate, and control others. By threatening with blame, we expose people to their deep-seated human feelings of shame.

Picture yourself coming into a meeting in this reptilian fashion:

You: "Damn it, we lost another client! Who did this? How could this happen? Do you know how hard I work to get these clients? Marketing, did you not communicate with them?"

Marketing: "We communicated well but the product wasn't set."

You: "Engineering, what is that about?"

Engineering: "I told the sales team we weren't ready, but they decided to push the time line anyway."

It's not me, it's you. It's not you, it's them. What we're doing here is passing the buck of shame. Our shame comes up because somebody's blaming us, and when it's triggered, our defenses go up, and we're not easy to talk to. We're not going to be constructive because that's not where our energy is going; it's expended on worst-case fears of rejection and incompetence. At the end of that meeting, nobody has moved to a solution because they're passing the buck of blame or getting overwhelmed and shutting down, freezing, and playing dead.

But there's another way. You come at the problem with mammalian leadership. Boundless leadership provides the tool to bear and work through feelings of shame and self-attack so you can be compassionate and firm, open to understanding and willing to take your share of responsibility. In this scenario, you walk into the meeting, and you announce, "We lost another client. This is not good. In thinking about it, I realize I need to take responsibility because somewhere along the line I have not communicated our values enough for you to fully understand what we need to do to keep these clients." Once you've set a tone like that, everything flips. What's the team going to do? You're not blaming anybody, you're modeling how enlightened leaders take responsibility.

A different social contagion will set in and someone might say, "I didn't follow up on an email, and if I had I could have caught this." Then somebody else might volunteer another possible glitch, and so on. What's happening? People are working together to figure out the truth of the problem and step directly toward a solution even though it's difficult, even though it goes against our business-as-usual conditioning. It is a powerful positive move that far outweighs our conditioned obstacles—solution-focused rather than stuck in the problem, building trust and team spirit rather than fraying at the fabric of collaboration and unity. It is also creating a strong basis for lessons learned so these errors are not repeated as often. That's the power application of the discipline of heart. To get there, we must develop empathy and be more resilient and prepared to engage and inspire.

Taking the path of empowered responsibility is not the easiest step, because it leads through our conditioned memories and fears of shame, but it's this path that can free us up to step into and model showing up as boundless leaders and impacting positive change we may have thought unattainable.

REVIEW

We began by exploring the basis of the discipline of heart—the vital importance of developing compassion as a social competency that enables us to understand and communicate skillfully with others, eventually supporting the boundless leadership trait of authentic engagement.

We defined compassion as the active response to empathy, the wish to help and the urge to act that follow from an accurate understanding and genuine concern for the internal experience of others. A basis in accurate, unbiased empathy ensures that compassion is objective or realistic and impartial or equanimous. The genuine wish to help makes compassion authentically engaged, and the active urge and skill that grow out of that clear-eyed intention to help are what make compassion dynamic and effective.

We learned that the cultivation of empathy and compassion in the discipline of heart requires us to confront and overcome ingrained obstacles—the mental blocks imposed by our survival-based implicit bias and emotional blocks imposed by our instinctive, stress-driven emotional reactivity.

We explored the key qualities of heart (empathy, resilience, engagement, and inspiration) that support the cultivation of compassion and linked them to practices (equal empathy, self-compassion, wise give-and-take, and evoking and emulating mentors) that help us build those heart muscles.

We examined one way to put the impartial, problem-solving heart and mind to work, through the application of empowered responsibility—the art of manifesting and modeling the confident open-mindedness that engenders participation and collaboration, supporting effective teamwork and deepening creativity and trust.

Part Four

THE DISCIPLINE OF
BODY, HEART, AND MIND
TRAIT OF EMBODIED FLOW

23 THE AWAKENED BODY

Reimagining and Rewiring Ourselves

In the discipline of mind, we focused on clarity—our ability to see reality and ourselves in a complete way, unobstructed by judgments and biases and freed to make better decisions. The discipline of heart was about our relationships—starting with our relationship with ourselves and based on that, extending to our connections with others and the world. Just as the mind is more than the brain, and the heart is more than a muscle, in this discipline—body—we focus on the power of the intimate, subtle depths of our physical being. This discipline allows us to unify mind, heart, and body so we can fearlessly shape who we are and how we impact the world.

The discipline of body is profound and surprising because it challenges conventional wisdom. While our common conception of the body is to think it has no role in how we know reality outside and inside ourselves, relate emotionally to ourselves and others, or envision and impact the world, the body in the context of boundless leadership is one of the most potent factors in these domains of leadership. Our approach to the body—based on new science and proven mind/body practices—shows how and why it's a key dimension of our way of being and leading. In this discipline, we'll explore the science of the body and its qualities and reflect on their synergy with mind and heart. In the course of our journey, you'll understand how the key trait of the discipline of body, embodied flow, and its core competency, fearlessness, enable us to consciously access and harness vision, energy, and expression to embody our purpose as boundless leaders.

WHAT IS A BODY?

Most of us think of the body as a known quantity and come to see it and treat it in a reductive, one-dimensional way. We are taught to see our physicality much as Newton's physics saw all material things: as a fixed, solid system, made up of anatomical parts that function in simple, mechanical ways. Even doctors view bodies as complex machines, like automobiles, and often see themselves as expert mechanics who keep the human body running well. As part of that vision, we treat our body as a living vehicle—we fuel it up with healthy food, keep it tuned through regular exercise, protect it by following medical advice, and take it in for routine checkups.

Boundless leadership conceives the body less as a physical object than as a lived, expressed experience, an interior universe—there's body and then there's *body*. We normally encounter our body as an object we see in the mirror or bump up against when we exercise or get sick. That doesn't address the felt sense of inhabiting a living, breathing body that happens to be not only sensitive but filled with a complex terrain of mind/body states. There's a line from James Joyce's *Dubliners* about a Mr. Duffy: "He lived at a little distance from his body, regarding his own acts with doubtful side-glances. He had an odd autobiographical habit which led him to compose in his mind from time to time a short sentence about himself containing a subject in the third person and a predicate in the past tense." We're all a bit like Mr. Duffy, living a little distance from our bodies, more in our mental representation of them than in their pulsing energy and immediate felt sense. We not only mistake our mental image of our body for the body *itself* but objectify and reify that image so we're no longer aware that it's not reality.

In this discipline the body is consciously experienced from the inside out. It's not the gross anatomical form, it's the subtle, mutable inner state and felt sense. It is about integrating a depth of inward perception that is normally hidden from consciousness by thoughts, words, and images that fill our waking lives. Perhaps dancers or athletes are consistently aware of this depth of inner experience, because they're always bringing awareness to the subtleties of their bodies, but most of us gloss over the nuances and take our bodies for granted.

This idea that our body is a façade rather than an inner dimension of how we feel is especially true in the modern West, which has increasingly split our minds from the lived emotional and visceral depths of being. Our experience of body relates to the oldest part of our brain, which dates to our evolutionary heritage as reptiles, followed by our social-emotional brain, which is linked with our hearts and our heritage as mammals. These are older than our newest, symbolic, and executive part of our brain, our primate heritage, which we typically identify exclusively as "mind."

If you read the work of sixteenth-century French philosopher René Descartes, one of the originators of modern Enlightenment thought, you'll find he saw the mind and body as separate, identifying the self exclusively with the thinking mind, hence, "I think, therefore I am." Descartes encouraged us to disidentify with and abandon our lived experience of the body and to conceive of it as a mere mechanism or physical container. But what scientists, especially neuropsychologists, are discovering is that splitting mind from emotions (the heart) and visceral embodied experience (the body) makes no scientific sense and flies in the face of the mounting evidence that mind, heart, and body are continually interacting and mutually cocreative.

This means if we're not consciously tuning in to our body, it's impacting us without our being aware of it. It's conditioning us with its needs, feelings, and reactions. For instance, we might grow discouraged and irritable when we're hungry or tired, yet optimistic and patient when we're rested and well fed. In addition, under stressful or traumatic conditions, we often experience our bodies activated in intense ways—hearts pounding in fight or flight, surging adrenaline and steroids, while in states of well-being like love or flow, our bodies feel activated in positive ways, and we feel euphoria, joy, and ease. This is in essence what Freud meant when he spoke of an unconscious mind, which he connected with our bodily needs and instincts. Current neuroscience sees the disconnect between normal waking consciousness and the emotional and visceral levels of our experience, which we call heart and body, respectively, as reflecting the split between conscious, explicit information processing in the primate brain and unconscious, implicit, procedural information processing in the mammalian and reptilian brains. We are wired to pay attention to our explicit level of waking experience and processing, while compartmentalizing our implicit emotional and visceral experiences, including factors that motivate and shape our way of being.

In the discipline of heart, we explored implicit biases and some of the subliminal emotional factors that unconsciously shape our motivation, from our inner critic and experience of core shame to the healing emotions of self-acceptance and self-compassion. When we bring consciousness to the implicit, felt sense of living in our body here and now, we discover a nuanced level of motivation and conditioning that acts as a powerful and consistent driver of our emotions and mindset.

Twentieth-century British economist John Maynard Keynes used the term *animal spirits* to describe these deeper drives and states we normally don't pay much attention to. In defining such a spirit as "a spontaneous urge to action" that colored our emotional disposition and mindset, Keynes was anticipating recent findings of behavioral economics.[20] The phrase is apt since primal emotions that drive our behavior—panic, greed, envy, shame, love, joy, awe, and rage—are fueled by energies we share with other social animals, energies that emerge as embodied, visceral instincts from the deepest layer of the human nervous system—the brain stem. The more intense, forceful, and all-consuming these common human emotions are, the more deeply they tap into the primal energies and dynamic states of the living human body. Thanks to the autonomic nerves that connect the brain stem with every one of our internal organs and tissues, these deeper "animal spirits" fill our bodies with an electrochemical charge meant to prepare us to respond to life-or-death challenges and opportunities. It is because of these nerves—arousing sympathetic and calming vagus—along with related nerve cells in our heart and gut, that we feel our strongest emotions throughout our bodies. When we get fearful, our heart may flutter, chest tighten, or gut knot; and if we feel panic or dread, our heart may pound or we may hyperventilate or feel overwhelming nausea. Stress emotions have their own visceral signatures, including envy, greed, shame, pride, and rage.

Happily, our embodied experience of animal spirits and embodied emotions isn't all stress related. We are also wired to feel different states of visceral intensity around bliss, joy, awe, and flow. That's why positive social emotions like compassion can have a wide range of expression, from reflective attitudes like empathy and concern to heartfelt feelings like love and care, and deeper still, the embodied forces of altruistic resolve and unconditional love.

The emotions we know in the social world at the heart level also have visceral depth and energies in the body. If we're unaware of the mind/body states underlying our emotions—whether stressful or social—we'll never be able to bring the deeper emotional and embodied intelligence of boundless leadership to them, and hence our gut feelings and reflex reactions will drive our moods, mindset, and behavior. We'll become upset without knowing it, charged with cravings without being mindful, or driven by forces we're unaware of.

That's why the discipline of body cultivates the trait of embodied flow. Since our primal animal intelligence lives in the deepest, embodied layer of our nervous system, the source of the potent forces that drive us, we can't afford to ignore or live at a distance from it. This subtle energetic body provides the fuel that runs our nervous system—the engine of our life. If we want our lives to run as cleanly and optimally as they can, we must bring our awareness to that layer and tap into the cleanest, most efficient fuel possible—the energy and chemistry of embodied flow. Tapping and harnessing that optimal fuel is no trivial matter. It not only requires bringing attention and awareness to normally unconscious levels of the mind and brain but also learning how to disarm and transform the energy of stress and trauma that block states of fearlessness and flow. Once we learn to transform the stress energies that drive us in survival mode into the fearless, thriving energy of embodied flow, we'll be ready and able to sustain the embodied presence, engagement, play, and joy that empower us to live and lead fearlessly in mind, heart, and body.

We tend to be attached to the familiar energy of stress, which can be compared to fossil fuel. Given that stress is the energy that drives our default survival mode, we know how it works. Fear does drive us, but as with fossil fuel, it has major costs and limits. Fear, rage, and shame are not sustainable sources of human energy because they're nonregenerative, high-cost, short-term fuel that involves a toxic, polluting effect on our internal environment. Yes, fear can drive us, but it also wears us out through the stress our minds, brains, and bodies sustain. When we work with our clients, we help them dig deeper than reactive stress energies to access the clean energy of flow, describing it as a system upgrade, replacing fossil fuel with renewable energy.

The intensity of our drive does not change with this upgrade, because both energies are sourced from deep inside us. When we learn to run our minds, hearts, and bodies on the clean energy of flow, we can access more drive and are able to sustain higher levels of performance more efficiently, because we're not wasting energy on stress reactions that block performance and erode our basic capacities. That clean energy is there if we can tap into it, and as boundless leaders we need to learn how to access and harness the embodied flow of unconditional love, altruism, joy, and play to lead effortlessly, effectively, and efficiently.

This is a key topic for Elazar and his clients, since he has found we can't fully succeed and thrive if we don't have access to the potent positive energy of embodied flow. Our dependency on fear-driven energy runs deep, even when we cognitively understand its limitations. Like most dependencies, we are constrained by our inability to imagine that we can experience a different way of being. Elazar's clients meet this juncture, almost without exception, with some variation of a simple question: "But if my fear of failure is not driving me, what will get me out of bed?" Given the depth of and familiarity with our need for extraordinary performance as the prerequisite for our happiness, it's an understandable question. The answer is equally simple: pure passion. As leaders we can feel the difference between a worker who is driven by outcome and another who is driven by craft. As colleagues and teammates we're drawn to this passion for learning and innovating; it's the clean and renewable energy that fuels us without the toxicity of stress and fear that make up conventional energy sources. To be clear, our dependency on the fossil fuel that relishes power can be mistakenly construed as a passion for winning, but that disguise is exposed when we lose. Passion for craft and love of doing it better have a more muted response to loss, as our energy is placed more on process than outcome.

To better understand the dynamic, think about it in terms of the evolution of our nervous system and brains. When we discuss embodied learning or leadership, we're referring to the reptilian part of our brain, specifically, how we can upgrade and integrate it with the newer mammalian and primate parts. In this work, we're acknowledging and leveraging the reality that our brain has two sides, two operative modes: stress and survival mode and social thriving mode. That bimodal structure applies not just to our newer social brain regions—the primate and mammalian—but also to our oldest, reptilian brain, which has a mammalian upgrade that allows it to operate in either primal self-protective mode or socially engaged thriving mode. You can think of this upgrade as an extra chip or a friendliness switch. Stephen Porges, the neuroscientist whose autonomic research we discussed earlier, calls this upgrade to the brain stem "the social engagement system."[21] It evolved to keep our bodies and nervous systems in social mode—calm, present, connected, caring, and playful. When it's activated, it effectively switches the primal energy and chemistry sourced from our brain stem from the self-limiting fossil fuel of stress to the expansive and connected clean energy of flow. As boundless leaders, we learn to activate that switch so we can clean our energy source and tap the boundless potential of embodied flow.

While flipping that switch in any one moment supports fearless states of embodied flow, the *trait* of embodied flow involves a natural, abiding capacity to keep that switch on as a new default. Within the trait, *embodiment* refers to how the primal energy and chemistry of the brain stem shift our mind, brain, and body into social mode, while *flow* refers to the unblocked access to primal clean energy that expands our emotional and mental capacities beyond habitual limits and boundaries, making us boundless. When we choose that clean energy, we can source our life in an embodied way, show up in the world, and pursue our dreams and goals.

24 LEADING FEARLESSLY

The Body Language of Flow

We've all encountered people with remarkable passion or ease with themselves and thought that could never be us. The reality is this ability to tap into our internal flow network is a natural capacity, and it can be learned! Through practice we can learn to tune our autonomic nervous system to the frequency of clean, embodied flow. We build to this level by cultivating the qualities of boundless vision, empowering speech, natural flow, and fearless embodiment, which help support states of fearlessness.

We learn to do this by taking up practices of embodied flow. We say "embodied" because, unlike the practices of attention training and compassion training, these are directed at controlling the autonomic nervous system that regulates the brain stem and bodily organs. They do so through two complementary pathways: one influencing our subtle body state from the top down through imagery and speech, the other influencing it from the bottom up through breathwork and movement. Together they empower us to gain conscious influence over the normally unconscious mind/body states that drive our bodies, hearts, and minds. On our path to boundless leadership, our natural capacity for fearless states of embodied flow gradually deepen into the trait of embodied flow.

Embodied flow is a vital trait, an enduring way of being that goes beyond a temporary peak experience or altered state. When we are involved in flow—balancing motion and stillness, viscerally open, intuitive, creative, and expressive—we tap into that clean energy of our reptilian brain. This allows us to channel the intense positive social emotions deep within our embodied selves and direct them to ease and joy, an actualized naturalness that supports the profound state of openness, intuition, and creativity. When we're in a state of embodied flow, it seems to transcend anything fleeting or transient. We feel utterly present, awake, and alive—as if we're where and as we should be, able to manifest the right vision, words, and expressions. Yet as wonderful as flow moments are, they don't arise spontaneously or accidentally. For them to emerge, such states require a competency—the competency of fearlessness.

FEARLESSNESS AND FEAR

Reshaping our understanding of fear is not a simple thing since it's a basic part of the human condition. Embodying fearlessness is not about rejecting or overcoming fear but understanding that fear is a projection of our primal self-protective mindset, based on an instinctive, insidious, and reinforced habit of worst-case misperceptions. To arrive at true fearlessness, we must address the primitive, instinctive roots of fear: our perception of the world as threatening, overwhelming, or scarce, as well as our perception of ourselves as inadequate, separate, or alone. Only when we override and reset the negativity bias in our default survival mode can we disarm the basic state of chronic hypervigilance and guardedness that keeps our fight-flight-faint-freeze reflexes activated in our bodies. Fearlessness is a competency that frees us to reimagine and rewire how we see ourselves, the world, and our relationship with it, empowering us to shift out of the reptilian mode of self-enclosed guarding into our higher mammalian mode of flowing, open, playful, confident embodiment.

When we speak of fear, we're not discussing individual differences, as if some of us are cowardly and others brave. We're discussing the hardwiring installed in us over millennia to maximize our ability to survive under the worst conditions in the wild. That hardwiring connects to our primal reptilian brain, which in its survival mode supports a mind/body state of hypervigilance that drives fearful emotions and thinking like *Are they out to get me? Can I outsmart or outproduce them?* The insidious thing about this fear-based way of being is that it's so chronic and pervasive that we are unaware we embody it, as if guarding, vigilance, and reactivity were facts of life with no practical alternative. Fortunately, there is a real alternative open to us since as mammals our reptilian brains have the upgrade that allows us to switch out of primal stress and survival mode into the embodied social mode of fearless thriving. That fearless mode is what supports our ability to see ourselves clearly and in context—as secure and connected beings in the abundant world that human cooperation and cultural creativity offer. When we are open to seeing, feeling, and tasting the fundamental social safety and connection to others that supports real fearlessness, we are ready, willing, and able to enter states of embodied flow.

When it comes to fear and fearlessness, the new science is good news, but there's a hitch. The reason we can go so long living in a mode wherein fearlessness and flow are rare peak experiences and we slip into the embodied guarding and vigilance of fear-based stress is that our reptilian brains and autonomic nervous systems are preset to a negative default of fearing for our survival. That is why the only possible way for us to shift to fearlessness and thriving as a new default is through repeated, persistent practice. Thanks to neural plasticity, however, when we understand our natural capacity for fearlessness and embodied flow and engage in persistent practices that evoke them, there is no doubt we can make this shift and wind up in a new default mode where fearlessness and flow become second nature.

Exercising our competency for fearlessness is not only a joy in itself, it also allows us to live and lead from our peak potential, our ability to be aware, engaged, connected to our passion, and flowing in our activities and way of being. That is because fear—conscious or subconscious—is the anchor of our limitations. It's what locks our minds, hearts, brains, and bodies into a rigid and draining defensive mode that shuts down our positive qualities of self-confidence, vision, expressiveness, passion, and innovation. If we want full, consistent access to these life-affirming forces, we must commit to a path of consistent embodied practice to rewire our brain stem and autonomic nervous systems.

THE FOUR QUALITIES OF BODY

Like the competency of clarity in the discipline of mind or compassion in the discipline of heart only more so, fearlessness requires deliberate training. Our reimagining and rewiring of self are concurrent with the four qualities within the competency of fearlessness that boundless leaders bring to any group dynamic:

1   Boundless vision: the capacity to envision a larger, more meaningful and impactful way of being, living, and leading for oneself, breaking out of the preconceived limits imposed by fear-based childhood images of self, others, and the world

2   Empowering speech: the capacity to conceive and inhabit a more meaningful and empowering narrative for oneself and one's impact on others and the world, breaking out of the default narrative established by fear-based beliefs about self and world formed in early childhood

3   Natural flow: the capacity to access, enter, and abide in a natural mind/body state of peak concentration and embodied well-being based on a stress-free energy that balances fearless arousal with blissful relaxation

4   Fearless embodiment: the capacity to relax somatic guarding and stress reactivity and to access and embody a way of being and moving that springs from a fearless bodily experience of safe connection, easeful expression, and fundamental well-being

More vigilant training is required for these four qualities because the discipline of body is the quantum leap to the potential of your boundless leadership. Until this point, despite the power and finesse of our training in the mind and heart disciplines, we've been expanding the boundaries of our habituated capacity, incrementally accessing a better and more capable version of ourselves. In discipline of body we recreate ourselves, birthing a new and boundless leader from our expansive and unbridled potential.

When Elazar leads workshops on innovation, he flips the paradigm from "Where is the farthest we can go from where we are?" to the more aspirational "Assuming there are no limits, where do we want to arrive?" This shift from starting with our limitations and trying to innovate outside the box to starting at the potential of our possibilities and not seeing a box is at the root of the four qualities of body. Boundless vision not only allows us to see more but to see more clearly, without any artificial lens to obscure the view. Empowering speech rewrites our story with an intentional and encouraging tone, leading to a wise and triumphant ending. Natural flow enables us to synthesize specific and seemingly opposite energies of intense arousal and excitement with a deep and abiding calm, allowing the visceral aspect of a true and unshakable self-confidence to emerge. Fearless embodiment grounds us in a stance that claims the potential of who we are meant to be.

This level of boundless leadership delivers on the "what" and "how" of higher productivity, cultures of collaboration and innovation, and a team of trusting partners inspired to achieve beyond their conditioning. However, the discipline of body also demands a laser-focused cultivation of the "why" of leadership, elevating our purpose and meaning to match our new boundless capacity. What would our organization be if profits were the strategy not the objective? What if our goals were process-driven and passionate about win-win activities reflective of an interconnected world rather than designed for self-benefiting outcomes based on debunked myths of scarcity and isolated individuality? What if rather than worshipping greater efficiency for better margins, we upended the hierarchical systems of exclusivity and entitlement that concentrate the wealth among a few to reveal systems powered by the regenerative and unbounded human potential organized around equity and generosity for the benefit of the whole?

This is a tall order, but one that easily fits within the field of our realized potential, which you'll see as we delve into understanding and training in these qualities and continue on our path to boundless leadership, starting with boundless vision.

25 BOUNDLESS VISION

Evoking a New Reality

As a quality of fearlessness, boundless vision means having the ability to remove the blinders our default survival mode has imposed upon our imagination and perception. These blinders are composed of self-limiting biases and beliefs we create and get locked into—interpretations, assumptions, fear-based views, and prejudgments—all things that narrow the frame through which we see ourselves and the world, obscuring the unbounded possibilities open to us. Boundless vision is what is revealed when we remove these blinders systematically and completely as we practice seeing ourselves, others, our organization, and the world through the wide-angle lens of infinite possibility. That's a simple explanation of a formidable process.

The power of our minds and the active role of our imaginations have more to do with what we see than what we think or believe. Their ability to construct what we perceive goes beyond framing or filtering what we see as possible to actively defining and producing what seems to be simply how things are. Neuroscientific research increasingly demonstrates that most of *what we think of and experience as actual perception* is an artificially generated virtual reality that we mistake for the truth of how things are. [22] Much of the time our unconscious minds and brains are hard at work producing a self-generated virtual reality that we take for the real deal. This ability to project our expectations onto our vision of ourselves and the world can be useful as an inner GPS system or simulation of what we anticipate. The problem is, if we don't know it's a movie or a GPS, then we're stuck in a limiting script or program, and we remain bound by our familiar routes, rerunning the same scenarios.

Our work as boundless leaders is to see past the limiting matrix of our lived assumptions. To activate boundless vision we must first become aware of our blinders, our limited and habitual vision of who we are, where we're from, and where we're going. From a leadership perspective, unnoticed self-limiting views tend to be one of the biggest obstacles to continued development and optimal performance. The inability to take a new perspective on the content and context of our life and work may be the greatest limitation to our capacity to see and realize our potential in our development and impact.

Yet, because of learning and conditioning it's hard to remove the blinders. Most of what we see is shaped by what we've previously learned—so what seems to be the way things are is how they appear in the mirror of our experience, conditioning, and training. When we enter into a particular situation—a meeting, negotiation, or review—we're looking at what seems like a new circumstance, but what we're not seeing is everything we bring to the situation that is distorting the lens through which we filter the realities and possibilities of the present moment.

What do we bring?

Most important is our preconceived sense of who we are: *What's my identity? My capacity? My goal? My work?* We also bring assessments of the reality outside us and a range of preconceptions about other people: *What is the environment I face? What is my team capable of?* These preconceptions reflect decades of conditioning, starting from our childhood, education, and community and culminating in our professional training and the consensus mindset of our current organization. Our filtering process is not conscious; it reflects an unconscious, implicit map of ourselves, other people, and the world—one which was conditioned unwittingly, often under duress, when we were anxious, insecure, or worried about ourselves and our place in the world. Given the fear-based logic of our default survival mode, we assume a filter that is negatively biased, muddying our capacity to see things from a fresh, optimistic perspective.

The challenge is to bring a fresh, open capacity to envision our possibilities or those of our team. We must return to our unconscious premises and default maps of ourselves and the world and learn to purge old habits as we expand the scope and reach of our imagination until we can conceive of a new vision of who we are and what reality holds. How do we undo our unconscious habituation to our default maps of self and world?

The good news is, thanks to the new science of self-regulation and neuroplasticity, we know we can bring awareness to processes that have become automatic and consciously revise and rewire them. To understand how we can undo our self-limiting mental maps, we must explore how those maps come about and how they impact our routine perception of our world and selves. We tend to think of our brains as operating like cameras, capturing reality, reading what's out there, and representing it faithfully. We also tend to think this happens in real time. In other words, we're always noticing what's out there and responding to it. This assumption is false. When it comes to processing information from our senses, including vision, our minds are more like projectors or virtual-reality generators than cameras.

Neuroscientist Rodolfo Llinás studied how our brains process perception and developed what he called the "quantum theory of consciousness."[23] His research showed that our brains are not passive sensors but dynamic generators of electrical activity, constructive processing, and virtual reality simulation. Within the reptilian part of our brain there's a structure known as the basal ganglia that serves as both our relay station for sense information and our generator of neural energy/brain wave activity. This structure sends a constant stream of electrical activity through our brains. This wavelike activation pulses through our neural networks, setting up a moment-to-moment snapshot of reality as it connects segments of our brain. These momentary snapshots are aggregated over time, with one blurring into the next, creating an experience of continuous perception like a movie. That may not seem surprising, but the startling fact Llinás found is that the movie our brain produces that gives the illusion of stable perception is a virtual reality, generated more by our canned memory and accumulated fantasies than by the sense input we're receiving from the outside world. He found the perceptual processor in our brains works almost exactly the same in the waking state as it does in a dream, when the brain receives little or no information from the outside world. The only real difference between perceptual processing in the waking and dream states is that when we're awake the brain gets bits of information from the senses that it uses to update its virtual reality several times per second. That's how we end up going through the world actively projecting a mental map of what we think is happening and why perception is deceptive, routinely locking us in reruns of our unconscious preconceptions, implicit biases, and habitual expectations.

That's why the first thing we practice as we embody boundless leadership is to become mindful of and release that self-limiting tunnel vision. This is vital not just to expand our capacity for bold imagination and fresh, creative vision, but also because the virtual realities we mindlessly live in, like the films we watch in theaters, trap our minds, brains, and bodies in a straitjacket of experience. This is because the brain *and* body experience imagery in the same way they experience reality. For example, if we see an image of an apple, our brain is in the same configuration as if the apple were really out there. That is why one study shows that the brain grows in the same way when people imagine playing a keyboard as when they actually play one.[24] As part of our survival mode, the human brain is wired by default to take what passes through the mind as reality. That way, if our primitive selves even imagined seeing a saber-toothed tiger, our brains and bodies would be primed to act as if it were really there.

While we're projecting, we're actively looking for what we want in the world and avoiding what we don't. While we're projecting our map onto the world, we're still not recognizing that it's a map. We're not "seeing" how much of it we created, and so we can delude ourselves. In other words, we can get trapped in a movie or nightmare that distorts reality in an impactful way. Unfortunately, given our default negativity bias, what this means is that our brain can not only narrow our ability to see what's out there, it can create worst cases out of thin air and skew our sense of ourselves and the world toward the negative. Before we can stop the horror rerun or awaken from the nightmare, we must recognize that what we're seeing *is* a rerun, that it's only a dream. Boundless vision starts with our unlocking the power of our imagination to influence our perception in ways that counter our negative trance and liberate our potential for quality control and creatively changing what we see.

When Joe teaches visualization or imagery, he often hears, "When I was a kid, I had a vivid imagination but now I don't. I can hardly see anything in my mind's eye." He challenges that self-limiting belief by pointing out it's not that we no longer imagine, but rather the experience we have of ourselves and reality is in effect a detailed imagination frozen or ossified into what *seems* like reality. Think about it: if you watch a scary movie, your body doesn't know you're not being chased by bad guys. That's why you startle, your heart races, or you may even sweat. However, if you watch a romantic comedy, you may have entered the theater stressed and tense but leave feeling at ease and one with humanity. The same effect comes from the mental movie we produce and watch in the theater of our minds and brains. That's why we must break out of the matrix and become writer, producer, and director of our mental movie. In essence, that's what boundless vision is about—editing out the worst-case biases, limiting habits, and default settings rooted in survival mode and reinforced by our nightmares of childhood helplessness and the scarcity thinking of most families and societies.

To see reality in all its abundant possibilities instead of a projected, limited version, we must return to the roots of our perception and retrain our brain. Through the science of neuroplasticity, we know we're not hardwired, so however much we're prone to perceptual conditioning, we have the capacity to shift it through repeated practice. The only reason the world continues to appear as it does in our mind's eye is because of repetition. Think about it: when you look in the mirror in the morning, you don't see the twenty-year-old self you see in your mind, you see somebody else, maybe now with gray hair or wrinkles.

Fortunately, when it comes to the science of mind/brain transformation, imagery turns out to be a powerful way of rewiring to perceive nuances or install capacities to respond in skillful ways. That's why flight simulators work to train astronauts and pilots before the high-risk activity of flying for real. *If we repeatedly practice positively reenvisioning ourselves and our world*, going through the motions as in a video game, we can fundamentally change how our brains our wired and operate.

One key element that may be a surprise in terms of the specifics of imagery practice is that it doesn't start with changing our map of the external world but rather with changing our image of ourselves. Once we rerun a fixed, limiting sense of who we are, it establishes the context and perspective from which we see everything else. To change our perspective, we must change our image of who we think we are. Why does that seem somehow impossible or impractical? We hold on to our image of ourselves as if it *really is* ourselves, as if it's our body, our life, even though it's only an image in our minds. But even if we recognize that our mental image is not who we are, and that it could be liberating to change or transform it, that image is so entwined with our habits and way of being, it seems impossible to change it, and we hardly know where to start.

It's not difficult to change our self-image. It's just that the best place to start is about as far from us as we can get—that is, with an image of another. When we're infants, the first consistent image we develop is that of our mother or primary caregiver. That image is the original teddy bear or blanket—what psychologists call a "transitional object"—since it enables us to hold on to a mental reminder that we *have* a caregiver, even when they're not in sight, when they've left the room. This enormous mental achievement is called "object constancy," and it's the seed from which our security as dependent infants and children grows. That image of our caregiver also turns out to be a mirror, because by watching how they see and respond to us, we "learn" who we are. Hopefully, they see something basically good, because otherwise we're going to learn there's something wrong with us.

When we looked toward caregivers in childhood as reference points of our reality and mirrors of our identity, it was without any ability to assess or choose what was admirable about them versus what was limiting and problematic. As a result, our sense of ourselves based on that formative experience is at best unexamined and provisional and at worst distorted and limiting. If we want to bring awareness and intention to updating our default self-image—the starting point of all our mental maps—we must revisit the interpersonal process of identity formation in a conscious and empowering way. This is why coaching and psychotherapy are vital contexts for our growth as leaders. But it's also possible for us to create a similar transformative dialogue in the space of our minds by using the practice of role-modeling imagery.

As we practice role-modeling imagery, we tinker with our sense of reality by re-mirroring or recreating our sense of self. We do this by choosing a mentor who embodies who we want to be, who helps us get in touch with and see who we want to be. Based on that pivotal shift, we can open ourselves to a new universe of possibilities and rehearse the qualities, way of being, and leadership style that will allow us to expand our impact and embody our deepest purpose, cultivating boundless vision.

Another key element of the science that makes role-modeling imagery so effective is that envisioning the confident, caring, and enthusiastic facial expressions and body language of positive mentors stimulates our mirror neuron system as well as our archive of facial and bodily expressions in positive ways that activate the social autonomic nervous system based on the newest branch of the vagus nerve. This has the effect of engaging the part of our brain stem autonomic system that calms and regulates the primal stress reflexes to promote an embodied social safety and connection. In other words, the practice sends top-down cues of safety and connection from our imagination (right brain) to our mammalian and reptilian brains, shifting our emotional and bodily tone from stress to fearless social engagement. This is one of the reasons we consider imagery an embodied practice.

Before we turn to a sample practice, its vital to review some of the key elements so you can understand and engage it optimally. At the heart of the practice is the role-modeling relationship wherein the process of enlarging our habitual self and world is imaginatively simulated and rehearsed through the positive influence of a mentor. The practice relies on open awareness to detach from our habitual sense of self and world and to envision an encounter with a congenial role model who mirrors our vision of an expansive self and world of possibilities. It rehearses a process of admiring, internalizing, and integrating the empowered way of being we see in mentors and models. Most important in the selection of role models are the qualities of genuine trust, admiration, and inspiration we seek to develop.

Real mentors are complex human beings with limits and quirks, who often elicit complex emotions. The intention here is to connect with the positive influence the mentor can have on our minds and lives, not to overlook the mentor's human limitations or differences but to intentionally harness the aspiration or inspiration they stir in us to guide and speed our insight, development, and transformation.

The imagery in this practice begins by prompting us to envision our body in its lighter, clearer version. This helps make us receptive to influence from our chosen role model, giving our sense of self the plasticity to try on and take in a more boundless way of being.

Practice

ROLE-MODELING IMAGERY

1   Settle into a comfortable posture and envision your
     body as translucent and luminous.
2   Tune in to body mindfulness and open your mind to
     make space for mindful awareness.

3   Into that space, invite a congenial mentor who embodies the qualities and ways of being you want to emulate.

4   Open yourself to their influence.

5   Imagine sharing your experiences with them.

6   See them welcoming all parts of you with deep confidence in your potential.

7   Ask for their inspiration, guidance, and commitment.

8   Envision them sending that freely as a wave of positive energy and light.

9   Take in their guidance and blessing, allowing these to dissolve your limiting sense of self.

10 Touch the core of your being and stir the positive qualities that are dormant within you.

11 Internalize their image and qualities as a catalyst for growing your expanded self.

12 Dedicate yourself to transforming into the most empowered version of you—for your sake and the sake of those you impact.

As we mentioned in our evoking and emulating mentors discussion in chapter 21, if you doubt your ability to meditate with imagery, the trick is not to expect too much right away but to work with whatever you can, trusting that the process will bear results just like a new exercise regimen. At first you may need to content yourself with reading or listening to guided imagery practices, as if they were poems or stories. Gradually your imagery will become almost as clear and real as normal perception, while retaining the transparency that comes from consciously creating and evoking a specific mental picture. Eventually, this skill will help alter the building blocks of perception, including your habitual sense of yourself and others. These shifts will open new doors in your mind, experience, and response to the world around you and inside you.

Practice

THE FLIGHT SIMULATOR OF
ROLE-MODELING IMAGERY

1   Settle into a comfortable posture and envision your
    body as translucent and luminous.

2   Tune in to body mindfulness and open your mind to
    make space for mindful awareness.

3   Into that space, invite the image of a role model who
    inspires and empowers you.

4   Focus on them as a model or mirror of the way of being
    and life you want for yourself.

5   Share your strengths and challenges, then own the
    potential your mentor sees in you.

6   Imagine the mentor's empowering vision and energy
    entering and transforming you.

7   See yourself embodying a new way of being and leading
    that mirrors your mentor's.

8   Enlist your mentor's full support and dedicate your
    efforts to a changed self and world.

9   Return to the practice, ideally at a regular time and place,
    three to seven days a week.

10 Tune in to this practice to refresh your vision when you
    feel blocked in daily life.

26 EMPOWERING SPEECH

Rewriting Our Role

Empowering speech is the next key quality that builds fearlessness and embodied flow in the discipline of body. This is the act of affirmative speech that evokes the potential for positivity in ourselves and others. Just as boundless vision is not about putting rose-colored glasses over our fear-based views but requires us to expose and change self-limiting images etched in our unconscious, empowering speech is not about talking over our ingrained fears and doubts. It is not to be confused with "the power of positive thinking" or positive affirmations. While empowering speech begins with facing and revising the negative self-talk of our inner critic, it goes deeper and further than revising our familiar narrative or inner monologue.

As we develop our earliest images of ourselves and the world, embedded with those primal images is an implicit, often preverbal set of linked assessments of who we are in relation to our caregivers and the world. These assessments comprise our basic constructs or beliefs about our identity, ability, and value, as well as about what the world is and how it works. Unfortunately, given how relatively small, helpless, and confused we are as infants and children, these first assessments tend to be negatively biased toward our worst-case fears of being unacceptable, unworthy, or powerless in relation to the adults upon whom our lives depend and the adult world that feels overwhelming. While we may soon outgrow these assessments and develop positive concepts of ourselves and our role, they have been wired into our images of self and world as core negative beliefs that shadow us in the form of inarticulate feelings of shame and self-doubt. It is these preverbal core beliefs that form the basis of the explicitly verbal inner critic, which tries to protect us from feelings we misperceive as facts by pushing us to drive ourselves to improve or prove our worth.

Empowering speech is the quality we need to rescript our explicit self-talk and implicit negative beliefs that anchor our preverbal ideas of who we are and can be in the world. We can change the rigging on our vessel, raising larger, more expansive, colorful sails, but imagine trying to set sail on a new adventure when the boat is still anchored in the harbor. One of the crucial things empowering speech does is to unhook what's anchoring our inner critic and limiting our ability to think expansively about ourselves and our lives. But that's not all. Empowering speech is not just speech that directly addresses and calms our primal fear and shame-based assessments, it also involves a powerful shift in tone that profoundly impacts our brains and bodies.

Speech is so much a part of our everyday lives that we don't recognize that it's a potent social action and interaction, and it delivers a strong internal message as well. From the time we're infants, one of the primary ways we connect to our caregivers is by monitoring tone of voice. We may not understand a lullaby, but we understand the tone. Hearing a warm tone calms our mind, body, and even our brain stem to make us feel, *I'm safe. I can relax. I am connected. I can be free. I can play.* Hearing or vocalizing a warm, caring, and resonant tone of voice— whether that of an imagined role model or our voice addressing ourselves or others—stimulates our auditory and glossopharyngeal nerves along with our archive of remembered vocal tones in positive ways that activate the social autonomic nervous system based on the newest branch of the vagus nerve. This has the effect of engaging the part of our autonomic system that calms and regulates the primal reflexes to promote embodied social safety and connection. In other words, along with role-modeling imagery, the practice of empowered speech sends top-down cues of safety and connection from the right brain and our auditory and glossopharyngeal nerves to our mammalian and reptilian brains, shifting our emotional and bodily tone from stress to fearless social engagement. This is one of the reasons we consider empowering speech an embodied practice.

In positive terms, empowering speech evokes and articulates the potential of individuals and groups in any situation. It allows us to draw attention to untapped capacities—ours and those of others. From a leadership perspective, most of our clients struggle with turning their inner speech and narrative from critical to encouraging and empowering. Often given the stress-driven mode of conventional business, what passes for an inner coach is laced with fear of failure or inadequacy. While it may sound like a pep talk, the tone may be fear-based or shame-based—more about avoiding the bad than encouraging and empowering, accentuating and evoking the positive.

Just as boundless vision can help us see through our negative habits of perception to the bigger potential, empowering speech gives voice to that vision, communicating, affirming, and evoking it with words. And when we're speaking from this empowering place, we're not just using positive words and ideas but a deeper, warmer, and more connected tone. We're taking care not to let our speech be tainted by stress, fear, failure, or worry. Instead, we're giving voice to fearless positivity—exclamations of care, joy, or wonder—which is what makes empowering speech so resonant. This is possible because we've exposed and rooted out false core negative beliefs that anchor shame and social stress reactivity and so freed ourselves to articulate our vision of the boundless potential within and around us in inspiring and transformational narratives for ourselves and others. This is how the evocative quality of speech releases the force of inspiration and aspiration within us and among those around us—our speech gives voice, tonality, and resonance to our boundless vision. Once we learn to use empowering speech effectively, it allows us to encourage and inspire ourselves and others to realize a bigger vision, to create a new shared reality.

Because our social lives are in large part coordinated by speech, words can powerfully affirm or even change things in our consensual social reality. Some language philosophers have described the power of spoken words to define, shape, and change our lived reality, referring to such world-creative words as "performative speech acts." The classic example is when the officiant at a wedding says, "I pronounce you married," and those words make it so. Empowering speech is one such performative speech act—an intentionally creative mode of expression that articulates a reality.

There are three final dimensions that make empowering speech more than just a positive inner coach or voice. One has to do with the performative power of speech to create reality, and it involves taking responsibility for that godlike creative power to shape who and what we really are. When we can clear our preverbal mind/brain of negative beliefs about ourselves and the world, we effectively open the space for reconceiving and redefining our identity to align with the expanded and empowered self-image we evolve through boundless vision.

The single best use of empowering speech is to pronounce our identity intentionally and repeatedly with that expansive self-image, effectively recreating ourselves in and through that one performative act. This pronouncement typically takes the form of an affirmation: "I can lead with clarity, compassion, and fearlessness" or "I embody self-awareness, authentic engagement, and flow." In this final act of taking responsibility for choosing and naming our identity lies the liberating and consequential impact of empowering speech. The key is taking responsibility for who we *say* we are. Once we realize we can change the frame of our identity and the story that comes with it, we've empowered ourselves to transform and also found the key to unlocking the boundless potential the people around us have to transform as well.

The second way empowering speech is more than self-coaching is that it adds a deeper register to our ability to convey vital messages to ourselves and others. Since 80 to 90 percent of our communication happens under the radar of words themselves,[25] how our tone and body language resonate with those words adds depth and power to our voice. Joe had a voice teacher when he was young who used to say, "Sing from your pelvic floor." At first, he wondered, "What the heck?" Joe began to realize his whole body was involved in making a full and resonant vocal sound.

Since our bodies make the sound we call speech, they are the medium and words are the message. Since, as Marshall McLuhan famously said, "The medium *is* the message," speech that engages our warmest, open tones is a truly empowering medium of communication. This deeper register of speech—called prosody—is the songlike dimension that caregivers intuitively use to help regulate the nervous systems of their preverbal infants and children. It also helps us as leaders to speak directly to the deeper, preverbal levels of our brain and the brains of others, giving speech the power to change not just minds but mind/body states.

The third way empowering speech allows us to transform our embodied experience of ourselves and the world lies in the dimension of time. This relates to how it enables us to revise the dramatic narrative that tells the story of who we are in real time: where we come from, where we are, and where we're going. In our early development, once we understand the use of words, this understanding gives us a powerful command over our experience and environment. We use requests rather than cries to communicate, we experience how speech has the power to invoke change, and we discover how stories or narratives help us weave our experience. With the science of vision we saw how our minds constantly interweave snapshots of mostly mental, mostly remembered imagery into a movie. Part of how they do that is through aggregating them into a narrative or story: *This is who I am. Here is where I'm going.* Similarly, speech has the power to give coherence and order (or fixity) to our internal perceptions and emotions. Because of its tonal element, it has the power to convey a deeper emotional quality—positivity, fear, or trust.

In that sense, we must understand that speech has a powerful role in our experience of ourselves and the world around us; it's not just a way to share information. It's performative, like the wedding pronouncement. It has the power to interweave a new identity and story that puts that identity into motion and action by adding dialogue and a story line. In our social environment, it creates a shared reality. Speech is probably the best way humans coordinate our diverse imaginations of what's happening. Just as dolphins squeak and somehow convey vital messages that help them connect in pods, we humans squeak at each other to connect in groups. When we create and share a set of goals, plans, steps, and measures with a group, our imaginations and actions tune in to the same frequency, allowing us to work as a team.

Using boundless vision, we reenvision who we are and what we are capable of and help others do the same, but our vision won't be complete or readily shared unless we can put words to the images. If you think about cartoons, they're just drawings, but what makes them feel like there's somebody there? If you're watching but you're not hearing the speech of the character you're probably not going to relate much. Same with silent movies—you don't know what's happening until you see the subtitles that describe the dialogue or the inner experience. That's what speech does. It solidifies and clarifies the internal experience and tone we're receiving.

Empowering speech enables us to inhabit our vision of being a larger version of ourselves in a more expansive field of action. It then goes further to help us weave that larger vision into an ongoing story or narrative that conveys its unfolding in social expressions and actions over time. The last act of empowering speech rewrites our familiar, limiting story into a more empowered, triumphant narrative that recounts the path of action by which we intend to have greater impact and purpose.

Practice
EMPOWERING SPEECH ONE

The practice of empowering speech is embedded within the practice of role-modeling imagery. It involves the same following twelve steps with performative speech added to steps 7 and 11:

1   Settle into a comfortable posture and envision your body as translucent and luminous.
2   Tune in to body mindfulness and open your mind to make space for mindful awareness.

3   Invite a congenial mentor into that space who embodies the qualities and ways of being you want to emulate.

4   Open yourself to their influence.

5   Imagine sharing your experiences with them.

6   See them welcoming all parts of you with deep confidence in your potential.

7   Ask for their inspiration, guidance, and commitment, including an empowering message such as "Be the example in your own life and world."

8   Envision them sending that freely as a wave of positive energy and light.

9   Take in their guidance and blessing, allowing it to dissolve your limiting sense of self.

10   Touch the core of your being and stir the positive qualities that are dormant within you.

11   Internalize their image and qualities as a catalyst for growing your expanded self, sealing it with an empowering pronouncement such as "I embody the larger way of being we all need!"

12   Dedicate yourself to transforming into the most empowered version of you—for your sake and the sake of those you impact.

Practice

EMPOWERING SPEECH TWO

1   Settle into a comfortable posture and envision your body as translucent and luminous.

2   Tune in to body mindfulness and open your mind to make space for mindful awareness.

3   Into that space, invite the image of a role model who inspires and empowers you.

4   Focus on them as a model or mirror of the way of being and life you want for yourself.

5   Share your strengths and challenges, then own the potential your mentor sees in you.

6   Imagine the mentor's empowering speech and tone entering and transforming you.

7   Affirm the new identity and story that embody your mentor's empowering message.

8   Enlist your mentor's full support and dedicate your efforts to a changed self and world.

9   Return to the practice, ideally at a regular time and place, three to seven days a week.

10   Tune in to this practice to revise your story when you feel stuck in your limiting one.

27 NATURAL FLOW

Harnessing Pure Passion

One of the much-touted yet poorly understood elements of leadership is flow. Brought into prominence by positive psychologist Mihaly Csikszentmihalyi,[26] flow refers to that peak mind/body state when our awareness, experience, and action arise from the core of our well-being system as an embodied experience of unhampered, unbridled flourishing. Accessing and cultivating flow are a natural way of living in possibilities, a critical aspect of being in deep harmony with our potential as humans and as boundless leaders.

We all experience states of flow—those moments when noise, distraction, and negativity give way to presence and immersion in what we're doing. These states invariably evoke positive mind/body conditions of well-being—wonder, joy, bliss, and equanimity. While there are many flavors of flow experience, we tend to compartmentalize or wall them off, reserving them for parts of our life where we feel we have control, like our favorite hobby, recreation, or sport. Whether it's swimming, dancing, cooking, or playing an instrument, we tend to feel these are the moments we live for, experiences that help us feel present, embodied, and alive.

Typically, work feels like another thing all together. We approach our jobs with a warrior mentality, a me-against-the-world feeling that anticipates how we may need to protect, defend, and prove ourselves—as if our work life is a just a struggle for survival. Given how our nervous systems are wired, once we bring that fear-based energy into the workplace, we're going to be blocked from our capacity for flow, since we're basically feeling embattled and stressed. Not only isn't this good for our well-being and performance, it isn't effective for the rest of the team because they're likely to end up tuning in to our stress-driven mind/body state and feel the same way. Remember social contagion?

The thrust of the discipline of body in boundless leadership is that it's eminently possible, even vital, for us to change our embodied approach to work. When we relegate our experience of flow to our nonprofessional, personal lives, we don't allow generative states of being with all their positive energy to be available to us as alternate modes of our nervous system. Just as an athlete or a performer can train to tap into flow states at will, through the practices of boundless leadership, we can learn to tap into flow energy and use it in all aspects of our work and lives. As with an athlete or performer, learning how to do this requires training: practicing exercises that empower us to switch out of stress states—with their embodied guarding and reactivity—and return us reliably and repeatedly to a positive energy and mind/body state.

When Elazar works with clients, he often asks, "Are you coming from a place of guarding against risk or opening to opportunity?" Understand that these two modes of our being are always accessible, depending on whichever is dominant in the moment. Then understand that whichever mode is fueling your mind/body state in the moment will critically shape how you handle a decision, meeting, conversation, or investment. Pause and remind yourself that you have the natural capacity to switch your fundamental mode of being to meet the situation as effectively as you can. When your start paying attention to your mind/body state in this critical light, you'll feel how habituated you are to guarding against risk and appreciate the practice of learning to switch your brain into natural flow—that exceptional state where we feel safe and hence free.

Energetically, this is the rut we're in as leaders, as an economy, as a culture. We've overemphasized the struggle part, the warrior energy of bracing for combat. We have an exaggerated sense of the importance, value, centrality, or necessity of struggle, of the zero-sum game where winner takes all. When we examine human nature and understand that work is fundamentally a social activity, we realize we must do it together, in a boundless way that creates value, productivity, and even joy. It makes sense that if we want to harness the clean energy of bonding and play, even if it's fierce, competitive play, we need to learn to switch out of fight-flight-faint-freeze states into flow.

As we change our relationship with economics, especially behavioral economics, and recognize the importance of balancing competition within safety and connection, we'll realize that there's nothing to be lost by bringing that playful, joyful energy into work. We're not giving up our competitive edge, we're honing it for a win-win culture where everybody contributes to the game, because we're releasing what's limiting us and going with a positive flow energy that unleashes our personal and collective best. Not only do we have nothing to lose when we release out limiting stress-driven energy and mind/body state, but we access the potential of human synergy and creativity—creating a whole that is greater than the sum of the parts. As leaders, and certainly as boundless leaders, this is the energy and culture we want to create. We want to generate a team, an organization, a field that is so much bigger than its component parts, and this is only possible within a culture fueled by natural flow.

THE PSYCHOLOGY AND BIOLOGY OF FLOW

There is a common misconception that flow involves the same energy and chemistry as the endorphin high associated with aerobic exercise like running or cycling or high-impact sports like soccer, tennis, or basketball. But it's crucial for leadership to understand that high arousal states are not monolithic and that flow states in particular involve a specific and unusual arousal based on a neural energy and chemistry that is quite distinct from what fuels conventional exercise and sports. While the endorphin high linked to aerobic exercise activates the stress response and hormones like adrenaline, norepinephrine, and steroids, flow depends on an exceptional form of ease-based arousal associated with meditation, yoga, chanting, dance, and qigong that mixes endorphins with the relaxation response and wellness hormones like serotonin, vasopressin, and oxytocin. As a result, the quality of arousal in conventional exercise runs on what we've called the dirty energy of our stress-driven survival mode, while the arousal of flow depends on the clean energy of our social flourishing mode, prompting the fearless social engagement of bonding and play.

This matters because when we source our leadership from the hard-driving energy we activate through hard-driving exercise and high-impact sports, we're coming from a stress-tainted place that will throw our leadership off balance, building a foundation of scarcity instead of abundance. However, if we source our leadership from the clean energy of flow, we'll surely be coming from a place of core well-being, thriving in abundant possibilities. The clean energy of flow will support mind/body states wherein arousal is balanced with calm self-awareness and authentic engagement, allowing us to express our full boundless capacities, have more impact, and be more at ease and effective. This is because natural flow involves not just a distinctive clean energy but also fuels the "animal spirits" of prosocial emotions—empathy, compassion, joy, and equanimity—as well as peak levels of self-awareness and authentic engagement, sustaining the key traits of boundless leadership.

Given this potential to shift our mind/body state toward boundless living and leading, it's vital we understand the basic nature of flow. In his book *Flow*, Csikszentmihalyi defined the term in a way that brought the idea into popular consciousness. He said that flow is a "state of concentration or complete absorption with the activity at hand and the situation. It is a state wherein people are so involved in an activity that nothing else seems to matter."[27] As a result, the idea of flow came to be associated with the peak experiences people have in a wide range of settings—from creative and performing arts to meditative and athletic highs. Based on this growing interest, psychologists began a decades-long effort to clarify the underlying biology of flow, combining research from a range of fields. What has emerged is a picture of peak experiences of arousal wherein our default neural processing is shifted at all three brain levels out of survival mode and into a state of mind/body flourishing.[28]

Normally, the symbolic, chatty, and fantasy-driven parts of our brain—related to the neocortex or primate brain—are directing our experience. If we're constantly thinking and playing memories and fantasies through our minds, we often don't sense our emotions or our bodies. We get carried away in a split-off mode of mind/brain processing. Flow is the opposite—as if the priorities of the brain are flipped. The chatty, fantasy-driven brain is decentered and quieted. Instead of being suppressed as usual, the older mammalian and reptilian parts of our brain dominate in an embodied positive experience where we feel whole and alive. Our bodies, our spirits, our energies, and our positive emotions all seem to have an extra intensity and focus, and everything feels easeful and natural, without the usual chatter of our inner critic or the disturbing emotions of fear, frustration, and doubt. It's like we're riding a wave of positivity that's coming from deep within us.

To understand the biology of this extraordinary state we return to our reptilian brain, specifically its mammalian upgrade and that extra chip that gives us new abilities to modulate and integrate the functioning of the reptilian brain and body. The old reptilian brain stem is engaged in basic life support and self-protection, and its reflex functions are primitive—fight or flight (sympathetic arousal), faint or freeze (parasympathetic arousal). Those are our extreme reactions for extreme circumstances, when we sense danger. The brain stem is activated in this way in states of stress and trauma, for instance. When our newer mammalian brain feels swamped, overwhelmed, and can't take in what's happening to us, the older reptilian part of the brain steps in with these primal reflexes to protect us. That leads to a high arousal state wherein our reptilian brain is driving our higher brain processing in a way that feels anything but easeful or pleasant.

While flow and stress are states in which the reptilian brain is dominant, the biology of stress and trauma is the direct opposite of flow. This is because in flow states our mind/body state is being run by the newer upgrade in our reptilian brain. This is the "switch" we evolved when we became mammals. It is connected to the new branch of the calming parasympathetic nervous system some call the "smart" vagus nerve. What we mean by "smart" is that it operates faster and voluntarily—within our conscious control. There are some functions of this newer part of our reptilian brain—like breathing—that we can consciously regulate.

The smart vagal system, or brain stem social engagement system, is based in new nuclei in the front-facing part of our reptilian brain. It gives us the capacity to activate our reptilian brain from within a fundamentally social mind/body state. When we do so, we don't feel threatened, we don't feel alone or disconnected. Instead we feel fundamentally, powerfully safe and connected and can calm and balance the older reptilian reflexes of fight or flight/faint or freeze, tuning the autonomic nervous system to get the best of both. This newer part of our brain has a way of creating a mixed arousal state that pulls excitement in from the sympathetic system along with the calm presence of the vagal system and mixes them with mammalian bonding and play hormones oxytocin and vasopressin in a special cocktail that feels like, *Wow, I am so alive, yet safe! Fully myself, yet connected to others.*

That cocktail modulates the older blissful chemistry of endorphins, dopamine, and serotonin in a novel way that empowers us to enter a special mammalian flow state in which we are aroused and calm in a balanced way. This flow state supports an embodied social engagement that allows us to stay present with others in a connected, caring, expressive, and playful way. This is our simple model of the biochemistry of flow. It's as if our new brain is tapping into the best in our older brain and calling forth a deep primal energy we're normally only using in exceptional mind/body states of bliss, growth, and well-being. For example, after a deep sleep, we don't remember much, but we awake refreshed and energized, even though we may have gone to sleep stressed and fatigued. Other primal states that share this restorative biology are hibernation (which we humans don't do), orgasm, and near-death experiences. Among these, the closest naturally occurring analogue to flow is orgasm, since it's the one primal regenerative state in which we are fully awake. In flow, however, we enter the same state not by attraction or physical stimulation but by focusing our minds on something that rouses both interest and calm.

One of the distinctive features of flow is an unusual mind/body state in which our bodies are pleasantly relaxed yet our hearts and brains are present and aroused. Socially, such flow states empower us to maintain fearless presence together with authentic engagement and exceptional levels of self-awareness, even when those around us may be fearful, angry, or shut down.

If natural flow states are beneficial and powerful, can we train ourselves to tap them routinely, and if so, how?

The good news is that flow states, like positive social emotions, can be systematically cultivated through contemplative practices that combine positive imagery and vocalization with deep abdominal breathing, in unusual embodied practices traditionally called tantric meditation and yoga. In some experiments done on advanced Buddhist and Hindu experts, imagery and vocal recitation combined with intensive breath-holding practices allow these practitioners to reduce the rate of their metabolism (the amount of energy bodies consume) by more than half, while maintaining exceptionally high, peak levels of heart-brain activation. Suppose you could go through your day using half the energy you normally do, while being at your peak, best, and most positive, emotionally and mentally? That's why being in a state of natural flow is like tapping into our brain and body's innate fusion power. That's why natural flow is the cause and payoff of leadership with a quantum differential.

In terms of the discipline of body in boundless leadership, controlling our breathing is our gateway to this natural flow capacity we have as mammals. Once we learn how to tap these regenerative mind/brain states using our new mammalian upgrade, we can access a steady current of this boundless clean energy source and bring this quality of being alive and present and yet ready to play and engage socially with others into our everyday lives and work.

The practice of breathwork is what allows us to learn to regulate our reptilian nervous system and shift gears at the level of our brain stem. This is because the vital rhythm of breathing is intimately connected to the autonomic nervous system in a way that allows it to act like the joystick or gearshift for our brain stem. In particular, the capacity to consciously control our breath activates our smart vagal nerve that serves our upper body, while the capacity to slow and hold deep abdominal breaths activates the older branch of the vagus nerve that serves our lower body. By learning to work with the breath, we develop the ability to shift out of risk-adverse reptilian "dinosaur gear" into connective, friendly "mammalian gear."

As we make this fundamental shift, we'll practice enjoying and embodying natural flow.

THE OXYGEN OF FEARLESS ENERGY: BREATH AS CATALYST

Breathwork is the practice that helps us develop the quality of natural flow. Our breathing is something we do automatically and don't often think much about. Sometimes we notice it, most of the time we don't. The power of conscious breathing can serve as an anchor for our stress-reactive default mind/body state, return us to a calming awareness of the present moment. It can protect our nervous system from the disruptions of social stress reactivity, and it can also empower us to shift gears in our autonomic nervous system and give the older part of our brain and body the message that we're safe, can be fearless, and can enter into a state of flow.

Before we practice, it helps to appreciate how to engage breathwork over time, acquainting ourselves with the process and developing a facility for new modes of conscious breathing that support and energize new ways of being. The first thing we learn in any breathing practice, like yoga or Lamaze for example, is that the breath has different parts, and we need to be mindful of breathing with our body. When we're distracted or anxious, our bodies tend to constrict, restricting us to shallow, quick breathing centered in the chest. With conscious breathing we usually relax as the axis of breath shifts deeper toward the belly, where the older part of our calming nervous system slows and regulates the breath while we sleep. What we try to do in beginning practice is learn how to integrate these parts of the breath and move toward a deeper, slower, and complete rhythm. We do this by using our hands as a natural biofeedback mechanism as in the exercise below:

1   Sit comfortably and close your eyes to get centered.
2   As you bring awareness to the rhythm of your breath, consider whether you're breathing with your whole body.
3   You can do this by putting your hands on your chest. Feel what it's like to breathe into the upper body, feel your chest expanding. This tends to be the shallowest breath.
4   Follow the breath and see how deeply you're breathing as you move your hands downward to the bottom of your rib cage. Is it expanding? Contracting? Is it cut off or constricted? Relax any tension you feel using your hands to gently send energy or a gentle massage.
5   Relax and breathe slower ... deeper. Can you take a full diaphragmatic breath? That is a breath with your diaphragm moving into the belly. Your belly may bulge out, but that's the point. Can you feel your entire abdomen moving down to the pelvic floor?

While there are many common ways to train to bring a centered and balanced poise to our breath energy and rhythm—such as deep abdominal breathing or alternate nostril breathing, where we breathe in one nostril and out the other using our thumb and knuckle as nose plugs—the main breath exercise we use to tap into natural flow is a practice of holding the abdominal breath called vase breathing or pot-belly breathing. This practice is widely used in the Indian and Tibetan yoga traditions to deepen abdominal breath holding in ways that activate the older branch of the vagal nerve while simultaneously activating the sympathetic system.

The practice begins as in role-modeling imagery by envisioning the body as a luminous bubble. Within that body we can optionally envision three channels like thick straws of light that run along the central axis of the nervous system from the nostrils (two side channels) and mid-brow (central channel) together up to the crown and then down toward the brain stem and spinal cord into the abdomen and pelvis. These symbolize the sympathetic, parasympathetic, and smart vagal branches of the autonomic nervous system, respectively. In this particular practice, the side channels join the central one at a point between the navel and pelvis and then feed into a luminous vessel shaped like a vase whose mouth opens to the central channel and whose base rests in the pelvis. This "vase" symbolizes the capacity of the autonomic nervous system to gather and store flow energy as a clean energy source for running the central nervous system.

The practice is done in the following steps:

Vase Breathing Practice

- Breathing gently in through both nostrils, completely filling the vase in the belly
- "Pressure sealing" the vase from above by nodding and swallowing, and from below by squeezing the muscles of the pelvic floor upward
- Gently holding the breath for a count of three, five, seven, or twenty-one, while holding the pressure seal from above and below
- Before any discomfort, releasing the pressure seal and forcefully exhaling some, but not all, of the breath, imagining it flowing up the central channel and out the mid-brow while keeping a reserve of breath energy "stored" in the vase, which helps sustain a deep-abiding flow of calm aroused energy

By holding the breath and stimulating the pelvic floor, this practice activates both parts of the autonomic nervous system, prompting a mixed energy of arousal and calm that provides the ideal energy for natural flow.

Like the practices of empowering narrative, the practice of breathwork is embedded within the practice of role-modeling imagery and involves adding vase breathing to the imagery and affirmation process as a preliminary practice in step 1 and again as a final "linking and sealing" practice after step 7 in the role-modeling practice.

Practice

SEALING ROLE-MODELING IMAGERY AND NARRATIVE WITH BREATHWORK AND NATURAL FLOW

1   Settle into a comfortable posture and envision your body as translucent and luminous.
2   Tune in to body mindfulness and open your mind to make space for mindful awareness.
3   Into that space, invite the image of a role model who inspires and energizes you.
4   Focus on them as a vessel of the positive energy and flow you want for yourself.
5   Share your strengths and challenges, then own the potential your mentor sees in you.
6   Imagine the mentor's flow energy and chemistry entering and transforming you.
7   Mix them with your own natural flow energy and seal them in with three to seven vase breaths.
8   Enlist your mentor's full support and dedicate your energy to a changed self and world.
9   Return to the practice, ideally at a regular time and place, three to seven days a week.

Tune in to this practice to tap your natural flow when you feel stuck in stress energy.

28 FEARLESS EMBODIMENT

The Stance of True Leadership

Empowered vision, speech, and flow culminate in embodied fearlessness—the ability to become less guarded and reactive while expressing a fluid, open, and playful stance and movement in your life. Together with our vocal tone and the energy behind it, our facial expressions and body language implicitly signal to ourselves and others whether we're uptight and reactive or joyful and playful. Whether consciously or unconsciously, we register these embodied signals and reflexively react or respond. That's why the quality of embodied fearlessness carries so much weight from a leadership perspective.

There are two main reasons why embodied stance and movement, however key, may strike us as surprising or novel leadership qualities. First, the revolutionary nature of the new science has clarified the role of the body in shaping our state of consciousness. Second, science clarifies how our facial expressions and body language broadcast our internal state to others.

The first breakthrough involves the discovery of what some call embodied cognition. That is the surprising fact that, despite the modern consensus based on the scientific philosophy of Descartes, mind and body are *anything but* independent realities. They are two sides of one completely interactive mind/body system where our minds impact our bodies, while our bodies—including our posture and movement—shape our states of mind. Instead of two disjointed parts in a hybrid machine, mind and body are like two constantly interactive and interdependent systems linked in an open and ongoing feedback loop, or like two compounds in the constant interchange of a dynamic equilibrium. A cringing posture makes us anxious; an expansive posture engenders confidence. Smiling makes us feel safer and happier; frowning makes us angry or sad. Likewise, moving any and all parts of our bodies in guarded versus graceful ways sends bottom-up messages (thanks to so-called *interoceptive feedback* via the vagus nerve) about our fundamental level of safety and social connection. Even the cerebellum, the most densely packed part of our brains long thought to coordinate fine motor movements, has been found to coordinate and direct all the skilled cognitive and executive operations of the new brain as well.

Considering the feedback our bodies give us led Elazar to recall one of the first corporate jobs he had. He was sent to Dallas as part of his executive training. It was his first time in Texas, and although he was pretty busy with work, on the weekend he decided to embrace the experience. He wanted to buy an authentic pair of cowboy boots. He went to a store, tried some on, and liked them so much he wore them back to the hotel. When he went out in Dallas that night, he felt like a different man! His demeanor changed; how he sauntered into a room changed. Although he's normally a pretty easygoing guy, that night he almost got into a fight. In retrospect he reflected, "It was all because of those damn boots!"

We're mostly in our heads as a culture and in business. We don't value how important what's happening in our body is to our nervous system, emotional tone, or state of mind. This is a new area of potential growth for leadership and for us as individuals.

This leads to the second reason mentioned above that the new mind/body science is so surprising: it clarifies how our facial expressions and body language transmit our internal state to others. Our bodies are not just in constant two-way communication with our minds, they are also constantly communicating with the mind/body systems of others. A vital part of our evolution as mammals is that we developed so that our nervous systems would be born, live, and die in constant two-way interaction with those of others. As we discussed earlier, we have mirror neurons, which are specialized neurons that scan the body language of the people around us and call up memories of how we felt when our body was in a similar posture and movement. This mirroring allows us to try to match what we see in others' facial expressions and body language with our best guess about what they may be feeling. This process of reading the minds of others must have been vital to our survival. If you're an impala and you sense the other impalas in your herd getting restless, you'll want to take notice, since their inner state may hold vital information about your environment like say, there's a lion coming out of the woods. If your herd-mate is anxious, you might need to be anxious, or if there's a beautiful oasis nearby and the herd is moving toward it with eager anticipation, you would want to notice and move with them.

As we've seen, such social contagion via facial expressions and body language is usually the main way emotions and mind states get transmitted back and forth between mammals. And this doesn't happen only in the wild, but in the conference room and boardroom and on Zoom as well. Unless we bring consciousness to how we're expressing our emotions and holding our bodies, we'll remain clueless about the implicit messages bouncing around the room, including those we're broadcasting. Whatever it is we feel, whether we're uptight, frustrated, or joyful, people will notice and respond, regardless of what we're saying or think we're saying via speech.

The numbers are surprising. Roughly 51 percent of any communication, more than half of the impact you have, comes from facial expressions and body language including your posture, gestures, and stance.[29] That in itself is enough to subvert the paradigm of modern economics that says we are *self-interested rational animals*, that what we think in our own heads is what matters, not what we feel or what our body or others' bodies are doing. It turns out, it's the opposite, as behavioral economics shows, making it quite plain that our training as professionals, especially leaders, needs to be reconsidered and revolutionized.[30] We should understand ourselves in the way of performers or athletes, who use their bodies to do something special, namely, achieve our fullest potential and broadcast a message, a way of being, optimism, or direction. This is an important shift.

Unfortunately, our modern disembodied mindset has become a way of being—we've lost touch with our bodies, especially in Western culture. It's natural to privilege the higher levels of mind—our mental processing or brain processing—and identify with them. It's easier to solve a problem in your head than to do the experiment or solve the problem in real life—mind, heart, and body.[31] We tend not to pay much attention to our bodies, which end up carrying the lion's share of our learning experiences, so our bodies live in the shadows of higher awareness, education, and professional training. As a result, our bodies tend to be stuck in childhood or the Stone Age, while our minds have been catapulted into a digital world. We can train ourselves to bring awareness to our body and shape how it impacts our energy, hearts, and minds as we learn to "speak" the language of expressions and gestures it broadcasts. The question is, how?

Fearless embodiment practice is a simple and direct way to return awareness to the body and use that attention to enrich what we normally take for granted. The practice begins by extending our body mindfulness to our posture and movement, so we can observe how it makes our minds feel. For example, if we're nervous, we might feel it in our belly. If we're stressed our shoulder might ache. When we understand embodied stance, it's like a mind hack—by shifting our bodies we can change our minds. We then can explore the dimension of impact on others by complementing our body mindfulness with equal empathy practice—that is, cross-checking the interoceptive input from our bodies with the visible reactions of those around us. As we become proficient in this basic language, we will notice how often our bodies are locked in stress guarding and reactivity and appreciate how that default setting impacts our capacity for boundless competencies like clarity and compassion. Based on this self-assessment of our embodied default mode and its impact on ourselves and others, we can then begin the work of fearless embodiment—freeing our body from the reptilian grip of fear and shifting it into fearless mode, so we can inhabit it in a fully mammalian way.

To varying degrees we all need repeated practice and conscious nudging out of our default survival mode, which keeps us guarded and stressed. As we repeatedly work on body awareness, we'll come to recognize the link between our mind/body energy and how we feel living in our body on a moment-to-moment basis. That's why throughout this discipline of body, we've explored practices that speak to the reptilian brain from the top down—like vision and speech—as well as breathing practices that work bottom up, from the body to the reptilian brain. The practice of fearless embodiment is the final step, adding a second bottom-up way to shift your autonomic system and mind/body state.

SCIENCE OF FEARLESS EMBODIMENT

What do we mean by fearless embodiment? We know that evolution wired us for survival—or rather it picked out the more squirrelly and vigilant of our ancestors—which led to our present nervous system, which comes out of the factory set to anticipate and avoid danger. We also know we have this deep survival conditioning within us, and as with natural flow, this is still wired in the reptilian part of our brain.

If we examine the biology of our brains in terms of fear versus safety, we evolved three neural systems of self-protection over the ages to shift from one state to the other. Our oldest pattern of self-protective wiring that's ingrained in our brain stem is the freeze response. It's basically feigning death—fainting, freezing, or shutting down. When animals feel cornered by a much bigger animal, fighting and flying are out of the question and this protective reflex kicks in to fool our predator into missing or mistaking us for dead. Although we're no longer in the wild, this still happens to us in many if not most cases of trauma and even in the milder form of shutting down our life force by accommodating social pressure.

The next layer of self-protective reflexes we developed in our evolution—the sympathetic nervous system reflexes—allows us to mobilize to cope with less overwhelming physical threats. If we think there's a chance we might be able to escape or fight danger, our heart accelerates, pumping blood away from our brain and gut and to our muscles instead, so we can mobilize—fight or fly. Again, although we're no longer in the wild, this reflex can get triggered at any time we feel socially threatened with shame or exclusion. This is why we are often somewhat tense—with our heart racing, butterflies in our stomach, or a knot in our throat—or feeling guarded and reactive.

The newest part of our equipment for dealing with stress is our smart vagal nerve. That's especially powerful in setting the tone of general calm, confidence, and engagement in our primate way of life. Once we fear nobody on the team likes us, or we're overly challenged by a task, we may become self-preoccupied, drifting into worse-case thinking and feeling socially isolated and negative emotions like fear. This can trip the rest of the cascade into fight-flight-faint-freeze. Although this is ingrained and wired into our system, we can combat and transform it.

Part of what the new science of the autonomic nervous system has shown is that as mammals we have an upgraded ability to calm our old reflexes, as we saw in the science of natural flow. We can do this by looking for safety cues like smiling faces and gentle voices, generating more cues like imagining ourselves as confident, speaking to ourselves in an assured tone, working with our breath, and assuming postures of well-being and ease. These send calming messages to our brain stem that allow us to stay present, to mobilize without fear. This is how mammals learn to be caretakers and leaders. A normal reptile isn't going to stay around to nurture its young. It's off and running and trying to get food or avoid danger. But mammals have the extra ability to stop running and to stay present, to calm their fears, and in calming their fears, to be able to connect with others in a deep and lasting way.

In embodied flow we saw how to send bottom-up messages by regulating our breath and tuning our autonomic nervous system to a balanced state that allows us to bring a fearless—fundamentally calm and confident—energy into our way of being. Now we'll practice fearless movement and see how holding and moving our bodies with open social stances and easeful gestures can calm our bodies, hearts, and minds. This ability to calm our bodies is fundamental to all the unusual cultural and social activities we do. Not only does it provide the capacity to stay present with others without freaking out if things seem difficult or intense, but it allows us to operate, execute, and perform with grace and ease.

There's an element to the science of how our brain stem upgrade and the new smart vagal nervous system are tuned in to the extra brain that coordinates our movements with grace and skill: it's the cerebellum. Since the cerebellum also coordinates mental activity, moving gracefully not only smooths demeanor but simultaneously lends ease and skill to our higher processing, including expressions of emotion, critical thinking, and task execution. That's why it's vital to every aspect of our leadership that we learn how to live in our bodies in this fundamentally fearless way.

Planting a New You: Fearless Movement

On a basic level, posture practice involves bringing awareness and balance to all levels of the mind/body system, head to toe. These practices not only help free up the head, shoulders, and pelvis where unconscious tension and shielding accumulate, they also relax and mobilize the torso for deeper, fuller breathing and balance and tone the autonomic nervous system. As a result, they deepen and enhance the impact of deep abdominal breathing on grounding and balancing the nervous system to support stable presence and embodied openness.

Practice

FEARLESS EMBODIMENT

Here are some breath and posture practices to relax and open the head, neck, heart, navel, and pelvis and stimulate and connect a balanced state of autonomic arousal throughout the body. Together they help spark a mind/body flow state and harness that state to fuel the quality of fearless embodiment. All posture practices may be added to vase breathing or done as simple mindful movements. Here are the top-down steps:

1   Five senses: Soothe and balance your sense organs by gently massaging your ears with thumb and forefinger; rotating your eyes counterclockwise and clockwise and then covering both eyes with your palms; massaging both nostrils between thumb and forefinger; moving your tongue from side to side, then up and down; pressing your lips together and parting them three times.

2   Head and neck: Rotate your head gently in a counterclockwise direction between three and seven times, then reverse the rotation for an equal number of turns clockwise. Nod your head gently and deeply forward between three and seven times, while interlacing your fingers behind your head and leaning it gently backward between three and seven times. Finally, with fingers interlaced behind your head and elbows opened wide, twist your head, neck, and upper body gently from side to side seven, twelve, or twenty-one times.

3   Shoulders: Circle each arm overhead three times clockwise and then throw each arm forward like hurling a lasso three times on each side; rotate each arm backward around the shoulder three times like doing the backstroke; extend both arms out to the side and switch from palms facing up to palms down three times.

4   Chest and heart: In a seated posture with forearm and hands crossed over the heart, take a deep breath into the belly and pelvis and hold it for a count of three, seven, or more. Exhale forcefully as your lean the chest and shoulders forward and down, shaking the heart and arms open, and making the roaring sound: *Hah!*

5   Abdomen: With your hands on your knees, actively rotate the abdomen like a belly dancer, first counterclockwise three, seven, or twelve times and then clockwise for the same number of rotations. For a subtler version, take a deep breath into the belly and hold it as you subtly rotate your

abdominal core three, seven, or more times counterclockwise as if stirring the breath, then stir clockwise the same number of times and forcefully exhale as before.

6   Pelvis and legs: Sit on several stacked cushions or a chair with back upright, forearms and hands crossed over your chest, and legs half extended and crossed in front of you. Leaning back slightly, alternately extend one leg almost fully while simultaneously retracting the other in toward your seat, repeating the movement seven to ten times.

As we mentioned above, the practice of fearless embodiment is most effective at grounding our stance and movement in a fearless way of being when it's embedded within the role-modeling imagery practice along with empowering speech and breathwork. This integrated body practice allows you to combine top-down and bottom-up methods, shifting your autonomic system and mind/body state so that fearless embodiment becomes installed in the body.

Practice
FEARLESS STANCE AND MOVEMENT

1   Settle into a comfortable posture and envision your body as translucent and luminous.

2   Tune in to body mindfulness and open your mind to make space for mindful awareness.

3   Into that space, invite the image of a role model who embodies fearlessness.

4   Focus on them as a model of the fearless stance and movement you want for yourself.

5   Share your strengths and challenges, then own the potential your mentor sees in you.

6   Imagine the mentor's embodied fearlessness and grace entering and transforming you.

7　Dissolve them into your own fearlessness and seal them in with three to seven vase breaths.

8　Enlist your mentor's support and dedicate your every move to a changed self and world.

9　Return to the practice, ideally at a regular time and place, three to seven days a week.

Tune in to this practice to shift into fearless embodiment when you feel stuck in stress.

29 APPLICATION

Embodying Meaning and Purpose: The Integrated Leader

Each of the disciplines of boundless leadership has an application, a way of putting the work of the discipline into action in your everyday life and work. We explored aligned intention as the application for the discipline of mind and empowered responsibility as the application for the discipline of heart. In the discipline of body, the application is embodied purpose. Once we've begun the work of embodying our larger way of being—the expanded vision, tone, energy, and stance we want—and hence we can access some fearlessness even in tough situations, it's time to start building a bridge from practice to daily life. How do we integrate what we're learning into how we show up at work, so we can optimize our positive impact on our living network—from self to team to company, from our inner life to our family, community, and planet? In other words, how do we apply what we've learned, felt, and embodied to create positive value and change, to cultivate what positive psychology calls our life meaning and purpose?

The greatest discovery of positive psychology is that real well-being, success, and happiness for us humans come not from achievement or external forms of success but from feeling connected to others socially, in an authentic and positive way. That means that the rewards of boundless leadership—for us and for others—come from how we connect our potential with the potential of those around us. All the qualities that build fearlessness and contribute to embodied flow—boundless vision, empowering speech, natural flow, fearless embodiment—are boundless precisely because they stretch our self-limiting images and stories and our self-protective energy and stance to make room for the larger potential we have to evolve in and through our connections with others and the world we share. We apply the discipline of body by envisioning, expressing, and embodying how we want to show up at key points in our day, connect ourselves and others to our optimal potential here and now, and make the greatest possible contribution we can in a moment-to-moment, real-time way to our future, our team, our organization, and the world.

One way to think about this application is as conscious realignment of our embodied mind/energy around the axis of our potential and optimal contribution, as revealed by our mentor. It's as if you were to ask yourself, "How would I show up today/in this meeting/on this project if I were my mentor—if I were embodying *their* qualities in my way of being?" To home in on this more precisely, we don't have to remain content with a vague generic boundless way of being but can break it down to the levels of being—mind, heart, and body—that we can align with our intention and purpose. The first two levels—aligned intention and empowered responsibility—relate to the disciplines of mind and heart, respectively. They allow us to check that we're clear about our positive intention for showing up, say, to be at our best for the sake of our team and shared aim and that we're taking responsibility for how we're showing up and not projecting any expectation or blame onto others. The next four levels relate specifically to the discipline of body:

1 Vision: Are we seeing ourselves and the world from our expanded self-image, emulating our mentor's way of being and impacting the world?

2 Tone: Are we correcting self-limiting beliefs and affirming our identity and role?

3 Energy: Have we toned our autonomic nervous system with the breath to prime flow?

4 Stance: Are we sensing and moving our body in ways that open us to fearlessly engage?

This application assumes a fundamentally social intention and responsibility, aligning our mind, heart, and body around an altruistic motive that links our self-realization to a specific contribution to others and the world. This is how it helps line us up with our potential for servant leadership and hence for embodying a core alignment with our prime prosocial motive and purpose: to fulfill our potential by contributing as much as we can to the well-being of others and the world. What makes this a key leadership application is that we're harnessing our practice of the discipline of body in a day-to-day way to shape and reshape our way of being in the world. This harnessing involves a practice of aligning and realigning our mind, heart, and body with our short-term aims and long-term purpose. This happens through the following actions:

Setting: We start each day by setting our vision, tone, energy, and stance in a morning practice of role-modeling imagery enhanced by empowering speech, breathwork, and posture, dedicating the practice to showing up aligned with our aim and purpose.

Resetting: We take mind/body pauses throughout the day to reset to our purposeful mode of being through briefly refreshing our vision, tone, energy, and stance.

Strategic presetting: We take the opportunity before any high-impact meeting, presentation, or creative project to align our mind, heart, and body with our aim and purpose.

By integrating the four practices of the discipline of body, embodied purpose can be a powerful application, helping shift our core vision, tone, energy, and movement to align our way of being and acting with boundless leadership.

Having completed our survey of the key insights, science, and tools of the disciplines of boundless leadership, we turn to the work of individualizing the method for your personal growth and transformation.

Part Five

A COMMITMENT
TO PRACTICE

30 MANIFESTING YOUR VISION AND PURPOSE

The Big Picture

We've explored the disciplines of mind, heart, and body and the practices that empower us to initiate change, but how do we sustain and magnify the change within ourselves? In this part of our journey, we invite you to envision and plan your path of practice and transformation. What is your boundless vision for yourself, your organization, and the world we share? As in all good business, if we wish to truly thrive, it's important to move beyond theory and experience to integrate the best practices and real-world applications into our lives. Each one of us will need a plan of action—including short- and long-term goals, a practice plan, and outcome measures—or nothing will be fully realized.

Typically in business when people ask, "What's your plan?" they want to know, "What do you hope to achieve? What are you going to do and when? What resources and time will you need?" Of course, what we're referring to here is vastly different from a conventional business plan in that it begins as a plan for our transformation as leaders, including the *why*, our deepest personal motivation and purpose. A practice plan is about having clarity about your final destination: where do you most want to find yourself as a leader? It also includes clarity about your motivation, *why* you're moving in that specific direction, as well as a plan or map of *how* you're going do it—what practices and qualities will get you to who, what, where, and how you want to be. Once you have this map, you can then plan for the resources or supports you'll need (the *what*) as well as the timing of how to progress, step by step (the *when*). The plan does not need to be perfect—we need progress not perfection—but to be alive rather than dead on arrival, the plan must always be in motion. Unlike conventional plans that are outcome based, your boundless leadership plan is process based, identifying and addressing the blocks and patterns that keep you from achieving your full potential. The map is all about opening up channels—accessing your vulnerability, unblocking your process—whatever creative form that takes for you. There's no right or wrong around it.

HITTING THE GROUND RUNNING: FIRST LOCATE YOURSELF ON THE PATH

In parts 1 through 4, we completed our high-level survey of the road map of boundless leadership. As we review that survey now with the aim of getting our feet on the ground and to get moving, we have to remember that the map is not the terrain. That's why the first small step toward getting on your way for real is to locate where you are on the path and figure out your most immediate obstacles and what practices you need to start moving through them. You do that by identifying the stress-driven obstacle or gravity that is slowing or stopping you in your tracks and then deciding how the disciplines can give you the leverage to break through and get moving. When we revisit the road map from this on-the-ground vantage, we see the journey to boundless leadership in terms of three strategic pivots away from the conventional path of living and working in survival mode toward the road not taken, the road that leads toward our boundless way of living and working in thriving mode.

At the level of mind, this means a strategic pivot that turns us away from a fixation on the external data or noise, especially as seen through the negative lens of scarcity and risk avoidance. That then turns us toward a focus on our internal mind state, maintaining an expansive awareness that can see boundless possibilities and stay radically open to learning. At the level of heart, this means a strategic pivot away from the social survival mode of denying fear-based biases and controlling shame-based emotions toward a social thriving mode of emotional equanimity that can accept and engage our own and others' emotional needs with unbiased empathy and authentic compassion. At the level of body, this means a strategic pivot away from limiting self-images and narratives—and the stress energy and stance they interlock with—toward a boundless vision of self and world that unleashes the embodied clean energy and motion of fearless flow. In short, the path to boundless leadership proceeds through three successive turns: from a critical mind to an open mind; from a careful heart to a caring heart; and from a guarded energy and stance to a fluid energy and stance.

Hopefully as you've read this book you've found which of these pivots is the most difficult and which of the three main blocks—negativity bias, shame avoidance, or embodied stress energy—is where your struggles lie. Likely the themes we covered in the discipline that corresponded to where you're stuck resonated and opened new angles for approaching and breaking through your current obstacle. If so, in all likelihood you found the practices that helped build the qualities you needed to make that pivot felt unburdening and empowering in a tangible way. Here is where you most likely will need to start your practice plan.

THE FOUNDATIONAL PRINCIPLES OF BOUNDLESS LEADERSHIP

Once you've located where you are on the path and have determined what you need, there's another step you need to take to get to work crafting your practice plan. That step is to be sure the goals you set for your practice and the specific methods you adopt are grounded in the three foundational principles of boundless leadership. Those principles are the essential science and business insight that form the basis for the disciplines. If you feel your work lies in the discipline of mind—in making the pivot from letting your mind contract around external factors to turning inward to the boundless potential of your capacity to notice and learn—the foundational principle you must leverage is that the biggest variable in what you see and notice is your mindset and mind state, not the conditions you face. If your work lies in the discipline of heart—in pivoting from guarding against blame and shame to opening yourself to engaging with care—the foundational principle you must leverage is that positive social emotions rather than rational self-interest and emotional self-control are the primary sources of confidence, social effectiveness, and the ability to influence others. Finally, if your crucial work lies in the discipline of body—in pivoting from limiting self-images, narratives, and stress-reactive energies to expansive visions, empowering narratives, and fearless flow energies—the foundational principle you must leverage is that embodied practices like prosocial imagery and breathwork can completely switch the whole mind/brain/body from survival mode into thriving mode.

DEVELOPING YOUR PRACTICE PLAN FOR BOUNDLESS LEADERSHIP

Once you have a sense of the pivot you most need to make to get moving, you can start setting short- and long-term goals and establishing the day-to-day elements of your practice plan. For instance, if your mind gets contracted and closed around external conditions, you may want to set as goals noticing when you're stuck in fixation or developing the presence of mind to turn inward and open. At the same time you may want to set long-term goals like identifying and clearing the negative biases your mind is contracting around or developing the qualities that stabilize clarity and eventually install it as the trait of self-awareness. This location and trajectory would suggest you'll need to get serious about attention training through establishing a regular practice of one or more of the four modes of mindfulness. And it would also suggest you'll need to weave into your workday compressed practices like taking time-outs for three or more mindful breaths or three to five minutes of open, mindful awareness at key intervals.

Likewise, if your heart is the place you tend to get stuck, and you find yourself defending against others who seem to trigger reactive emotions or your inner critic, you may want to set goals like correcting the social biases and shame-based inner critic that lock you into social survival mode or learning to access and expand the prosocial qualities that grow compassion and eventually install the trait of authentic engagement. This location and trajectory would suggest you'll need to develop your practice plan around compassion training through the regular practice of skills like self-compassion or invoking and emulating mentors. And that would suggest you'll also need to weave into your day brief practices like self-compassion breaks or calling mentors to mind at social stress moments.

Finally, if you're stuck at the level of your body, having trouble making the pivot from limiting self-images, narratives, or stress energy and guarding, you will want to focus on revising your self-image and story around role models or shifting your body energy out of stress into the clean energy of flow, building the qualities of embodiment that promote fearlessness and eventually get installed as the trait of embodied flow. This location and trajectory would suggest you'll need to build your practice plan around the embodied practices of role-modeling imagery and narrative as well as breathwork and fluid posture/movement. And it would also suggest you'll need to find brief daily practices like invoking mentors to expand your self-image and vision and taking three vase breaths or doing some self-massage at moments of bodily stress and guarding.

When you set out to develop a provisional practice plan, you'll want to be sure it includes the following seven elements:

1   The pivot you most need to work on
2   The obstacle that's most blocking you
3   Your prime short-term objectives for three months,
    six months, and nine months
4   Your principal long-term goals for one year, two years,
    and five years

5 Your regular weekly practice plan, including practice(s), duration, and frequency
6 Your brief practices for everyday life and work
7 Your outcome measures, such as less distraction, reactivity, fatigue and more flexibility, resilience, clean energy

Clearly, most of us need to work on all three disciplines to achieve our full potential. The caution here is to work on them one at a time, folding in the next one as we gain proficiency in the preceding one. It's vital that you not set overly ambitious goals that can discourage you or cause burnout.

31 INTEGRATING THE APPLICATIONS AND ORIENTING TOWARD GREATER PURPOSE

Once you get into a regular practice rhythm and start to feel its impact on getting you through blocks and building key qualities, it's time to focus strategically on the application practice that will help leverage your inner progress for your on-the-ground leadership capacity. Remember, each discipline of boundless leadership has its own application:

Aligned intention for mind
Empowered responsibility for heart
Embodied purpose for body

You may begin by focusing on the application most related to your immediate blockage. Or, if you've begun to make some movement on your worst obstacle, it might make sense to progress sequentially, since the applications, like the disciplines, build on one another. This is because by learning to clarify and align, we become more intentional in our everyday life and work. It is that greater sense of agency and direction that enables us to take empowered responsibility for our part in the complex interplay of real-world events, including our impact on others. That agency and responsibility carry over into our big-picture intentions for ourselves and empower us to take responsibility for the single greatest source of leverage we have as leaders:

our own development. This growing momentum toward intentional agency and empowered responsibility for our overall impact on our growth, as well as on others, our teams, our organizations, and the larger world, is what naturally brings us to a more intentional and responsible sense of our purpose as people and as leaders. This is where our momentum leads to the application of embodying purpose.

The final application of embodying purpose in a real sense reflects the culmination of our practice plan—leveraging our practice, including the discipline of body, to the deepest and widest possible contribution or impact we can make as leaders. When we can set our intention and actually take empowered responsibility for how we show up in the most fundamental way—as living, breathing, embodied beings—we are aligning every aspect of our humanity from our vision and tone to our energy and stance with the impact or difference we want to create. In so doing, we are making the ultimate use of our primary instrument as leaders—ourselves—to maximize the leverage we can exert in any given interaction or context by modeling the way of being we believe will best contribute to our goal in that interaction or context. If the medium is the message, the ultimate medium of human self-expression, communication, and influence is how we hold ourselves at the deepest level—the level of what we see, say, feel, do, and are in our moment-to-moment, living, breathing, energy bodies.

Of course, the application of embodying purpose focuses on bringing that alignment as leverage into our everyday work lives, on sustaining it through the day, and on applying it strategically to specific divisions, meetings, presentations, or projects. But what building momentum looks like on the level of this last application is that, as this process becomes more intuitive and natural, we extend it to the larger horizon of embodying our purpose not just in the moment, day by day, but in the aggregate, as our optimal, whole life vision of what impact we would like to have at the end of our careers—our consummate purpose as people and as leaders.

This natural extension of the application of embodied purpose to the final horizon of our biggest possible life purpose brings in the final dimension or version of our practice plan. While getting started with an initial plan is all about where we are located now, in a real sense the process of integrating the applications leads us to a radically different take on our plan—one that looks at our practice and measures progress from the standpoint not of where we are but of where we aim to be—of our arrival point. What do we ultimately aspire to as people and leaders? What impact on others, our organization, and the world reflects the largest possible purpose, difference, or contribution we intend to make? In this last dimension of our plan, we start from our final destination and work our way back, filling in what needs to be done to get us from where we are to where we aim to be. Since developing this final form of your plan can be hard to grasp, we offer an unconventional template for fleshing it out: your leadership mandala.

32 THE MANDALA OF LEADERSHIP

When you close this book, the boundless leadership program hasn't ended, it has only just begun! That's why we'd like to offer one more tool that will especially help with your commitment to practice: your mandala of leadership. Think of it as a way to assemble and personalize your plan and your vision from the standpoint of your final destination, coalescing the tools we've offered through the previous chapters into a blueprint for creating and becoming, a tangible guide to manifest your vision.

THE MANDALA

We've created the boundless leadership mandala to help you engage and actualize your plan going forward. Perhaps you've seen images of Tibetan mandalas. These are not static works of art but cosmic maps meant to help practitioners focus in a multidimensional way on the embodied integration of their contemplative practice and purpose. *Mandala* is a multilayered and nuanced term. On one level it means an environment, a sacred circle or experiential horizon where transformation occurs. In our case, we're creating an inner imaginative space where we're envisioning our transformation as individuals and leaders. Of course, beyond that imaginative level, our mandala is also a crucible for our actual, embodied transformation over time. That means the transformation of our stress-driven mind, heart, and body into the mind, heart, and body of boundless leadership. While our mandala begins as a visual learning aid, a model for imagining our journey of transformation, it also symbolically represents how our minds, hearts, and bodies over time will become crucibles for transformation as we practice and master the disciplines of mind, heart and body.

What does a mandala look like? The classic mandala is a square placed within a circular protective perimeter reinforced by a firewall and set within a larger environment. The square represents the blueprint of a virtual learning space—an inner home base for transformation. In it there are four quadrants, one on each face of the square, which all converge on a circle in the center. Each quadrant is accessed by one of four gates that open the space to the outer world. The idea is that this is the virtual workspace wherein we're going to be transformed. It's a metaphor for the mind/body state or way of being we want to inhabit and embody.

Your Mandala of Boundless Leadership

As for the four gates, they are facing the four directions—east, south, west, and north—usually oriented with the east on top and west on bottom. Each gate and quadrant combination is also associated with a specific color—white for the east, red for the south, yellow for the west, and green for the north—while the circle in the center where the quadrants meet is blue. These five sectors of the mandala are further associated with times of day, seasons of the year, parts of our mind/body process, challenges to be overcome, insights to be gained, and phases of our overall transformation. In effect, the basic architecture of the mandala allows for the embedding of rich, multilayered symbols designed to help give us a sense that we have everything we need all around us and are ready to transform every aspect of our being and lives on the path of boundless leadership.

INTRODUCING THE MANDALA OF BOUNDLESS LEADERSHIP

The point of framing your plan as a mandala is to visually represent the embodied fruition of your plan in a way your right brain can see it, to create a visual architecture for your understanding and practice. Bear in mind that the mandala specifically represents the final fruition of your practice plan in an embodied way of being. It is a map of your work in the discipline of body. Of course, since the path to boundless leadership is a journey of cumulative step-by-step learning and practice, your mandala assumes as a context that you've done your work in the disciplines of mind and heart. You can remind yourself of this by symbolically identifying the circular perimeter, or firewall, that usually surrounds and "protects" the mandala as having two layers—one is made of the clarity and self-awareness that protect your mind from being caught up in negative biases or the noise of inputs from the outer world, the other is made of the compassion and authentic engagement that protect your heart from being triggered into reactivity by the disturbing emotions of people around you.

As you work on bringing your final plan to life, you can use words, images, objects, colors, and symbols to understand and represent your vision (at the eastern gate), your new narrative (at the western gate), the energetic flow you want to command (at the southern gate) and your way of moving as the boundless leader (at the northern gate). This all culminates in a full embodiment of the transformed you (in the center).

There are no right or wrong versions of your mandala. It is a learning aid like a vision board to help combine your left-brain verbal plan with a right-brain kinesthetic image, created to better integrate your vision at a deeper level of mind and brain. In this way, it offers a skillful means of installing cues for a new way of being, just as a visual image can help etch a key idea into your memory. The insights and skills represented in the mandala get installed in your deeper psyche and nervous system and become a sort of GPS for your transformation. Creating the mandala is all about your personal expression—there's no good or bad, right or wrong. Among the most crucial benefits of the mandala as a map for change is that it's not a disembodied, impersonal, abstract image but one that centrally includes you and graphically represents your final way of being and embodied purpose. In fact, the whole mandala is an image of who you want to be *when you get where you want to go*, including the final way of being that embodies how you want to impact the people, organization, and world around you. This is what makes it such a powerful learning technology.

At this point, we suggest engaging with the mandala as a liberal arts experiment. Get a big piece of paper, find some colored pencils or markers, get on the floor, and start messing around. Or feel free to approach the mandala as a collage project, cut some images out of your favorite magazines and paste them on. It's about having fun and trying to see what naturally comes up around it. As you develop your mandala and see how it anchors your practice and accelerates your transformation, you'll find it can provide a virtual workspace wherein you can process key decisions and transitions in ways that help guide and speed your transformation as a person and leader.

THE DIMENSIONS OF TRANSFORMATION
SYMBOLIZED IN THE MANDALA

To help stimulate the creation of our leadership mandala, we offer some cues to illustrate what we mean by boundless vision and the other qualities inscribed in the generic mandala model. We hope these cues will connect with your lived experience in ways that spark an intuitive sense of your fully embodied transformation. Specifically, we align the four gates and center with five key aspects of your lived experience and offer five simple prescriptions to indicate the work involved in transforming those aspects—as raw materials—into the four qualities and practical application of embodying boundless leadership.

East: See It!

The east targets how you habitually see yourself, your body and your place in the world. It locates the work you need to do to reenvision yourself and the world, to *see* your expanded potential and impact. The challenging question it poses is, What is your larger vision for yourself, and how do you *see* yourself and your life when you've arrived at your ideal destination? The color white linked with this quadrant represents the light of dawn and emergence of spring, when the vibrant fullness of embodied life appears most vividly. It is also linked with the obstacle of survival bias, which fixates on how things seem at face value, and with the reflective intuition that allows us to see through the apparent solidity of things to recognize the deeper way they are always changing and evolving.

West: Say It!

The west targets your default identity and story, what you normally think and say you are, where you come from, and where you're going. It locates the work you need to do to revise your identity, role, and narrative, to *say* what your expanded role and destiny are. The challenging question it poses is, What is the affirmative declaration and empowering story you will own as yours, and what will you *say* to empower yourself to realize your vision? The color red linked with this quadrant represents twilight and the vivid colors of autumn, when we readily appreciate the precious distinctiveness and individuality of all people and things. It is also linked with the obstacle of fear-based clinging and with the expressive intuition that allows us to discern and articulate the distinct potentials and destinies of ourselves and all others.

South: Feel It!

The south targets the normal gut feeling of your sensitivity, what your default felt sense of being in your body and daily life is. It locates the work you need to do to transform your bodily energy and chemistry, so you *feel* the inspiration and flow that will enable you to embody your expanded vision and narrative for yourself, others, and the world. The challenging question it poses is, What kind of energy flow do you need to tap and harness on your path of embodied transformation? What will you need to *feel* to power and sustain your boundless vision and way of being? The color yellow linked with this quadrant represents the light of day and effulgence of summer, when the warmth of embodied life enhances our sensitivity. It is also linked with the obstacle of scarcity thinking and with the empathic intuition that allows us to see beyond our immediate sensations to recognize the common sensations and needs of all.

North: Do It!

The north targets the default way you stand, move, and behave in your body, your normal facial expressions, body language, and way of acting. It locates the work you need to do to physically embody and express the vision, story, and energy of your expanded way of being and impacting others and the world. The challenging question it poses is, What rhythms and forms of expression do you need to inform your posture, movements, and actions so that you'll physically inhabit and convey your boundless way of being and leading? The color green linked with this quadrant represents dusk and the regenerative power of winter, when we tap into the most primal creative urges of life and nature. It is also linked with the obstacle of jealous competition and with the executive intuition that allows us to work skillfully and dynamically with others toward shared success and common good.

Center: Be It!

The center targets your default mind/body state, the familiar context or gestalt of your lived conscious experience of self in the world. It locates the work you need to do to integrate the expansive vision, narrative, energy, and stance you've been cultivating into a whole new sense of who, what, how, and where you are. The challenging question it poses is, What fundamental shift in embodied consciousness do you need to make to own and hold the new way of being and embody the larger purpose you're growing into? The color blue linked with this central circle represents midnight and the constant season of the now in which we must continually deepen our grounding in the timeless power of presence. It is also linked with the obstacle of shame/pride and the existential intuition that guides us to take our place in this ever-changing reality and embody our full potential and purpose in relation to others and the world we share.

WHAT BELONGS IN YOUR MANDALA?

Given the generic lay of the land, what kinds of personal reminders or symbolic elements might you want to put in your mandala?

Images of Mentors or Role Models

The most potent images that orient our imagination and energy at the level of embodied learning are images of people or archetypes—mentors or figures that personify the qualities you seek to develop, inspire you to move through the obstacles you face, and evoke the intuitive wisdom you need to transform.

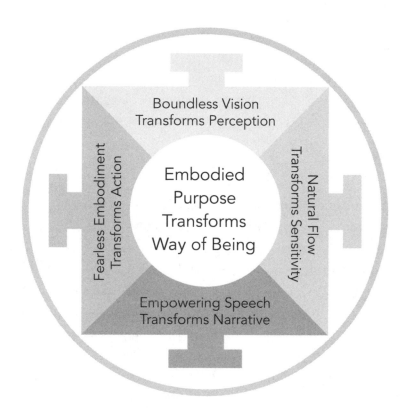

The Mandala of Embodied Transformation

Affirmative Words or Phrases

Affirmative words or phrases could range from affirmative messages you received from mentors to commitments you've made to yourself and include pronouncements of your expanded identity or narrative, like "I embody the compassion we all need now."

Names or Symbols of Specific Practices

Names or symbols of practices may include reminders or commitments to continue specific practices you've found helpful in overcoming obstacles or developing the qualities you need in whatever quadrant of your mandala.

Evocative Symbols

Evocative symbols could include any image—perhaps a gemstone, tool, animal, plant, lake, mountain, ocean, sun, moon, constellation—that evokes in you a felt sense of one of the qualities or the larger way of being you're trying to develop.

Organizational Impact

While your leadership mandala is first and foremost a map of your transformation, the application of your transformation to specific contributions to others—your organization or the world at large—is an integral part of embodied purpose. For instance, you might place trusted advisors or your inner circle of peers in various quadrants of the mandala to represent your intention to engage or empower them in specific ways. Likewise, you need not limit your mandala to your inner work or intimate circle of teamwork. Outside your inner mandala you could include one or more larger horizons of the mandala that represent your impact on others, teams you lead or interact with, or even on your larger organization. Bear in mind that you don't want to dilute, distract, or overtax your inner work by jumping to these levels of practice application prematurely. We advise that you start with a simple practice mandala that addresses your personal aims and aspirations, independent of current professional roles or challenges, and then move on to more specific applied impact when you're truly ready to do so without obligation or stress.

Larger Social and Environmental Impact

While your mandala is meant to guide your transformation as a leader, your vision of your broadest possible impact will hopefully include some specific intentions regarding your social impact on the world at large as well as the impact you have on the natural environment. These broader impacts are usually represented as lying outside the firewall of your mandala, in the larger social and natural environment. For instance, you could envision your personal or organizational transformation as impacting people in the larger society by envisioning people at various levels of fortune around the globe benefiting in specific ways from your efforts. Or you could represent the natural environment on which your mandala and the outer world beyond your firewall rest and envision your transformation protecting, preserving, and restoring aspects of nature like wildlife, oceans, forests, or air. Here too, we suggest you bear in mind that you don't want to dilute, distract, or overtax your inner work by jumping to these levels of practice application prematurely. Start by modeling how you'll transform yourself and then move on to a broader social and environmental impact when you're truly ready to do so naturally, without undue burden or stress.

33 COMMITMENT TO REAL PRACTICE

Implementing the Plan

Once you have your plan and have personalized it to dovetail with your highest intentions, vision, and purpose, you must commit to using it, and that means fully committing to yourself. Consider your goals and ask yourself, "What do I want to achieve for *myself* and what impact do I want to have on my business, my life, and the world around me?" Remember that boundless leadership is a way of being, not a fad diet or quick fix. It's meant to impact how we show up in the world. It takes time to implement the processes we've explored in this book and even more time to make them new habits and, eventually, second nature. Unless we are appropriately humble in our expectations of ourselves and in our willingness to reach out to mentors, peers, learning materials, and communities of practice, we are at risk of burning out once our enthusiasm or willpower fade.

Your practice plan can be quite varied and complex. It doesn't mean one practice every day. It can be, "I'm going to keep an eye on where I am. If I fall into negativity bias, I'm going to _____, and if I notice my reptilian brain dominating my decisions, I'm going to use _____." In this book we've given you the tools—like R.A.I.N. and mentor practice—and your job is to select the best one for each situation and apply it.

Are you clear about the obstacles that you need to work on and the potentials that you want to activate? To what extent? It doesn't have to be clear in the sense of being able to write them down in a sentence. Going back to the discipline of mind and the importance of clarity, focus your attention on what it is that you feel is stopping you and proceed from there to heart and body. When you look inward, what do you feel you need to cultivate?

Whether we go inward or not has a lot to do with intention. As a society, especially in the high-achieving West, we tend not to turn inward as much as we should. And when we do, guilt, almost a perceived selfishness, often arises. A way to check on this is to ask yourself, "What's the intention?" Be aware you need to stabilize and strengthen this foundation of purpose and consider what you have to give. If nothing matters other than yourself, it's a different intention from one that applies the actions of boundless leadership to the team, the company, the people in your life, and the world.

The second thing to remember is your plan must be solid and balanced. If you don't have a sustainable structure for practice—a plan to practice X, at Y time of day, for Z time, and Q days per week, until you get U result—your efforts may be haphazard and all over the place. But if your structure is too rigid, and you're not prepared to evaluate your progress or lack of progress and adjust your plan accordingly, then you're not addressing what's happening in real time. Finding the balance between rigidity and flexibility takes time, experience, and often checking in with peers and guides. One metaphor Elazar likes to use with his clients is drilling for oil. If you only drill one well no matter how deep you go, you're minimizing your chances of striking oil. Similarly, if you're drilling random shallow wells, you're not going to get deep enough to strike oil. This balance of depth and scope, rigidity and fluidity is individual and done by feel—it's a dynamic, organic process. Our plan can help us bring self-awareness to the scope.

Our self-awareness can indicate if we're hiding from ourselves or going deep and revealing our vulnerability. For example, in applying self-awareness you might ask yourself if you're bringing shame to what you're doing or not doing. And you might then ask, "Is the shame helpful?" As things like this arise, with your enhanced clarity based on applying boundless leadership you can make adjustments based on what you find.

Likewise, perhaps the most essential vital ingredient in a practice plan is compassion for and authentic engagement with others and ourselves. We must be able to engage our practice not out of an aggressive urge or drive but out of a genuine acceptance and care for our own well-being and human development. This is especially important when you realize that long-term practice is not linear; we can get in the flow and fall out of rhythm repeatedly. This is why accepting the vicissitudes with self-compassion is critical. In addition, one of the best ways to determine whether our practice is working is to check in with others about how they experience our presence and energy. Often others can affirm whether our practice is really changing our way of being for the better or we're just driving ourselves or kidding ourselves and need to ask for more guidance, inspiration, and support.

Finally, one of the most accurate measures of the effectiveness and progress of our practice plan is how we are inhabiting our bodies. To what extent are we caught up in driving or ignoring our embodiment? Here we sincerely ask our bodies whether they are moving toward the feeling of fearlessness and singular taste of embodied flow. We may be focusing on our preliminary work in the disciplines of mind and heart—the challenges of finding clarity and compassion that are a constant life work for us all—but even if we've not yet extended our practice plan to the discipline of body, or started working on our leadership mandala, our bodies should be feeling a beneficial impact from our practice. If we're on the right track, we should find it easier to breathe and feel a tangible softening in our bodies. If not, no shame or blame, but we probably need to go back to the drawing board and seek out the personal, caring help and support of learning guides and/or communities. When it comes to deep and real transformation, we're all on a level playing field—we're all bozos on the evolutionary bus. We have enormous untapped potential, but we also invariably need the help of others to encourage, inspire, and empower us to embody real change. As the poet T. S. Eliot wrote in *Four Quartets*, "Humility is endless."

AFTERWORD

As we complete our upgrade to a boundless leadership default mode, we not only transform our way of being and make drastic shifts in how we lead but taste the *why* of leadership.

In an ever-deepening world of interconnectivity and interdependence, the clear choice is to embrace the whole and not solely our part in it. It is evident that if we win by making others lose, then in a real sense no one wins, and we all lose. If one part of the world is ablaze, then the whole planet coughs. If we use manipulation and exclusion to manage others, then none of us will ever feel safe. If wealth creates wealth to concentrate resources in the hands of the few, then we are diminishing the likelihood of what Charles Darwin referred to as the greatest human trait—compassion—to be the guiding principle of that wealth.

There are many intentions that can benefit from the power of boundless leadership. One that resonates for us is to apply our full unleashed potential to creating a kinder, more caring world for our children and children's children. And to do so with abundant gratitude and fearless confidence. Good luck on your journey—and don't hesitate to reach out for help!

ACKNOWLEDGMENTS

We begin by acknowledging the exceptional team that made *Boundless Leadership* possible. We are both deeply grateful to Alice Peck, our editor par excellence who worked patiently to rein in our free-flowing banter and shape it into digestible food for thought. We also want to express our heartfelt thanks to Stephanie Tade, our extraordinary agent, who right away saw the potential and need for boundless leadership and led us and the book to its rightful home at Shambhala. There we have thoroughly enjoyed working with our incredible in-house editor Beth Frankl, who also instantly recognized what we were up to and who has shepherded the book through the labyrinth of publication with humanity, humor, and care.

ELAZAR'S ACKNOWLEDGMENTS

In acknowledging those who helped me find my way to boundless leadership, I must first of all thank my father for his decision to transplant our family from the small and tightly knit community of Iraqi Jews in Iran to America, which reflected his quest for boundless possibilities. No longer living with the external threats and constraints of religious persecution in this new land of opportunities, I began to bump up against my self-limiting habits and beliefs, launching my life's journey to boundless leadership.

My path was further energized by recognizing the limits of the conventional business mindset and was full of stumbling forward and stubbing toes in the dark. Fortunately, this leaning into the unknown led me to discover silent meditation retreats, which gave me a way to turn inward, so I could face my obstacles and see my untapped potential. Eventually, the practice brought me to the gracious hearts and wise teachings of Sharon Salzberg and Joseph Goldstein. I will be always grateful for the time I spent with them at the Insight Meditation Society in Barre, Massachusetts. Soon their "home" became my second home, as the power of the noble silence we shared allowed me glimpses of the light that shines inside us all, introducing me to the first key milestone on my path to boundless leadership: insights into awareness and clarity.

As my search continued, I forsook religion to embrace the religious experience and traded my pride of being among the chosen for the humility that comes of understanding that I was one among many, interconnected with all. A fervent advocate of this view, His Holiness the Dalai Lama, began reshaping my life, teaching me that boundless leadership springs from authentic kindness and wise compassion. My understanding of this heart practice deepened as my path crossed with Lama Losang Samten, once His Holiness's personal attendant, who became for me a living example of fearlessness and grace in action. I feel deeply indebted to both these exceptional leaders, as well as other mentors Denma Locho Rinpoche and Gelek Rinpoche, for enabling me to better access the second key of boundless leadership: compassionate engagement.

Fortunately, my professional life was also honored by guides and mentors. I am grateful to Linda Fayne Levinson, the first female partner at McKinsey, for mentoring me on the vital role of clarity of mind in leadership; to Kenneth I. Chenault, the former chairman and CEO of American Express, who elegantly married business effectiveness with the humanity of business; and finally, Brad D. Smith, chairman of the executive board of Intuit, who reaffirmed the primacy of the human potential movement, long before it became fashionable.

For *Boundless Leadership* and more, I am ever grateful to Joe Loizzo without whose tireless efforts this book would not have been possible. A collaborator, colleague, mentor, and friend, our journey of giving life to this book was, for me, telling evidence of the power of marrying the art of transformation with the science of enlightened leadership. I remain indebted to his sharp mind, wise heart, and steady hand.

My gratitude also runs deep for my wife, Vimukti, who, among other things, helped me turn the third key of boundless leadership—embodied flow—bringing her deep knowledge as a highly trained yoga therapist to recalibrate the subtle messaging buried in my body. And I give thanks for my daughters, Carolina and Alejandra, who as recently adopted teenagers are for me both the ground and sweet fruit of the path of boundless leadership. Together they all have helped keep the flame of inspiration burning, reaffirming that love—by definition—is forever boundless.

JOE'S ACKNOWLEDGMENTS

Words never fail as fast as when the time comes to acknowledge those who have shown us the greatest kindness. I think I speak for both Elazar and myself when I say that our journey to *Boundless Leadership* has been far longer and more convoluted than either of us could have imagined. Yet here we are—at a milestone that evokes a deep sense of fulfillment and gratitude. What makes the journey that led to this book feel so meaningful for me is the memory of the mentors, friends, and loved ones who have guided me on the way.

As first-generation immigrants on the eve of World War II, my parents brought me into the world at a turning point in their American dream. At two months old, I was sailing to Europe with my four older sisters, heading toward our great adventure. I spent my early years in Switzerland, watching my father realize his deferred dream of becoming a doctor. Yet when we returned to Long Island for him to complete his training and start practicing psychiatry, I felt like an immigrant in my native land. As I saw him succeed at the cost of his innate love of family, music, philosophy, even life, I got my first real lesson in the shadow economy of our stress-driven culture and leadership.

As one of the many who passed through Ellis Island, my mother had a deep sense of that shadow economy and the toll it can take.

Not only had she been uprooted from her ancestral home in Sicily to start third grade in Brooklyn without a word of English, she also had to watch her mother cry daily over the loss of her community and to suffer with her whole family the devastating loss of her older brother Johnnie in the war. I believe that was why, instead of accepting the university post she was offered after completing her master's degree, my mom stayed on teaching eighth grade history. It was not lost on me that she intentionally charted a path not often taken in our upwardly mobile culture, leaving herself time and energy to deepen her contemplative pursuits.

So first and foremost I'm grateful to my mother, Carmela Paula Napoli Loizzo, for offering me an early and vibrant example of how to thrive throughout the life cycle, while balancing the personal and professional, mundane and transcendent. While I admired my dad's intellect, ambition, and generosity, I realize that I found my way thanks to a series of mentors who embodied my mom's countercultural path.

In high school I met Father Phillip K. Eichner, who in addition to being my first philosophy teacher, served as president of three elite Catholic high schools and board chair of the Catholic League for Religious and Civil Rights and won a landmark patients' rights case governing end-of-life care. He became my first living example of Thomas Merton's "contemplation in a world of action."

At college, I met Robert A .F. Thurman, the first Western Tibetan monk, who returned to lay life as a professor, remaining a lifelong friend to His Holiness the Dalai Lama. Bob would go on to translate groundbreaking works of Tibetan philosophy, fill the first chair of Tibetan studies at a major American university, establish Tibet House US and Menla, and launch the Treasury of the Buddhist Sciences translation series with Columbia University Press. He was my next example of countercultural leadership, a living bridge between the contemplative wisdom traditions of the East and the competitive secular academy of the West.

Bob also introduced me to the Buddhist psychology preserved in Tibet, which stretches back to the world's first university at Nalanda in

North India, and from there to the transformational methods and egalitarian learning community of Shakyamuni. In that tradition, I found a wiser, more effective path of healing than the mechanistic one my dad and I were trained in. So I set out to integrate Buddhist contemplative science and practice into the nascent fields of mind/body medicine, contemplative neuroscience, and contemplative psychotherapy during my psychiatry training.

In those same years I found my first psychiatry mentor, Rolf Arvidson. Rolf was a Norwegian immigrant who had joined the resistance as a teenager and was forced to flee the Nazi occupation. Educated and trained in the U.S., he became the youngest training analyst ever at the Boston Psychoanalytic Institute, though his maverick interests in relational, creative, and embodied approaches led him to break away to cofound the Psychoanalytic Institute of New England. Rolf exemplified my ideal way to practice psychiatry—as a contemplative refuge from and countercultural alternative to the invasive system of modern surgery and pharmaceuticals.

In order to integrate Buddhist psychology experientially, I traveled with Bob Thurman to India, where he kindly introduced me to the Dalai Lama and his tutors Yongdzin Ling Rinpoche and Tsenshab Serkhong Rinpoche, as well as Ngawang Gelek Rinpoche. In the years that followed, I closely followed all four of these remarkable men, each embodying in different ways the exceptional methodology of contemplative leadership that is the Nalanda tradition's greatest contribution to our future.

While their compassionate leadership and far-reaching institutional and social impact are often seen as otherworldly attainments, these masters see them as the natural result of a reproducible method of contemplative training and integration that could transform anyone. That method dates back to the fruition of the Nalanda curriculum centuries ago—the path of neuropsychological transformation called the optimal integral process (*anuttara*-yoga-tantra). Unlike our modern universities, Nalanda and its sister institutions in Tibet never gave up on fully realizing our human potential. Instead of separating knowledge and power from the ancient disciplines of contemplation and ethics, as we have, they trained all their leaders in the integral process, to bring a fully realized humanity to guide all secular disciplines—science, technology, economics, and politics—toward collective well-being.

So it is neither an accident nor a miracle that the Dalai Lama has been at once a global thought leader, Nobel peace laureate, the political head of Tibet's nonviolent government, and the spiritual leader of a nation of six million. Likewise, Yongdzin Ling Rinpoche was not just the Dalai Lama's primary mentor, one of three leading experts on the most critical school of Buddhist philosophy, and the living master of a twelfth-century lineage of optimal integral practice, but also the academic head of a monastic university system that originally included a faculty and student body of some seventeen thousand. Finally, it was not a matter of luck or talent that my closest Tibetan mentor, Gelek Rinpoche, served as a scholar who personally preserved over 170 Tibetan texts from extinction, who became an inspiration to thousands of Western students including artists like Allen Ginsberg and Paul Simon, and who also acted as the entrepreneurial founder of a still-thriving global contemplative community called Jewel Heart.

As for the last leg of the journey, it coincided with my meeting Elazar Aslan at a time when I had just finished my doctoral studies with Bob, had begun clinical research on meditation, and was in the process of founding the Nalanda Institute for Contemplative Science. I am so very grateful for Elazar, a wise, skilled, and nurturing soul who shared my search for a road not taken in leadership and came primed for the dialogue that fueled our collaboration, our Boundless Leadership program, and this book.

It is with great joy that I come to my wife and life partner Gerardine Hearne Loizzo, who has shared every step on the path for these twenty years, encouraging me up the steep inclines, challenging me when I strayed, and waking me up to my privilege as an overeducated white male, given so many unfair advantages on the uneven playing field of our society. Last but not least, it is my pleasure to thank my two amazing young sons—Maitreya (Trey) and Ananda (Nandi)—who are developing into such fine men, I trust they will soon become boundless leaders.

For whatever errors, limits, and blind spots remain in this work, I take full responsibility. And for any help and value this book may offer those who like Elazar and me seek a more sustainable, equitable way of living and leading today, I dedicate the benefit so that all who share this precious earth may enjoy personal thriving, interpersonal compassion, organizational stewardship, and collective liberation.

May all be well!

December 15, 2020
Nalanda Institute for Contemplative Science
The Lenape Island of Manhattan

NOTES

1. Barbara L. Frederickson, "The Role of Positive Emotions in Positive Psychology: The Broaden-and-Build Theory of Positive Emotions," *The American Psychologist* 38, no. 2 (2001): 218–26, https://doi.org/10.1037//0003-066x.56.3.218.

2. Shelden Cohen, Peter J. Gianaros, and Stephen B. Manuck, "A Stage Model of Stress and Disease," *Perspectives on Psychological Science* 11, no.4 (July 2016): 456–63, https://doi.org/10.1177/1745691616646305.

3. Sara W. Lazar et al., "Meditation Experience Is Associated with Increased Cortical Thickness," *NeuroReport* 16, no.17 (2005): 1893–97, https://doi.org/10.1097/01.wnr.0000186598.66243.19.

4. Madhav Goyal et al., "Meditation Programs for Psychological Stress and Well-Being," *JAMA Internal Medicine* 174, no. 3 (2014): 357–68, https://doi.org/10.1001/jamainternmed.2013.13018.

5. Antoine Lutz, Lawrence L. Greischar, Nancy B. Rawlings, Matthieu Ricard, and Richard J. Davidson, "Long-Term Meditators Self-Induce High-Amplitude Gamma Synchrony during Mental Practice," *Proceedings of the National Academy of Sciences* 101, no. 46 (2004): 16369–73, https://doi.org/10.1073/pnas.0407401101; Antoine Lutz, Heleen A. Slagter, John D. Dunne, and Richard J. Davidson, "Attention Regulation and Monitoring in Meditation," *Trends in Cognitive Sciences* 12, no. 4 (2008): 163–69, https://doi.org/10.1016/j.tics.2008.01.005.

6. Federal Aviation Administration, "Aeronautical Decision-Making," in *Pilot's Handbook of Aeronautical Knowledge* (Oklahoma City: United States Department of Transportation, 2016), 2-1–2-32; Emil Persson, Kinga Barrafrem, Andreas Meunier, and Gustav Tinghög,

"The Effect of Decision Fatigue on Surgeons' Clinical Decision Making," *Health Economics* 28, no. 10 (2019): 1194–1203, https://doi.org/10.1002/hec.3933.

7. Shai Danziger, Jonathan Levav, and Liora Avnaim-Pesso, "Extraneous Factors in Judicial Decisions," *Proceedings of the National Academy of Sciences* 108, no. 17 (2011): 6889–92, https://doi.org/10.1073/pnas.1018033108.

8. Sheldon Cohen, Peter J. Gianaros, and Stephen B. Manuck, "A Stage Model of Stress and Disease," *Perspectives on Psychological Science* 11, no. 4 (2016): 456–63, https://doi.org/10.1177/1745691616646305.

9. James K. Harter, Frank L. Schmidt, and Corey L. M. Keyes, "Well-Being in the Workplace and Its Relationship to Business Outcomes: A Review of the Gallup Studies," *Flourishing: Positive Psychology and the Life Well-Lived*, 2003, 205–24, https://doi.org/10.1037/10594-009.

10. Rajendra Sisodia, Timothy Henry, and Thomas Eckschmidt, *Conscious Capitalism Field Guide: Tools for Transforming Your Organization* (Boston: Harvard Business Review Press, 2018.)

11. Theodosius Dobzhansky, *The Biology of Ultimate Concern* (London: Collins, 1971); Edward Osborne Wilson, *Sociobiology: The New Synthesis* (Cambridge, MA: Belknap Press, 2002).

12. Johanna Bick et al., "Effect of Early Institutionalization and Foster Care on Long-Term White Matter Development," *JAMA Pediatrics* 169, no. 3 (2015): 211, https://doi.org/10.1001/jamapediatrics.2014.3212.

13. https://www.adultdevelopmentstudy.org/grantandglueckstudy

14. Helen Y. Weng et al., "Compassion Training Alters Altruism and Neural Responses to Suffering," *Psychological Science* 24, no. 7 (2013): 1171–80, https://doi.org/10.1177/0956797612469537; Lea K. Hildebrandt, Cade McCall, and Tania Singer, "Differential Effects of Attention-, Compassion-, and Socio-Cognitively Based Mental Practices on Self-Reports of Mindfulness and Compassion." *Mindfulness* 8, no. 6 (2017): 1488–1512, https://doi.org/10.1007/s12671-017-0716-z; Susanne Leiberg, Olga Klimecki, and Tania

Singer, "Short-Term Compassion Training Increases Prosocial Behavior in a Newly Developed Prosocial Game," *PLOS ONE* 6, no. 3 (2011), https://doi.org/10.1371/journal.pone.0017798.

15. Adam M. Grant, *Give and Take: A Revolutionary Approach to Success* (London: Phoenix, 2014).

16. Joé T. Martineau, Jean Decety, and Eric Racine, "The Social Neuroscience of Empathy and Its Implication for Business Ethics," *Organizational Neuroethics*, 2019, 167–89, https://doi.org/10.1007/978-3-030-27177-0_12.

17. Tania Singer and Olga M. Klimecki, "Empathy and Compassion," *Current Biology* 24, no. 18 (2014), https://doi.org/10.1016/j.cub.2014.06.054.

18. Richard J. Davidson and Sharon Begley, *The Emotional Life of Your Brain: How Its Unique Patterns Affect the Way You Think, Feel, and Live—and How You Can Change Them* (New York: Plume, 2013).

19. Jim Harter, "4 Factors Driving Record-High Employee Engagement in U.S.," *Gallup*, February 4, 2020, https://www.gallup.com/workplace/284180/factors-driving-record-high-employee-engagement.aspx.

20. John M. Keynes, *The General Theory of Employment, Interest, and Money* (New York: Harcourt, Brace, and Company, 1936), 161–62.

21. Stephen W. Porges, *The Polyvagal Theory: Neurophysiological Foundations of Emotions, Attachment, Communication, and Self-Regulation* (New York: Norton, 2011), 191.

22. J. Allan Hobson, Charles C. H. Hong, and Karl J. Friston, "Virtual Reality and Consciousness Inference in Dreaming," *Frontiers in Psychology* 5 (2014), https://doi.org/10.3389/fpsyg.2014.01133.

23. Rodolfo Riascos Llinás, *I of the Vortex: From Neurons to Self* (Cambridge, MA: MIT Press, 2008).

24. Alvaro Pascual-Leone et al., "The Plastic Human Brain Cortex," *Annual Review of Neuroscience* 28, no. 1 (2005): 377–401, https://doi.org/10.1146/annurev.neuro.27.070203.144216.

25. Fatemeh Bambaeeroo and Nasrin Shokrpour, "The Impact of the Teachers' Non-Verbal Communication on Success in Teaching,"

Journal of Advances in Medical Education & Professionalism 5, no. 2 (2017): 51–59.

26. Mihaly Csikszentmihalyi, *Flow: The Psychology of Optimal Experience,* (United Kingdom: HarperCollins, 1991).

27. Csikszentmihalyi, *Flow*, 4.

28. Daniel Brown, "Mastery of the Mind East and West," *Annals of the New York Academy of Sciences* 1172, no. 1 (2009): 231–51, https://doi.org/10.1196/annals.1393.018.

29. Bambaeeroo and Shokrpour, "Impact of the Teachers' Non-Verbal Communication on Success in Teaching," *Journal of Advances in Medical Education & Professionalism* 5, no. 2 (2017): 51–59; Silvia Bonaccio et al., "Nonverbal Behavior and Communication in the Workplace: A Review and an Agenda for Research," *Journal of Management* 42, no. 5 (2016): 1044–74, doi:10.1177/0149206315621146.

30. John Conlisk, "Why Bounded Rationality?" *Journal of Economic Literature* 34, no. 2 (1996): 669–700, https://www.jstor.org/stable/2729218.

31. Silvia Bonaccio et al., "Nonverbal Behavior and Communication in the Workplace," *Journal of Management* 42, no. 5 (2016): 1044–74, https://doi.org/10.1177/0149206315621146; Robert A. Wilson and Lucia Foglia, "Embodied Cognition," *The Stanford Encyclopedia of Philosophy* (Spring 2017 edition), https://plato.stanford.edu/archives/spr2017/entries/embodied-cognition/.

INDEX

body mindfulness, 17, 61–62, 139
  fearless embodiment practice
    and, 218
body mindfulness meditation, 68
bottom-up processing, 18
boundless leadership
  developing your practice plan for,
    234–36
  foundational principles, 233–34
  reasons for calling it "boundless,"
    x–xi
  See also path to boundless
    leadership; *specific topics*
boundless leadership map, 25t
boundless vision, 191
  activating, 186
  defined, 182, 185
  empowering speech and, 195, 197,
    198, 200
  and mandala, 244, 245, 247f
  nature of, 183, 185, 189, 225–26
brain
  as social organ, 110–11
  See also neuroplasticity;
    neuroscience
brain stem, 8f, 16f, 32f, 207, 208, 219–21
  animal spirits and, 174
  breathwork and, 210
  embodiment and, 177–79
  See also reptilian brain
brain structure and function, three
    systems of, 8f
  stress and, 16
brain structures, 8f, 16f, 32f
breath as catalyst, 210–13
breathing, natural flow and, 209, 210,
    213, 214
breathwork, 210–14
bypassing, 126t, 126–27

caregivers, 128, 137, 138, 190–91, 195,
    196, 199
caretaking, 126t
C.A.T., 87–93
categorization of people, 121
center (mandala), 241–44, 246
clarifying intentions, 87–89. *See also*
    C.A.T.
clarity
  defined, 47, 171
  discipline of mind and, 46, 57, 74
  obstacles to, 47–52
  self-awareness and, 46, 54, 56–62,
    87, 94, 97
codependency, 126t, 128
cognitive appraisal (phase in cycle of
    stress and trauma), 13–14
Cohen, Sheldon, 13, 59
collective effort, a matter of, 98–99
collective productivity, 98, 99
compassion
  active components of, 132
  authentic engagement and, 30,
    97–103, 112, 113, 119–20, 123, 252
  benefits of, 105–8
  defined, 132, 166
  empathy and, 102, 105, 116–18, 147,
    148, 166
  evolution of, 120–22
  four criteria of authentic, 125,
    126t, 128
  four masks of inauthentic, 125, 126t
  importance, 252
  leading with, 99, 103
  nature of, 102
  neuroscience of, 116–18
  terminology, 131
  transformative, 104–5
  wealth and, 253

energy, 226

engagement, 143–44

  defined, 101, 143

  vs. disengagement, 145, 149

  See also specific topics

epigenetics, 10

equal empathy, 122, 133–34, 148–49

equal empathy practice, 121–22

  steps in, 133

equalizing self and other, 135

equanimous concern, 126t, 128

evolution, 120. *See also* survival of the

  fittest

extreme(s), 69–72

  loosening the hold of the, 73

fatigue, 49

fearless embodiment

  defined, 182

  the science of, 219–21

fearless embodiment practice, 218, 221

  steps in, 221–23

fearless energy, the oxygen of. *See*

  breath as catalyst

fearless mode, 181, 218

fearless movement, 220–21

fearless stance and movement,

  223–24

fearlessness and fear, 180–82

feeling. *See* south (mandala)

fight-flight-faint-freeze response, 15,

  60, 71, 72, 163, 219–20

  vs. flow, 173, 205

  negativity bias and, 180

  reptilian brain and, 71, 207, 208

  self-compassion, resilience,

    and, 142

"fittest" (Darwinism), 109

fixed attachment to outcome, 51–52

fixed mindset

  vs. growth mindset, 45

  See also unbiased awareness

flexibility, 8, 38–40

flow

  defined, 178, 203, 206

  psychology and biology of,

    205–10

  See also natural flow

freeze response, 219. *See also*

  fight-flight-faint-freeze

  response

gates, four, 241, 242, 244

Give and Take (Grant), 127

give-and-take, wise, 146–50

  steps in, 148

givers, matchers, and takers

  (salespeople), 127–28

Grant, Adam, 127

"Greed is good," 113

habits, 10, 24, 46, 76, 83

  purging old, 187

  stress-reactive, 10, 15, 17–20, 23, 24,

    28, 29, 59–62

  traumatic self-habit, 104

happiness, real sources of, 17–19

heart

  four qualities of, 100–101, 128

  See also discipline of heart; mind,

    heart, and body

heart muscles, building, 149

Hebb, Donald, 11

hierarchical design of reptilian

  organizations, 5–7

hippocampus, 116, 118

human nature, 113–14. *See also specific*

  topics

mindful attention training, 29, 44, 67
    four steps in, 61, 94
    and self-awareness, 61, 62, 94
    See also mindfulness: four forms of
mindful awareness, 17, 139
mindful insight, 17, 62, 82, 83
mindful self-compassion, 139, 140
mindfulness
    defined, 29
    four forms of, 17, 61–62, 94
    nature of, 61
    See also nonreactive mindfulness
mindfulness meditation, body, 68
misperception, 49–51
    defined, 49–50

natural flow, 204–6, 209, 210, 213,
    241f, 247f
    breathing and, 209, 210, 213, 214
    defined, 182
    nature of, 183
    See also flow
negativity bias, 20, 44, 137
    effects, 14–15, 17, 44, 143, 189
    overriding, overcoming, and
        resetting, 144, 180
    overview and nature of, 9–10,
        42–43
    reversing, 44
    stickiness of, 48
    survival mode and, 9, 29, 43, 67, 180
neocortex/primate brain, 7, 8f, 12, 16f,
    32f, 122, 177
neuroplasticity
    attention and, 28, 45, 46
    meditation and, 12, 18, 27, 28
    overview, 10–12
    significance and implications,
        10–12, 27, 43, 46, 61, 181, 187, 189

neuroscience, 9–10
    of emotion, 132
    of empathy and compassion, 116–18
nonreactive mindfulness, 17, 62, 72
    loosening the hold of the
        extreme, 73
north (mandala), 242, 243, 245–46
nurturing our hurts, 141. *See also*
    R.A.I.N.

object constancy (psychoanalysis),
    190–91
objective understanding, 126t, 128
open awareness, 41, 62, 78, 82, 155, 192
    bias and, 41, 52, 54
    meditation, 78–79

path to boundless leadership, 26, 99,
    179, 184, 242
    locating yourself on the, 232–33
perceptual stress habits, 59
performative speech acts, 198
polarization, 70, 72. *See also* extreme(s)
Porges, Stephen W., 65–66, 111–12
positive emotions, 113–16, 145
positive psychology, 8, 113, 115, 146, 225
positive thinking
    power of, 195
    See also affirmations
pot-belly breathing. *See* vase
    breathing practice
presence, 63–65
    balance and, 69
    and clarity, 65–67
    defined, 54
present moment, 29
    leverage is in the, 68
    starting fresh in the, 75
    See also mindfulness

primate brain. *See* neocortex/primate
    brain
pyramid design of reptilian
    organizations, 5–7

quantum theory of consciousness, 187

R.A.I.N., 139–41
recognition (step in the chain of
    awareness), 85
recognition of our hurts, mindful, 141.
    See also R.A.I.N.
reflexes, 7–8, 207, 219–20. *See also*
    fight-flight-faint-freeze
    response; visceral reflex
reptiles, evolutionary transition
    from, 120
reptilian brain, 71, 181, 207–8, 219
    breathing, breathwork, and, 210, 219
    nature of, 180–81, 207
    positive social emotions and, 115
    shifting out of, 180, 210, 218
    in social mode, 110
    stress and, 7
    survival and, 7–8, 58, 66, 181, 219
    and survival mode, 177, 180–81
    upgrading and integrating, 177, 180,
    207–8
    See also brain stem
reptilian leadership, xiv, 66, 164–65
    vs. mammalian leadership, 111–12
    See also us-versus-them view
reptilian organizations, 5, 6
    defined, 5
    hierarchical/pyramid design, 5–7
resetting, 227
resilience, 138
    defined, 100
    real sources of, 17–19

responsibility, levels of, 158, 159f
role-modeling imagery, 191–92, 212–14,
    233, 235
    empowering speech and, 196, 200
    flight simulator of, 194
    practice of, 191–93, 200
role models, 155, 192
    images of role models in mandala,
    246
Rosenzweig, Mark, 11–12

scarcity thinking, 6, 16f, 19, 21, 108, 245
    boundless leadership and, 20
    negativity bias and, 20, 29, 44
    reptilian organizations and, 5, 6
    stress-reactive habits and, 60
    survival mode and, 29, 82, 112,
    114, 189
seeing. *See* east (mandala)
self-awareness, 27, 32t, 45, 54, 58–59, 63,
    94, 251
    capacity for (*see* metacognition)
    clarity and, 46, 54, 56–62, 87, 94, 97
    defined, 38
    discipline of mind and, 23, 57, 97, 128
    flow and, 206
    intention and, 87
    mindful attention training and, 61,
    62, 94
    negativity bias and, 42–44
    trait of, 38–40
self-compassion, 30, 138–39,
    146–49, 252
    frameworks for, 139–42
    taming shame and, 142
self-image, revising and expanding,
    190–91, 198, 235
    imagery and, 156
self-interest, 108, 113, 152, 217

unbiased mindfulness, 134
unbiased understanding, 160, 162
unconscious mind, 18, 174, 175, 185–88
us-versus-them view, 54, 103

vagal system, 208, 212, 221
vagus nerve, 108, 191, 196, 210, 211, 220
vase breathing practice, 211–12, 212f
    steps in, 212–13
virtual learning space, 241
virtual reality, 185–88
virtual workspace, 241, 243

visceral reflex (phase in cycle of stress and trauma), 15–16
visceral stress habits, 60
vision, 226. *See also* east (mandala)

wealth, 253
west (mandala), 242–45
Wilson, Edward O., 109
win-win biology and psychology, 113
win-win culture, 205
wise give-and-take. *See* give-and-take, wise
words, 197–200, 247

ABOUT THE AUTHORS

Elazar Aslan is the CEO of Caterfly Solutions, a firm offering coaching, workshops, and rigorous programs to leaders and their organizations, so they can operate from their peak potential and have a positive and sustainable impact on their communities and the world. Before founding Caterfly, Elazar was a successful entrepreneur and restaurateur, as well as an executive at Kraft Foods, American Express, and ADP. He has an MBA from the Wharton School and a degree in organizational psychology from the University of Pennsylvania.

An avid believer in human transformation, Elazar has studied with some of the foremost teachers and scholars in various spiritual disciplines. His personal journey to boundless leadership is the why and how of all his work.

An Iranian-Iraqi-Jewish Buddhist, Elazar lives with his wife and two daughters in Philadelphia where he spends his free time serving on nonprofit boards, writing poetry, and leading mindfulness and self-inquiry workshops for youth and adults.

Joe (Joseph) Loizzo, MD, PhD, is a contemplative psychotherapist, clinical researcher, and meditation teacher who integrates ancient contemplative science and practice with current breakthroughs in neuroscience, psychology, and optimal health. After training in psychiatry at Harvard and completing a PhD in Buddhist studies at Columbia, he founded Nalanda Institute for Contemplative Science, a nonprofit that trains lay and professional caregivers in evidence-based methods of contemplative self-healing to empower themselves and others to reduce stress, build resilience, and cultivate lives of engagement and purpose in our interdependent world.

To learn more about our work please visit https://nalandaboundlessleadership.org.